OTHER BOOKS BY DAVID R. GROSS:

Animal Models in Cardiovascular Research

Travels with Charlize: In Search of Living Alone

Succeeding As a Student

ANIMALS
DON'T BLUSH

David R. Gross

BOOK PUBLISHERS NETWORK
Changing the World One Book at a Time

Book Publishers Network
P.O. Box 2256
Bothell • WA • 98041
Ph • 425-483-3040
www.bookpublishersnetwork.com

Disclaimer: This is a seriously fictionalized memoir. I changed the names
of most of the real-life people to save them, or their heirs, any possible
discomfort. The cases and events are real, but most did not happen in the
time or order presented. All the animals were actual patients, although I
forgot their names and made up new ones. None of the animals ever blushed
at anything I did to them.

10 9 8 7 6 5 4 3 2 1

Printed in the United States of America

LCCN 2015947881
ISBN   978-1-940598-81-9

Editor: Julie Scandora
Cover designer: Laura Zugzda
Typographer: Melissa Vail Coffman

DEDICATION

*Rosalie and I were married for almost fifty-three years.
I miss her everyday and will always do so. She never
read this book. I asked her, and she responded, "I lived
it. Why would I want to read about it?" Then she smiled
that wonderful, woeful smile.*

CONTENTS

INTRODUCTION

THE CONFLUENCE OF THE YELLOWSTONE AND MISSOURI RIVERS is a region of the United States steeped in the history of the northern upper plains nomadic tribes, fur traders, and the mountain men. I joined a veterinary practice there in 1960, directly out of veterinary school. Our clients included townspeople, river-valley farmers, high-prairie dry-land wheat farmers and ranchers, and North Dakota Badlands ranchers, the latter doing their best to wrest a living from government grazing leases and their too-small homesteads. All were determined, independent-minded folks who expected their veterinarian to be physically tough, knowledgeable about all species of animals, and skilled in the practice of the profession. Our animal patients were the same as they are today—prone to the same illnesses and injuries. They were for the most part stoic and never embarrassed by anything they did or that I did to them. The characters in this book are those people, those animals, and that time and place.

PART I:
SUMMER 1960

CHAPTER 1:
SKIPPER JONES

I GATHERED SOME OF THE THINGS I thought I might need—a bottle of pentobarbital, an IV drip set, a 500 ml bottle of sterile saline, and hair clippers. The clippers tugged when I tested them on the hair of my forearm. I scoured through several drawers and found a new set of number forty blades. I called my bride of fifty-seven days to let her know I would be late. While I was talking to her, a dark-green, 1952 Chevy pickup, covered in a thick layer of dried mud and dust, pulled into the parking lot in front of the hospital. A man got out of the pickup, reached over, and lifted a dog out of the bed. Three paws, wrapped in what appeared to be blood-soaked dishtowels, dangled loosely.

~

It was my first weekend on the job, mid-June 1960. "I'll be happy to handle the Saturday calls and any emergencies this weekend," I had told Dr. Schultz.

I was on the last scheduled call of the day when Dick Mathes reached me on the mobile radio. "John Jones is bringing in his cow dog, got caught by the mowing machine. His ranch is about thirty miles from town in the Badlands. He called about three, so he should get here soon."

When I arrived at the animal hospital, Dick met me at the garage door.

"Barbara and I are on our way to visit relatives in Glendive, so you're on your own. I expect all you'll do is put the dog down, anyhow."

◆

A petite, young woman, blond hair, dressed in clean but worn Levis, a denim shirt, and cowboy boots jumped to the ground from the passenger side of the pickup. She turned to lift down a young girl, her blond hair almost white. An older boy, another towhead, jumped out unassisted.

The way the rancher carried the dog into the hospital told of his gentle nature. His face was weathered, his hands were thickly callused, and his chest was massive. He had the beginnings of a potbelly but small hips and surprisingly short legs. He was in his mid to late twenties.

I held the door open and directed the Jones family into the exam room. Skipper, a two-year old border collie bitch, black and white with wide-set, expressive, brown eyes, thumped her tail on the stainless steel top of the examination table.

The man covered his guilt and anxiety talking fast. "I was mowing meadow hay and didn't know Skipper was following along. Just before I reached the end of the meadow, I made a quick turn and caught her. When she yelped was the first I knew she was even there. I picked her up and ran about a quarter of a mile to the house. I told Kathy to call while I wrapped her legs in some clean towels to staunch the bleeding. We all piled into the pickup and drove in as fast as we could."

Skipper raised her head, the rancher patted it, and the dog lay back down on the table with a sigh. There were lacerations on both front legs and the left hind leg. It appeared that some metacarpal and metatarsal bones were broken. The left hind leg looked strange. When I palpated it, the dog flinched. There was dried blood, dirt, and hair contaminating all the wounds.

Skipper's heart rate was fast, but her pulse was reasonably strong. When I pressed then released the mucous membranes over her gums, the capillary filling time was slow but not slow enough to indicate severe shock. The dog was stoic, but I could see the pain in her eyes.

"What do you think, Doc?" asked Jones. "Do we have to put her down? It looks awful bad, don't it?"

"Well, I think there's a reasonable chance we can save her. I need to clean up her wounds, control any infection, and set the broken bones. The major problem will be the extent of damage to the tendons. Tendons don't heal easily, and they are difficult to approximate."

The rancher frowned.

"Sorry . . . it's easy for sutures to pull out of tendons, so it's difficult to hold the cut ends together. If the tendons aren't cut all the way through, we can suture them, and they might heal enough for her to get around without too much trouble.

"First, I'll have to treat her for shock, then anesthetize her, and spend a lot of time cleaning up the wounds before I can start to put her back together. I can't really tell you how extensive the repairs will be until I get everything cleaned up. Certainly, the least expensive thing to do would be to put her to sleep, but I spent most of the last six years learning how to deal with this sort of thing. I am pretty confident I can save her."

Jones searched my eyes.

I did my best to look professional and self-assured.

"How much, Doc?"

"It would be three dollars to put her to sleep, probably at least a hundred if we try to save her. Here's the deal. I'm new. I'm anxious to prove what I can do, and I want the challenge of trying to save this dog." I glanced at the two children. "It appears to me that Skipper is pretty special."

He reached out and petted the dog's head again. Skipper responded with a single tail thump that seemed to resonate through the room.

"I'll tell you what, Mr. Jones—I'll make a hundred dollars the limit."

Jones looked at me and blinked his eyes, fighting tears.

"Well, I don't know . . . I gave twenty bucks for her, and she's one of the best cow dogs in this part of the country, but a hundred . . ."

"I'll do everything possible to keep the cost down, but I can't promise anything more than to limit everything to no more than a hundred dollars. Most of that will be drugs and supplies. I'm essentially donating my time, knowledge, and effort."

Both children were searching their parents' faces, first their dad's and then their mom's, their eyes and heads moving back and forth, almost in unison. Neither of the children said anything. Both reached up simultaneously and patted Skipper's head. The dog raised her head slightly. Her tail beat a rhythm on the tabletop.

"OK, Mr. Jones, how about this?" I said. "Let me start the intravenous drip and give her some anesthetic. We'll treat her for shock, and once she's anesthetized, she won't hurt anymore. If you decide you want to put her to sleep, we can go ahead and do that. The IV and the anesthetic will only cost you a couple of dollars extra."

"What do you think, Kath?" asked the rancher.

She shrugged. "It's up to you. It's a lot of money, and she might still be a cripple. Is that right, Doc?"

The boy couldn't stay quiet any longer. "Please, Dad." Then he clenched his mouth shut.

The little girl chimed in. "Yeah, pleath, Dad, we have to."

The rancher sighed. "OK . . . you guys understand this means no Christmas or birthday gifts this year?"

The boy and girl looked at each other.

"We know," the boy said.

"Pleath, Doc, make her all better," the little girl added.

The rancher gave his wife a questioning look. She nodded her agreement. No Christmas or birthday gifts for her either.

I clipped the hair over the cephalic vein, the large vein on the top of her front leg, occluded it with my left thumb, and slipped in a twenty-gauge needle. I hooked up an IV drip and secured the needle to the leg with adhesive tape. I ran in about two hundred milliliters of saline as fast as it would go and then slowed the drip to a drop per second. After the dog's heart rate slowed, I anesthetized her with half the normal calculated dose of pentobarbital and put in an endotracheal tube.

"The tube in her windpipe is to make certain she can breathe without any trouble," I explained, "just a precaution. I'll call you as soon as I finish with her and let you know how things go. It will probably take several hours, so don't worry if you don't hear from me until late. OK, Mr. Jones?"

"Look, Doc, every time you say "Mr. Jones," I look around for my dad, and he died five years ago. I'm John; this is my wife, Kathy, our son, Ferdie, and our daughter, Jenny."

"Hi, Kathy," I said nodding at her. I reached out my hand to Ferdie.

"Ferdie, how old are you?"

"I'm gonna be ten in a couple of months." The boy talked and looked like a miniature of his father, *sans* the potbelly.

"Wow, I thought you were at least eleven. Jenny, you're how old?"

"Thixth." She was missing her front teeth.

I smiled. "Well, I'm very happy to meet all of you, and I promise I'll do the best I can for Skipper."

The rancher put one meaty arm around Kathy's shoulders and gathered his children in with the other. "OK, group, we did everything we could for Skipper. Doc promised to do his best, and the forecast is for rain in a couple of days. I've got to get the hay in. Let's go home. Doc, you've got our phone number?"

"Got it," I answered.

"OK then. See you."

After they left, I called Rosalie. "I'm here alone, and I'm going to need your help to do some surgery on a dog."

"OK, I can stop dinner, put everything in the refrigerator, and be there in ten or fifteen minutes."

While I waited for her to arrive, I gathered all the surgical instruments I thought I might need, made up a pack, and put it into the autoclave. I had just started clipping the hair away from the wound on the left forelimb when I heard Rosalie enter the waiting room.

"I'm here. Where are you?" she called.

"Wait! Don't come into the exam room yet."

I went out to the waiting room. "Listen, this is not pretty. The dog got in the way of a mowing machine, and three of her legs are practically cut off. I'm going to try to patch her up, but I need you to get me anything I might need while I'm scrubbed in. Think you can do that?"

She nodded. I kissed her on the cheek, took her hand, and led her into the treatment room.

"Oh," she said, backing up. "It smells." She puckered and twisted her mouth to the left, wrinkled her nose, and squinted her eyes.

I had neglected to warn her about the odors that an outdoor dog, blood, and dirt would generate.

"Whoops . . . sorry. I'm so accustomed I hadn't noticed. Now that you mention it, the smell does kinda permeate the room."

She held her hand over her face looking directly at Skipper on the table. All four legs were sticking over the edge. The three injured paws hung down at right angles, pointing at the floor.

"You didn't notice? Peeugh . . . I don't feel so good!"

"Tell me what all you did today," I suggested. "Talk to me. Don't look at her; look at me. Do you need to sit down? What were you making for dinner?"

"You can't be serious? You want to talk about food?"

She went into the waiting room, dragged a chair to the doorway of the exam room, and sat down putting her head between her knees.

After fifty-plus years experience as a veterinarian, I've observed a basic difference between men and woman. When a woman is feeling light-headed or woozy while I'm working on their animal, they will go away and sit down until it passes. Men, and especially teenage boys, will grit their teeth and continue to watch until the back of their head bounces off the floor.

I clipped all the hair from the lower part of each injured leg and cleaned off the dirt and foreign material. I carried Skipper into the operating room and taped a small piece of cotton so it fell over the open end of the tracheal tube.

"Baby, you OK? Can you come in here now? I need you to watch her breathing while I'm doing other things. The cotton moves every time she takes a breath. See how regular it is?"

Rosalie joined me in the exam room.

"Yeah," she answered, nodding her head.

"OK, let me know if her breathing pattern changes or stops."

As I disinfected the skin around the wounds, I explained what I was about to do. "I'm going to have a surgical gown, gloves, cap, and mask on and won't be able to touch anything that's not sterile. Everything I might need is in this cabinet," I said, showing her. "I'll put everything I can think of on this sterile instrument tray before I start, but if I need something more, you'll have to get it for me. The most likely will be more suture material."

I showed her how to identify and open packs of suture and how to drop them onto the instrument tray without contaminating anything. I opened a pair of size eight-and-one-half surgical gloves and dropped them on the instrument tray. With everything arranged, I put on a surgical mask and cap, scrubbed my hands and arms, and put on a surgical gown. Rosalie, following my instructions, tied it in back, careful to avoid touching me. I put on the gloves throwing the sterile paper wrapping into a kick bucket.

I draped each wound with sterile towels and then put a large drape over the dog covering everything but the wounds. First, I cleaned the left forepaw carefully trimming away dead and injured tissue.

"This is good. The superficial flexor tendon is not transected."

"Transected?"

"Not cut all the way through. I can suture the part that's cut, and it should heal. I can also realign the metacarpal bones by palpation and splint them; that should work."

Rosalie smiled, "If you say so."

I closed the skin over the reconstruction and turned my attention to the right forepaw. As I dissected, there was a sudden spurting of bright red arterial blood. I applied pressure with a gauze sponge, searched for the end of the vessel with a mosquito forceps, found the artery, and clamped and ligated it.

"I don't know if there's enough blood supply to keep this paw alive, but it seems to be reasonably warm, and we're kinda in luck. Both the superficial and deep flexor tendons are intact; the suspensory ligament's just nicked. This might work." I was more hopeful.

I aligned the fractured metacarpal bones and closed the skin.

"This left hind leg isn't as badly cut. I'll align the tibial fracture when I have a Thomas splint ready."

"What's a Thomas splint?" Rosalie asked.

"I'll show you in a bit."

Rosalie put in a stellar performance. She reported changes in Skipper's breathing and twice followed my instructions and administered small additional doses of the anesthetic. As the surgery progressed, she watched with more interest as I cleaned and reconstructed the tissues. She started asking questions about what I was doing and why. I put in the last skin suture and stretched my back. It was after nine.

"OK, I'm putting sterile bandages over each skin wound, and I'll cut the hand off this plastic rectal sleeve like this and then cut what's left in half leaving two tubes."

"What's a rectal sleeve?" Rosalie asked.

"Oh, sorry, we use these to do rectal exams on horses and cattle. See, it pulls all the way up to my shoulder," I demonstrated. "Then when I take it off, I just invert it and the manure's on the inside."

"That's disgusting," she said.

"Not so bad. The amount of information gained from palpating the abdominal organs is essential. Anyhow, I'll slide each of these tubes over a foreleg to protect the wounds from getting wet when I build the plaster splint."

I dipped gauze impregnated with plaster of Paris into warm water squeezing out most of the water.

"I'm going to form a three-sided splint extending up here to the elbow," I lectured. "The front of the leg will be open, just covered with a light bandage and tape. That way I just cut the tape to check and treat the wounds and re-tape when I'm done."

Rosalie cocked her head to the side, smiling. "You just have to teach, don't you?"

"What are you talking about," I said.

"You're always lecturing. When we have kids, you are going to try to teach them something all the time."

"Is that bad?"

Her smile expanded, crinkling her eyes. "No, it's good. Continue."

After the plaster dried, I removed the splints, setting them aside to cure.

"I'll make the Thomas splint out of this." I showed her a three-eighths-inch-diameter, six-foot long aluminum rod.

"You still haven't told me what a Thomas splint is," she said.

"Hugh O. Thomas, in 1876, published a description of an apparatus consisting of a proximal ring that fits around the thigh with two long rigid rods extending beyond the foot. His invention places traction on the leg, stretching it so it holds the bones in place. He developed it to treat hip and joint disease in humans, but it works really well for upper leg fractures in dogs and cats."

"See, you're at it again, Professor," she laughed. "I feel like I'm back in a lecture hall."

"Never mind," I said. "I thought you were interested. You asked."

"I am, I am," she giggled. "Don't stop now; it hurts so good." She tickled under my chin with a forefinger.

I pretended to bite her finger, then took a gallon jug of disinfectant, and bent the middle of the rod into a circle around the jug, the two ends extending straight down on the same plane as the circle. I removed the jug, padded the portion of the circle between the two straight rods with cotton, and covered that with adhesive tape. Fitting the circle over Skipper's thigh, I fitted the padded portion between her inner thigh and abdomen bending the bottom of the circle to make the angle comfortable. After I was satisfied with the fit, I bent the rods in front and back of the leg to conform to the natural bends at the knee and ankle. I then bent the bottom of the two rods to form a platform two inches below her extended leg. Finally, I taped the leg in place inside the splint after palpating and setting the fracture.

"Oh, so now you're interested." Rosalie had moved in close to watch, and I nudged her with my knee. "You're blocking my light; back off, girl."

"Sorry." She smiled and leaned her head on my shoulder.

I put a thin layer of cotton in each of the hardened plaster splints and, after aligning the fractured metacarpal bones, fit the splints to each leg.

"I'll cut a small window in the tape each day," I explained.

"I know; you told me," she reminded.

Finally, I took radiographs of all three legs.

"Check it out," I told her, putting the X-ray films on the viewer and pointing to the fracture lines. "Everything lined up to perfection."

"Big deal," she replied. "Didn't seem to me you worked that hard at it."

I stuck out my lower lip.

"OK, Tarzan, you can beat your chest. I'm proud of you."

I gave Skipper a shot of antibiotics. Fitting the dog into a cage without banging the splints or pulling out the IV drip took some doing. When the dog was finally in the cage, I gave her a pat on the head and straightened up. Rosalie, standing behind me, gave me a big hug.

"I'm going to have to stay with her until she wakes up enough so I can remove the endotracheal tube," I said.

"So, it looks like you're under control here. How about I go home, finish making dinner, and bring back a picnic? I'm starving," she complained.

"That's a great idea. I'm hungry too. Isn't this a lovely way to spend a Saturday night?"

Rosalie left, and I cleaned up and put things away, checking on Skipper every five or ten minutes. Her pulse remained strong, and her breathing was regular and deep.

When Rosalie returned, I went to the car to help bring in our dinner.

"I made a new casserole called Rice Veracruz. It has ground beef, onions, rice, tomato sauce, black olives, chili powder, cumin, and some other seasonings in it. I hope you like it. I also brought a thermos of hot coffee. The Pyrex dish is cherry cobbler, and I have a salad and some iced tea. You take the food, and I'll take this paper bag of dishes and things," she directed.

We finished eating, and I checked on Skipper. When I jiggled the endotracheal tube, the dog swallowed, so I removed the tube. Skipper lifted her head and gave me a blank stare. I gave her a pat on the head.

~

The next morning, Skipper was banging around her cage, distraught. As soon as I took her out of the cage, she calmed down. I lifted her up so she could stand, but she was clumsy on the splinted legs. She gradually gained her balance, hopped forward two steps, lost her balance, and fell. She struggled to stand, wagging her tail in wide circles when I helped her up.

I carried her into the treatment room and put her on the exam table to check her wounds and give her more antibiotics. When I was done, she resisted my putting her back in the cage.

"Well, I'm sorry, Skipper. I forgot you've probably never been inside a house, never mind a cage."

I carried her out to the barn and left her standing on the concrete walkway while I put some clean straw into one of the box stalls. I called to her, and she hobbled over, went directly into the stall, and lay down on the straw with a contented sigh. I gave her some clean water and half a can of dog food. Still prone, she wolfed down the food and lapped with contentment at the water.

~

Over the next ten days, Skipper progressed remarkably well.

"Well, Skipper, old girl," I said, as I examined the second splint, "everything is dry." I put my nose close to the wound and sniffed. "No infection, you are doing great!" Skipper reached over and licked my face. "OK, OK, enough." She beat a staccato rhythm on the examining room table with her tail.

That evening, I thought a little extra air circulating through the barn would make the dog more comfortable, so I left the barn door open a few inches.

When I arrived the next morning, the stall door was open, and Skipper was gone. I searched throughout the hospital and all around it outside. Then I climbed into my practice truck and extended the search, driving ten miles in the direction of the Joneses' ranch. However, I found no sign of her. Dejected, I went back to the clinic and called the Joneses to tell them what had happened.

"It's OK, Doc; we'll find her. I'll take the pickup and travel the roads to town to look for her," Kathy said.

For the next week, I fought periods of depression. When out on calls, I drove slowly checking both sides of the road. John put an advertisement in the local newspaper, and the radio station did a human-interest story. I talked to a reporter doing a follow-up story.

"We can only hope she's making her way home," I told the reporter. "But with three broken legs, it's going to be very difficult for Skipper. I'm hoping someone will spot her and will call us or the Jones family so we can get her back."

The twelfth morning after Skipper's escape, I was in the office working on case records when the phone rang.

Dick Mathes answered. "It's John Jones," he called out.

My gut rumbled.

"Hi, Doc." The voice on the line was cheerful. "Skipper showed up this morning. She was at the door when I went out to do chores.

She's sorry looking, but the hind leg splint is still on. The casts on her front legs are worn down some, but she seems to move OK. She ate a powerful amount of food. What do you want I should do?"

"John, that's great news. Can you bring her here this afternoon? I'll check her over."

⁓

Skipper stood on the exam table smiling and wagging her rump, sneaking a lick to my face every time I got close enough. Her ribs protruded, but she seemed normal otherwise. John, Kathy, Jenny, and Ferdie all crowded around the table, each with a hand on the dog.

"Well, Jones family, I think we dodged a bullet. She's in great shape, considering what she must have gone through to get all the way home. Everything seems to be healing nicely. I'm going to replace these splints on her front legs, redo the tape on the Thomas splint, and give her a big dose of antibiotic. Bring her back in two weeks, and we'll take X-rays to make certain her bones have healed. She's one amazing dog."

⁓

Being able to help Skipper and her family is one of the reasons I became a veterinarian and the reason I continue to stay connected to it these many decades later. But I am getting ahead of myself. Let me start again . . .

CHAPTER 2:

IN THE BEGINNING

THE HOLSTEIN BULL RAGED in the steel stanchion, two thousand pounds of fury jumping, kicking, pushing, and throwing his head from side to side. The banging and clanging of the stanchion echoed in the barn. The bull's eyeballs bulged, his pupils dilated, and snot spewed from his nostrils. He jerked his head up and to the side ripping the nose tongs from my hand. Dr. Schultz jumped back as the steel tongs flew past, grazing his forehead and knocking off his Cubs baseball cap.

"Damn, Dr. Gross, that was close. Can you grab him and hold him, or should I let Don do it?"

I wasn't making much of an impression on the man I hoped would offer me employment.

There was a six-foot-long rope attached to one handle of the nose tongs. The rope passed through a hole in the other handle. When the rope pulled tight, it was supposed to hold the tongs closed.

I grabbed the tongs and returned to the fray. Wrapping my left arm around the bull's neck, I grasped his lower jaw and pulled my body into his head. He easily lifted my two-hundred-plus pounds off the ground, but I held on while he did his best to shake me off. I replaced the tongs in his nostrils, clamping down hard. I slid my free hand down the rope keeping the tongs closed tight while I wrapped the rope twice around the steel bars on top of the stanchion. Putting all my weight into the effort, I pulled the bull's head back up and to the side.

All we were doing was getting a blood sample for a brucellosis test. Don Gordon and the dairy farm owner had brought the milk cows into the barn and locked them, six at a time, into their stanchions. We had finished the thirty-five cows. The bull was last.

In 1960, veterinary medicine was male dominated and macho. Patients had a monetary value, and nobody expected veterinary care to exceed that value. Chemical restraint of animals was in its infancy. Choices of antibiotics were limited. Clients expected their veterinarian to be tough, wise, skilled, and able to handle any animal, any disease or injury, and any situation. There were no board-certified specialists, and advertising in any form, except for a modest listing in the Yellow Pages of the phone book, was considered malpractice. In my class of sixty students, there were only three women. All but a few of the class came from agricultural backgrounds. Today's veterinary school classes are 75–85 percent women, and almost everyone comes from a suburban background.

The summer of 1959, I was home between my junior and senior year in veterinary school, working for the Agricultural Research Service of the USDA. Most of the work I was doing was on the Navajo reservation in northern Arizona, but I spent weekends at home in Phoenix.

I stood on the front stoop dressed in clean Wrangler jeans, a starched, button-down collar, long-sleeved, light-blue Oxford shirt, the sleeves buttoned, despite the one-hundred-plus Phoenix temperature. I wore flat-healed cowboy boots and my silver Resistol 5X beaver cowboy hat pushed back from my forehead. I was a shade less than six feet three. The back of my shirt was wet. My five-year-old car was not air-conditioned.

I knocked on the door, and Mr. Bockserman answered. A blast of cool air from the swamp cooler running on high speed hit my face. He was about five feet ten, his dark hair cut in a flattop. He wore metal-rimmed glasses and a wrinkled short-sleeved sport shirt. The single pocket of the shirt held two cigars and a ballpoint pen. A curl of smoke rose from the cigar in his mouth, his right eye squeezed partially shut to avoid the smoke. His jaw was square and strong. I saw a small patch of beard he had missed just below his left ear.

"Hello, sir. I'm Dave Gross, here to take Rosalie out."

I extended my right hand. He took it and squeezed. I squeezed back. He smiled and let go.

"Rosie, your date's here. You did tell us he is Jewish, did you not? Come in; we're letting the hot air in."

The house was similar to the one I grew up in, both built soon after the Second World War. We entered directly into the living room. Opposite the front door was an open doorway into the eat-in kitchen. On the wall to the left was another open doorway to a hall, two bedrooms, and a bath.

Mrs. Bockserman came out of the kitchen wiping her hands on her apron. She was pleasingly plump, only a couple of inches shorter than her husband. She pushed stray strands of short gray hair back over both ears and offered me a soft, warm hand. Her smile was conspiratorial.

"I'm happy to meet you at last, Dave. Maxine has talked about you for some time."

It was a setup. Maxine was married to a friend, a student in the class ahead of me in veterinary school. Before marrying Phil, she had worked in the office of an insurance company where Mrs. Bockserman was the executive secretary. After Maxine had met Rosalie, she and Mrs. Bockserman had shifted into matchmaker mode.

"I'm concerned that Rosie is not dating Jewish boys," Mrs. Bockserman had said. "She says none of them are interesting."

"I know someone perfect," Maxine had responded. "He's tall, has dark, curly hair, blue eyes, and was captain of the swimming team in his second year of veterinary school. It's very unusual for anybody to continue to participate in a varsity sport and still make good-enough grades to stay in vet school."

Her mother had kept mentioning me to Rosalie, and Maxine had never missed the opportunity to tease me about the tall, thin, beautiful daughter of her friend.

Both Rosalie and I had finally given in to the incessant prodding and agreed to meet. I had called her and suggested we go out for a Coke. Neither of us had been willing to invest much in that first date.

Maxine had not exaggerated. A vision, five feet seven with long, dark-brown hair almost reaching to the small of her back floated into the room. High arching eyebrows accented wide-set, fawn-like, dark-brown eyes. There was just hint of blush on her cheekbones and wide smile. She came towards me moving like water down a gentle incline. I was mesmerized.

I bet I can span her waist with my hands, I thought.

I was driving a 1954 Oldsmobile, handed down from my dad. We walked to the car, and as I held the door open for her, I noticed the chestnut highlights in her hair. My German shepherd, Mister, was in his usual place in the back seat.

Before I met, Rosalie all the girls I had dated had made a big fuss over Mister, but he mostly ignored them. I held the car door open, and as soon as she sat down, Mister was all over her. She gave him a perfunctory pat on the head, but he would not leave her alone. He kept nuzzling her and pushing his head under her arm. He insisted that she pet him. I twisted in the seat to order him down and noticed he had an erection. The dog was always very discerning.

I drove to the corner, braked the car, and turned. When I accelerated again, something in the accelerator linkage stuck, and the engine started racing. I stomped on the brake with all my weight and managed to keep the car in control. In those days, few major intersections were without a gas station. I swerved into the one on the nearest corner, slammed the transmission into neutral, and turned off the engine.

Rosalie pushed her door open and leaped out. When she was ten feet away, she turned to stare at the car with her mouth open.

I exited the car with as much dignity as I could muster, in the process managing to knock off my hat.

The mechanic on duty unstuck the linkage, and I managed to talk Rosalie back into the car. We sat in a booth at the Carnation on Central Avenue and talked for almost an hour, each nursing a single Coke. Along with a lot of other information, I found out she was finishing a degree in elementary education at Arizona State and commuted from her home to Tempe every day. She had one more semester of class work, plus her student teaching, and would finish the following April.

The next night, we had a real date, went to a movie. We were together every night I was in town for the rest of the summer and wrote to each other every day after I went back to school.

When I came home at winter break, I gave her an engagement ring.

The second Tuesday in March, the secretary of the director of the teaching hospital posted a new three-by-five-inch index card on the bulletin board in the student locker room. Dr. Marcus Schultz, Sidney, Montana, was looking for an associate veterinarian. I called that night and arranged to visit the practice the coming weekend. Mister and I left just before noon Friday and arrived in Sidney eleven hours later, stopping only for gas along the way.

I drove north through town staying on Highway 200. Spotting a park that filled an entire city block and because the night was clear, I decided to save the cost of a motel room. I parked and rolled out my ground cloth, foam pad, and sleeping bag on grass, covered with a thin layer of frost. Mister curled up next to me.

It was dawn when the dog licked my face and well below freezing. A layer of frost covering my sleeping bag and the ground. I retrieved my pants from the bottom of the bag and put them on before emerging, stood on the bag to dress the rest of the way, and then sat on the bag to put my boots on. With Mister in the back seat, we explored the town. Four blocks north of the park, I spotted an open restaurant just off Central Avenue on West Main Street. There was a new Woolworth's store across from it.

The sun, brilliant in the clear sky, warmed the car as I drove slowly north. Most of the commercial buildings appeared to be frame construction from the 1930s, and they looked tired. The railroad tracks were on my right between the town and the river. West of town, the valley rose in undulating hills to bluffs and the high prairie. Occasional fields of spring wheat were green patches in the otherwise brown landscape.

Turning around, I went back through town looking for the Sidney Animal Hospital. I drove south to Fourteenth Street and turned east, following Dr. Schultz's directions. The hospital was set back from the street, and a large, leafless bur oak shielded the gravel parking lot in front.

My stomach rumbled. Mister sat up and cocked his ears.

"Hear that, boy? I am hungry. Let's get some breakfast at that place in town."

It was just past six, and the coffee crowd apparently arrived late on Saturdays. I removed some clean underwear, socks, Wranglers, and a shirt from my duffle bag in the trunk of the car. I was holding them under my arm when I walked into the restaurant.

A middle-aged woman wearing a pink uniform stood behind the sit-down counter. She glanced at the clothes under my arm and smiled. A large nametag announced that her name was Sue.

"Hi, Sue. I'm going to have some breakfast, but I've got a job interview with Dr. Schultz today. Would it be OK if I changed into some clean clothes in your restroom?"

"Sure, honey. You a vet?"

"Yeah, almost. I graduate the first part of June."

"Well, good luck. You'll like Doc Schultz. He's good people. Want coffee?"

"Thanks, yeah. I'll be out in a minute."

"Take your time. I'll wait to pour till I see your baby blues again."

❧

I was waiting in front of the hospital, Mister inspecting the premises, when a panel truck pulled into the lot and parked in front of the double garage. A small, slender man with horn-rimmed glasses got out of the truck, his left foot reaching for the ground. I walked towards him noting a face that matched his body. His gray eyes were taking me in, perhaps a little put off by my size.

"Dr. Schultz? I'm Dave Gross."

We shook hands, his grasp was assuring, welcoming.

"Dr. Gross, glad to meet you. Been here long? You should have rung the bell. Dick Mathes would have let you in. No need to be out in the cold."

"It's not that cold, and the sun is nice. My dog needed to run around some."

Mister came over. Schultz extended the back of his hand and then patted him on the head.

"Beautiful animal. Let's go inside."

Inside the hospital, he led the way to his office taking off his jacket and a Chicago Cubs cap as we walked. He was balding, and a fringe of light-brown hair was hanging over his shirt collar. He motioned me to the chair in front of his desk and sat down on the corner of the desk so he could look down at me.

"Well, Dr. Gross, what questions do you have for me?"

"I'm interested in the history of the mountain man, so I know about Lewis and Clark and the historical importance of the confluence of the Yellowstone and the Missouri and the importance of Fort Union in the fur trade, but that's all I know about this part of the country. What's the livestock industry like?"

"Well, let me say first off that as far as veterinary service this practice is pretty much it for most of Richland County and over into the Badlands in North Dakota. About five thousand people live in Sidney, and about nine or ten thousand in the whole area. The valley is part of the Lower Yellowstone Reclamation Project, started in the early nineteen hundreds."

"Are there any feedlots?" I asked.

"Not many, three I can think of off the top of my head, small operations. Most of the cattle are grass fed and shipped east."

"What about dairy farms?"

"No big ones, but some folks are just starting to get into that business. Most of the ranchers and farmers still keep one or two cows around for their own supply of milk, butter, and such. It's a traditional farm practice with some larger ranches north and west of us. In fact, the first call this morning is to test a dairy herd for brucellosis. You want to ride along?"

"Sure, that's why I'm here."

"Mornin', Doc." A moderately overweight man of average height stood in the doorway. He had a full head of dark hair just starting to gray at the temples and yellowed, uneven teeth.

"Mornin', Dick. Come in. I want you to meet Dr. Gross; he's the man I told you about."

I stood, and we shook hands.

"Couldn't run this outfit without Dick Mathes here," explained Dr. Schultz. "He's my hospital manager. He and his wife live on the premises. He answers the phone, schedules the calls, takes care of any hospitalized animals, and keeps track of the drugs and supplies inventory, all that stuff."

"Well," I said, "I'm happy to meet you, Mr. Mathes."

"Dick," he replied. "Glad to meet you. Hope you'll join us."

The phone rang, and Dick went to the reception desk to answer it. He wrote down some information. Immediately after setting the receiver on the hook, the phone rang again.

"Sounds like you've got a busy day," I remarked.

"All of them are. That's why we need somebody." Schultz was on his feet. "Let me show you around the hospital; then you can come with us. My other man, Don Gordon, should be here soon. Obviously this is the reception and waiting area."

We walked through the sparse examination room and then continued into a combination treatment, pharmacy, and laboratory room. The small animal surgery room was adequate, but there was no gas anesthetic machine.

"No clinical lab or X-ray?" I asked, opening a door to a large empty closet.

Schultz opened a cabinet door and took out an old microscope. "I use this to look at fecal specimens and blood smears. I've been thinking about getting an X-ray machine but haven't done anything about it."

"That closet would make a good darkroom. Is there any plumbing nearby?"

"Yes, as a matter of fact, the restroom is on the other side of the wall there."

A third door from the exam/treatment room led to the large office we had just vacated. The office had three doors—the one into the treatment room, the one that opened directly into the reception area, and the third opened into the garage. We looked into two small animal wards, each housing twenty-five stainless steel cages. Outside each ward was a covered and fenced-in exercise area.

The large animal wing consisted of a treatment and minor surgery room with another direct access to the two-truck garage. There was another large, empty room with a rough concrete floor and a center drain. Dr. Schultz explained that it was for his large-animal surgery. The barn had ten box stalls, a tack room, and a storage loft for hay, straw, and feed. Behind the barn was a working area for cattle with a loading dock, pens, handling chutes, and a squeeze chute.

We finished my tour of the hospital and went back to Dr. Schultz's office. A man, only a couple of inches shorter than I, was waiting for us. He was wiry with long thin arms and legs that I knew would translate to strength and endurance. His face was gaunt, his wispy blond hair cut short. He wore a bright-red plaid flannel shirt and baggy bib overalls.

"This is Don Gordon, my driver and right-hand man. He can teach you more about pulling calves than I can."

We shook hands.

"Pleased to meet you, Dr. Gross. Heard you're from Colorado State and an athlete."

"History," I said. "Finished up my eligibility two years ago."

"You got the truck all restocked and ready to go?" asked Dr. Schultz.

"Yep, all set."

Don drove to the first call, the three of us crowded on the truck's single bench seat, me in the middle. Dr. Schultz provided more information:

"The Lower Yellowstone Irrigation Project came about in 1934 and covers about seventy-five miles along the Yellowstone valley. The farmers with irrigated fields produce mostly corn, beans, and hay with sugar beets their major cash crop. Holly Sugar built their refinery here about 1925, and they control the beet crop allotments. The farmers use non-irrigated land for pasture, and there's quite a bit of dry-land grain farming, mostly wheat. Some of the farmers also grow vegetables, lots of different varieties of potatoes, fruits, and berries, and quite a bit of hay, mostly alfalfa."

"What's your average call distance? Lots of driving?"

"Depends. Some days we don't get more than three to five miles from the hospital; others I may go as far as forty or fifty one way."

After finally drawing blood from the bull, we spent the rest of the morning on an assortment of routine calls. While we were out, Dick Mathes was in contact over the mobile radio adding more calls to the list. It was almost two in the afternoon when we stopped at the Sidney Bowling Center for lunch. Dr. Schultz introduced me to Mrs. Kappel, who was in charge of the restaurant. I learned she worked for a group of five local businessmen who had recently purchased the whole operation.

During lunch, Don told me that his oldest son was the point guard on the high school basketball team that had won their fourth consecutive state Class A basketball championship the previous week. Later that afternoon, I found out that both Dr. Schultz and Don were Lutherans, although Dr. Schultz had been raised Catholic. Neither blinked nor seemed to care when I told them I was Jewish. I learned early in life to let people know I was Jewish as soon as possible. It forestalled the embarrassment of an unguarded bigot moment.

Dr. Schultz and his wife had four children, two boys, eleven and eight, and two girls, nine and six. Don had two sons, the basketball player was sixteen, and the other son, more interested in baseball, had just turned thirteen.

Dr. Schultz had a few questions for me, most of them regarding the cases we had seen that day and how I would handle them. He seemed satisfied with my answers.

We got back to the hospital well after dark having driven over two hundred miles that day.

"Do you work like this every Saturday?" I asked.

"Most every day; Sundays are usually a little slower. I'm wearing out."

"I imagine so," I said.

"So, when can you get here?"

I had passed muster.

"Well, graduation is June 4, but I'm getting married on April 23, and we won't have time for a honeymoon. I'm flying home to Phoenix on the Friday night, we'll be married Saturday night, and I have to be back in school Monday morning. I promised Rosalie that we would combine a honeymoon and camping trip before I report to a job."

"How long?" Schultz asked.

"Mid-June?" I responded.

"If you can be here by June 9, you've got a job."

I smiled. "What's the salary?"

"Five hundred a month," he smiled.

That was about average for the deals my classmates were making.

"That sounds OK," I replied, "but only for a fifty-hour week. I'm here to gain as much experience as I can as fast as I can, but after I've put in two hundred hours in a month, I want 40 percent of what I bill for the rest of the month."

He scowled, then took a long look at me, and smiled again. "You are Jewish. I like it. You'll be anxious to get in lots of hours and work your butt off."

He stuck his hand out. I took it.

"Deal," he said.

"Deal," I replied.

"No need for you to sleep on the ground tonight. I told Dick to pay for a room at the motel on the corner off Central." He reached into his right rear pocket, took out his wallet, and handed me a twenty. "Here's something for dinner and gas. I remember being a poor student, maybe a little too well."

"Thanks, I appreciate it, but it isn't necessary. I didn't expect it."

"I know you didn't, but it will make me feel better. I should have you to the house for dinner, but I'm certain my wife didn't wait for us. You take it easy driving back. We need you here. June 9."

"June 9."

Chapter 3:
On the Road

THE SUN HUNG JUST WEST of overhead. Steep canyon walls, and even steeper cuts leading into the canyon, cast short shadows. Aspens shimmered in the occasional breeze. Watched by a red-tailed hawk riding the warm updrafts, our two-door, 1957 Ford Fairlane, a wedding gift from my parents, glided through the switchbacks, the V-8 engine rumbling. We were climbing, heading north on Highway 287, the Cache la Poudre River rushing down the canyon on our left, Fort Collins disappearing in the rearview mirror.

The luggage rack affixed to the top of the car was piled high with camping gear. The trunk held four suitcases full of our clean clothing, competing for available space with cardboard boxes containing our wedding gifts and accumulated household items. The trunk lid closed only after I bounced on it.

More boxes filled the floor in back, stacked level with the coats and small boxes on the back seat. Soiled clothing in pillowcases filled corners and spaces. A tattered canvas tarp covered everything in back. Mister, all 105 pounds of black and silver German shepherd, was perched on the tarp enjoying being able to see out of the car while resting his head on his paws.

I had graduated the previous week. Rosalie, my bride of forty-two days, and I were headed to Sidney, Montana.

A three-quarter-ton Chevy pickup suddenly appeared around the curve. A wood stock rack, extending high above the cab, tilted drunkenly as the truck encroached on our lane. I slammed my foot on the brake pedal. The Ford fishtailed drifting left towards the canyon. The truck hesitated and then swerved towards the middle of the road. I abandoned the brake and jammed my foot on the accelerator, aiming the car as close to the edge of the left lane as possible. Metal screeched as the two vehicles touched and then parted. Separated by fifty feet, we pulled back into our rightful lanes and glided softly onto the gravel shoulders.

I reached over, pulling Rosalie close. "Are you all right?"

She tucked her head under my chin and murmured into my shirt, "I think so. . . . Yes . . . yes, I guess I'm OK. . . . I'm shaking!"

"Will you be OK if I let go so I can check on the guy in the pickup? You're certain you're OK?"

She nodded her head. "Go ahead; I'm fine." She let go of me, wrapping her arms around herself.

The other driver and I both exited our vehicles. "You OK?" I called.

"Yeah. . . . How about you folks?"

"We're good; nice driving. Sure glad you decided to switch lanes with me!"

The cowboy removed his sweat-stained, wide-brimmed Resistol with his left hand and wiped his forehead with the sleeve on the same arm. "I think we all got off pretty damned lucky this time. Any damage to your car?"

I walked around to the passenger side and checked a scrape with my finger.

"Just a little paint scraped, nothing serious. How about your truck?"

"Hell, it's so beat up I wouldn't know which dent is new."

We each waved an arm and returned to our vehicles. I settled again into the driver's seat and then pulled Rosalie close.

"You're OK?"

"I'm fine. What on earth was that guy doing? He was in our lane." Now she was angry.

"The road's narrow, his truck is top heavy with that stock rack, and we were both probably going a little too fast. I'm slowing down."

I started the Ford, checked carefully for other vehicles in both directions, and pulled back onto the highway.

Rosalie decided to swallow her anger.

"So, Dr. Gross, tell me again how much fun I am going to have on my first-ever camping trip."

Mister sat up and licked the back of her neck.

She pushed him away and twisted to face the back seat. "Well, what do you think, Mister? Do you want to go camping?"

The dog jumped to his feet, his tail wagging furiously.

～

The highway switched back and forth steadily upward, the big V-8 growling contentedly. We were driving in Wyoming's Medicine Bow range. We reached the pass, 8,500 feet above sea level, and stopped at a sign identifying the state campground I was looking for.

The sign was frail, weather beaten, but the rutted gravel road leading off to the north appeared reasonably dry and passable. I drove slowly and carefully for two miles in deep ruts. The oil pan scraped twice on the center mound before we reached the campground.

A clear mountain stream rippled its way along the north side of the narrow mountain meadow, gently meandering west to east. Across the stream, a precipitous, rocky cliff initiated the first of many rises leading, pyramid-like, to the snow-covered pinnacle of Medicine Bow Peak. The pristine campground was freckled with a dozen weathered picnic tables, benches attached. An equal number of rusting, dented, fifty-five-gallon oil drums, refuse receptacles, stood near the tables.

I stopped the car.

Rosalie, still sitting in the middle of the front seat, slid closer. She whispered, "Oh, Dave, it is absolutely beautiful! It's like a picture postcard."

"I'll pick a spot, get the tent up, and start dinner before it gets dark," I said.

We were a long way from any other campgrounds. I was anxious to get a camp set up before Rosalie noticed there were no outhouses. Reaching back into the car, I retrieved the most recent of my letterman's jackets. I shook off most of the dog hair and put it on. Mister was out of the car tracking back and forth across the meadow, nose close to the ground.

Choosing a flat spot near one of the better picnic tables, about ten yards from the stream, I started the engine to move the car, and Mister followed on a dead run with a worried expression on his face.

A curve-handled pump, sky-blue paint peeling, stood on a concrete slab about twenty yards south of the site. A small cluster of evergreens and aspens grew proudly ten yards north. Rosalie had not yet noticed the lack of sanitary facilities.

I'd worked diligently to convince my city-raised bride that camping out would be an inexpensive yet wonderful honeymoon experience. The clincher was that I had promised to see to her every creature need. She warned me that she intended to make the most of that promise.

I retrieved my families' old canvas umbrella tent, smelling of campfire smoke and pine needles, off the luggage rack, staked it out, put up the poles, raised it, and laid an extra ground cloth over the floor. Next, I rolled out and blew up an air mattress, laid a foam pad over it for Rosalie and another foam pad directly on the ground cloth for myself. Our sleeping arrangements were complete when I rolled out our two bags, one borrowed from my brother.

I rebuilt the loose-rock fireplace, scattered by previous campers. All the wood on the ground was soggy, so I collected a large stack of dead lower branches from nearby trees and started a fire. The sun dipped behind distant western peaks, but the fire was roaring, and the camp well organized. Rosalie sat facing out on one of the table's benches, hugging herself, and watching me work.

The dog shifted his attention to the stream and its near bank. Black mud reached halfway up his legs.

"I'll get him cleaned up," I murmured.

I walked to the well and tried the pump. After several minutes of futile effort, I decided the leathers were dried out and the pump wasn't going to work. It needed more attention than I was prepared to give.

"I'll wipe him off with a towel before we get into the tent," I told Rosalie.

One of my veterinary instrument purchases was a two-gallon stainless steel bucket, perfect for dipping water out of the stream. I filled it halfway and set it on one corner of the picnic table next to the Coleman stove. Opening our ice chest, I took out a large, inch-thick T-bone and a package, triple wrapped in aluminum foil, containing two parboiled potatoes, four parboiled carrots, a raw onion, and a handful of raw cauliflower. I placed a large, blue enamel coffee pot full of water on the Coleman stove. After the campfire burned down, I situated the foil pack of vegetables amongst the coals and rebuilt the fire. When the fire burned down again, I arranged a small wire grill over the coals, rubbed the steak with onion salt and coarsely ground black pepper, and put it on the grill.

The water boiled, and the steak was well done. We sat across from each other, and I served Rosalie the eye of the T-bone and some of the steaming vegetables from the foil package. We ate in gathering darkness.

Halfway through our meal, the campfire, built up a third time, faded to embers. Sparks drifted into the low-hanging clouds.

After we finished eating, I stripped the steak bone of all fat and meat and dumped that and Rosalie's leftovers into Mister's dish, adding two handfuls of kibble. The dog pushed the quickly emptied bowl over the ground with his tongue, licking it spotless.

Rosalie consumed three cups of tea trying to stay warm.

"OK, where do I go to the toilet?"

I took out a GI folding shovel and fixed the blade at a right angle to the handle. "You use it like this," I demonstrated, "to scrape out a hole. Then you squat over the hole. You need to tuck the TP inside your coat so it doesn't fall on the ground and get wet."

As my demonstration progressed, so did her frown.

I took her, unyielding, into my arms and rubbed the small of her back. "It's OK. It's not that bad. Indoor plumbing is a recent development. Outhouses are just a step above a hole in the ground."

She glared at me, remained stiff-backed, silent. I took the roll of toilet paper gently from her hands, tucked it in the front of my jacket, took the shovel under my arm, a flashlight in one hand, her hand in the other, and led her off into the nearby thicket.

Rosalie stood silently while I dug a shallow hole. I handed her the roll of TP and the flashlight.

"Call me when you're done. Come on, Mister."

After a few minutes, she returned, lips clenched. She retrieved her overnight case from the car and ducked into the tent.

"Do you want the Coleman lantern inside the tent?"

She nodded, her lips clamped tight. A single tear coursed down her left cheek.

I held my tongue between my teeth.

The wind, smelling of rain, kicked up and dropped the temperature another few degrees. I built up the campfire, then found a fair-sized log, manhandled it close to the fire, and laid the empty tent bag over it.

"Come on out, honey. It's not all that bad, is it? Come sit here. The fire's warm. I'll make certain all the rest of the places we stop at have restrooms, I promise. This is a state campground, not a national. It didn't occur to me that they wouldn't have at least an outhouse. Come on; don't pout."

She joined me on the log. We sat side by side staring at the fire. Mister sat and stared at us, his head tilted to one side. After a few minutes of strained silence, the dog nuzzled under Rosalie's free arm until she was hugging his head while he licked her cheek. She smiled, patted him on the head, and rubbed his ears. He rested his head on her knee. She continued to rub his ears while the dog gazed at her.

I was desperate to start a conversation.

"I sure wish I was able to zip our sleeping bags together. The damn zippers don't mesh."

"Do you ever think about anything else?" She feigned exasperation.

"You're giving me the business, right?"

"What do you think?" she said.

"Yeah, I think you're giving me the business. You're still pissed because you had to pee in the woods."

Mister stuck his nose under her coat and pushed aside her sweater.

"Yeeoh!" she shrieked jumping onto my lap, her arms around my neck. "His nose is freezing!"

"Yeah, it took me months to train him to do that."

⁓

Sleet pounded the tent while we dozed. The ground was hard and damp. Even with the foam pads, it was a long, uncomfortable night. The tent didn't leak, despite its age, but the dampness permeated. Light filtered weakly into the tent as we awoke, face to face.

"Good morning," mumbled Rosalie. "Are you awake? I didn't sleep at all."

I reached an arm out of my sleeping bag stroking her face with the knuckle of my right index finger. "Sure you did. I woke up several times during the night, and you were sound asleep each time. I'm getting up. I've got to pee."

"Me too, but I don't know if I can squat over a shallow hole in the ground."

When Rosalie returned from the thicket, I filled our cast-iron skillet with thick-cut bacon, fired up the Coleman stove, and started breakfast.

We finished, and she smacked her lips appreciatively and then took my hand.

"Well, big guy, that was very good. Let's take a little walk before you pack everything up and I have to sit in the car again."

Mister ran ahead, stopping to check on our progress every few minutes. We walked, holding hands, downstream about two hundred yards to a large sign I had not bothered to read the night before.

As we approached, I said, "It probably just identifies the campground with instructions about how to avoid starting forest fires and what to do with your garbage, that kind of stuff."

We found a skull-and-crossbones announcement. Bold lettering proclaimed:

NOTICE TO ALL CAMPERS. WATER FROM
THIS CAMPGROUND, INCLUDING THE
STREAM, IS CONTAMINATED. UNDER NO
CIRCUMSTANCES SHOULD WATER FROM
THE STREAM, OR FROM THE WELL,
BE USED FOR DRINKING!

Rosalie looked at me and shook her head.

"Well, Doctor, how bad is this? What do you suppose the water is contaminated with? Are we going to be sick? Why on earth didn't you see this last night?"

I tried to calm her. "Look at the notice. It's probably been there since last summer. The stream is full of ice melt and probably pure by now. In any case, we boiled all the water we used, so it's not very likely we'll get anything."

Her look told me she wasn't buying what I was selling.

We walked back.

Rosalie retrieved her makeup case and climbed into the front seat of the car. Before she closed the door, she inquired. "Will it be possible to pack up and leave as soon as possible? I would really appreciate finding a gas station or restaurant with a real toilet and running water, preferably hot, and, oh yes, safe to drink. I think I can feel an acute attack of diarrhea coming on already." She closed the car door more firmly than necessary.

We got back to the highway and drove to Saratoga where we found a combination gas station, sporting goods store, and restaurant. We went into the restaurant while a pimple-faced teenager filled the car with gas and checked the oil and tires. I ordered coffee while Rosalie rushed to the ladies' room. The teenager came inside, and I paid for the gas and then moved the car out of the way. Rosalie joined me in the booth, her hair in a long ponytail, but she was not smiling. I figured the restroom had to be gruesome, considering the condition of the men's room I had visited between my second and third cups of coffee.

Back in the car, she ranted. "Well, that ranks as the fifth worse experience in my entire life, and the other four also involved gas-station restrooms! Peeing in the woods was bad, but at least it wasn't so filthy I had to avoid touching anything!"

I said nothing.

We drove over Togwotee Pass arriving at the campgrounds at Coulter Bay on Jackson Lake in Grand Teton National Park. Rosalie went to check out the restrooms. She returned gushing.

"They are clean, very elaborate, flush toilets, hot showers, and ceramic tile. I can deal with this kind of camping!"

After spending another rainy night at Jackson Lake, we only had two days to experience Yellowstone Park. Stopping briefly at the South Entrance, we grabbed a handful of pamphlets, a map of the park, and continued in the rain. As we drove, I lectured Rosalie on the history of the Corps of Discovery, the fur industry in the northwest of the early 1800s, and especially of the Sidney area where the Yellowstone River joins the Missouri.

Rosalie smiled stifling a yawn with her hand.

"What . . . why are you smiling like that?"

"You are so sexy when you wax eloquent about the history stuff," she teased pushing up the short hair on the back of my neck.

We drove on, stopping at the various points of interest for a few minutes each until we reached an empty Madison Junction campground at the north end of Madison Valley. The main road into the campground branched into multiple loops with well-sited camping areas, looking south down a narrow, flat flood plain, covered with brilliant green grass and budding wild flowers. I set up camp while Rosalie and Mister checked out the facilities.

"Well, it's barely adequate compared to Jackson Hole—no tile, no hot water, no flush toilets—but the privies are clean and only about a hundred yards up this gravel road." She motioned with her head. "There's a pump near the outhouses, and I pumped it," she reported, "and water came out."

"Outstanding!"

"Yeah," she smirked, "and there were no signs warning of contamination; I checked carefully."

"You're just not going to give me a pass on that, huh?"

"Not for a very long time."

"Well," I said, changing the subject, "tonight's menu calls for chili."

I put bacon into a pot. When the bacon was crispy, I dumped a chopped whole onion into the grease and then cubes of round steak seasoned with garlic salt and coarse ground black pepper. After the beef browned, I added half of a disarticulated chicken. Once the chicken browned, I added what was left of the Coors I had been sipping and opened another. "You want one?" I offered, extending the can.

Rosalie took it, sipped, and made a face, handing it back. "I don't understand how you can drink that stuff."

I grinned. "Drinking the beer is the most important part of my recipe."

She watched, chin resting on her hands, elbows on the table, as I finished putting in the spices and vegetable ingredients.

"This is best if it simmers for at least two or three hours, but we probably didn't start early enough for that. Are you starving, or can you wait an hour or so?"

"Oh, I suppose I'll survive for an hour," she laughed.

A car with New Jersey plates pulling a pop-up camper drove up and stopped, a young man behind the wheel. A girl in her late teens sat in the middle of the front seat. The young man rolled down his window.

"Hi, any bears here?"

"We haven't seen any here, but there are supposed to be plenty of them around," answered Rosalie.

The young man looked around nervously and then spotted Mister. The dog, as was his custom, positioned himself between Rosalie and anyone he didn't know.

"Look at the beautiful German shepherd, Caroline. He's huge. Is he afraid of bears?"

"Nope," I replied.

Mister kept his eyes on the couple as they conducted a whispered conversation. The rest of the campground was empty, but they pulled into the campsite next to ours. Leaving the trailer hooked to the car, the young man raised the top of the camper, and the couple climbed inside.

We went for a long walk. After we returned, I wandered over to the garbage pit. "Look, honey, the garbage pit has this heavy, latched steel lid, designed to keep the bears out. You have to release this latch with one foot and then step on this pedal with your other foot to operate the lid."

"Aren't you hungry?" asked Rosalie. She pulled out the dishes and silverware, setting the table. "I'm starving. The chili smells wonderful!"

I served each of us a large bowlful. "Perfect," I declared, "picante but not enough to mask the flavor."

"For you," she laughed, waving her hand in front of her mouth, taking a large gulp of water, "but it is good." She took another spoonful.

There was still chili left when we declared ourselves full.

"Should we try to save it?" I asked.

"I don't think so. We have plenty of food with us. What would you put it in?"

"Well, it seems a shame to toss it." Nevertheless, I walked to the garbage pit, scraped the contents of the pot into the pit, and let the lid slam shut.

Clouds masked the stars, the moon not yet up. I lit the lantern. We played gin rummy sitting across from each other. While I was dealing out another hand, Rosalie thumbed through one of the pamphlets we had collected.

"Now look at this," she said holding up a pamphlet and tapping it with her right index finger.

SPICY FOODS ATTRACT BEARS. DO NOT PUT SPICY FOODS IN GARBAGE BINS.

"Oops . . . too late now," I blushed, shrugging.

It was half-past eight, but we were already yawning.

"It might be warm enough to open up the sleeping bags," I suggested.

"Might be," she smiled back.

Mister and I waited at the pump while Rosalie used one of the privies. After she came out, I pumped water while she brushed her teeth. I filled the stainless steel bucket halfway with water, carried it back, and put it on the Coleman stove to warm. Once it was heated, I poured some of the water into a dishpan and left Rosalie in the tent with it, the lantern, Mister, and her overnight case.

Throwing a clean towel over my shoulder, I made my way back to the privies, my shirt unbuttoned, the laces on my hiking boots untied, my kit with shaving gear, toothbrush, toothpaste, and soap under my arm. For an unknown but perhaps prescient reason, I also took the ax thinking to get more firewood on my way back.

After using the outhouse, I stood at the water pump, brushing my teeth. There was a loud metallic clang, as a garbage pit lid was ripped open. Rosalie screamed, and Mister erupted into furious, angry barking. I grabbed the ax and ran down the gravel road, toothbrush clenched between my teeth, toothpaste foaming out of my mouth. The towel flew off my shoulder. My toes grabbed frantically to keep my unlaced boots on as I ran. I saw Mister's silhouette, clawing at the tent flap.

A small black bear was standing over the garbage pit. Through the fabric of the tent, back-lit by the lantern, I saw Rosalie. She was screaming at Mister while trying to hold him back. The bear looked over its shoulder as it reached down into the garbage bin for more of my famous chili. I spat out the toothbrush and started shouting. "GET OUT! TAKE OFF! YEEOUH!"

I squatted down and unzipped the tent flap that was starting to tear from Mister's attack. "Let him loose, honey. It's just a small bear."

I grabbed the dog's collar as he lunged through the opening. The two of us now faced the bear, the dog growling.

"GO ON! GET OUT! SCRAM!"

The bear moved to face us, nonchalantly watching us directly instead of over his shoulder. He continued to fish out and eat the chili. When finished, he turned, glanced over his shoulder, and then strolled away, unconcerned by antics of man or dog.

As soon as the bear departed, the young couple erupted from their camper. The girl quickly unlocked the car door and climbed in, locking the door behind her. The young man scurried around the camper, got it folded back down, ran to the car, and knocked on the window, looking in all directions for the long-gone bear. The girl unlocked the door, and he jumped in locking the door. Gravel spewed as they swiveled down the road and out of the campground.

Rosalie came out of the tent and stood next to me hugging me around the waist with her left arm and patting Mister with her right hand.

"My hero and my hero," she murmured.

"However, you, husband, need considerable work on reading warnings. My God, for an experienced camper, you don't seem very aware of dangers!"

"OK, I get it. You and Mister better come with me while I retrieve my stuff. Do you see my toothbrush anywhere? Did you see those two make tracks out of here?"

Rosalie started laughing. "I just had a mental snapshot of you galloping down the road with your hiking shoes unlaced, your toothbrush in your mouth, your mouth foaming, your shirt flapping, and waving an ax. No wonder those two took off. They weren't afraid of bears; it was the madman they were escaping from!"

It proved warm enough to open the sleeping bags and continue our honeymoon. I intended to hug Rosalie all night, but after ten minutes, my arm fell asleep, my shoulder started to hurt, and I had to extricate my tingling arm. She spooned close, smiling in her sleep. Rain again pounded the tent.

Chapter 4:
The Sidney Animal Hospital

WHEN WE ARRIVED IN SIDNEY, Dr. Schultz was out on calls, but Dick Mathes had some news.

"I checked on furnished apartments for you to rent, but there's not much to choose from." He handed me a list of five rental property owners with their phone numbers. "Doc Schultz says you should spend the day finding a place to live and get moved in. He'll meet you here tomorrow morning at eight."

I used the phone in the office to contact the people on the list. Then Rosalie and I went around to have a look. The first place was an old motel. The advertised two-bedroom apartment consisted of adjoining rooms with two tiny kitchenettes and two less-than-stellar bathrooms. The second place was in an old fourplex featuring plumbing from the thirties. The third landlady informed us she didn't allow pets.

The fourth place was a two-bedroom basement apartment under a small, white frame house. The entrance to the apartment was through an outside door one step down onto a small landing. To the right from the landing and up two steps was a door.

"Where does that door go?" asked Rosalie.

"That opens into the kitchen of the upstairs apartment," the owner answered.

Down fifteen steep stairs from the entrance was a landing, three-feet square. The owner opened the door with Rosalie standing on the first step up and me, stranded several steps higher, my head bent forward and pressed against the ceiling of the stairwell. The door opened directly into a combined living room/dining room sparsely furnished with a well-used sofa, a round oak pedestal table, and four wood kitchen chairs, unfinished.

The landlady stayed in the main room while Rosalie and I inspected the place.

"All the windows are above my head," I murmured.

"Yeah, dark and gloomy." Rosalie smiled and faked shivering.

There were base cabinets and counters against two walls of the kitchen, a pantry under the stairwell, an apartment-sized gas stove, an old refrigerator, and a stained enamel sink.

"There's something weird about the kitchen," I whispered. "What is it?"

"There aren't any cabinets on the walls over the counters," Rosalie whispered back.

The bedrooms each sported a small closet, a single chest of drawers, and a sagging double bed, with open springs and cotton mattresses. I sat on each of the beds and bounced. They both protested with a horrific screech.

The bathroom separated the two bedrooms. I flushed the toilet, ran water in the tub through the showerhead, and opened both the hot and cold water into the sink.

"They drain OK; that's something."

"Two other couples have seen the place today. If you're interested you need to make up your minds," the owner told us. "The dog is OK; he seems well behaved, but I'll need a fifty-dollar deposit to cover any damage he might cause."

The fifth place was another basement apartment that looked to be thirty or forty years beyond its prime. We called and hurried back to the one place that was habitable and gave our new landlady a check for two hundred dollars, the first and last month's rent and the dog deposit.

We spent the first night in our new home trying to sleep with me wedged between the headboard and the footboard. My bulk depressed my side of the bed raising Rosalie who slid into me. I tried hugging her, my front to her back. Ten minutes passed.

"You're crushing me," she complained

I rolled onto my back. "Here lay your head on my shoulder."

She did and I hugged her with my left arm. After five minutes, I told her, "My arm and shoulder are asleep. This is impossible!"

We switched sides of the bed, but it didn't make any difference. We both finally lapsed into fitful sleep, each hugging our edge of the mattress.

"We could each use one of the beds," suggested Rosalie over breakfast.

"No way."

"But we can't afford to buy a decent bed."

"I have a solution," I said.

~

After breakfast, Rosalie delivered me to the Sidney Animal Hospital. It was ten till eight.

"Knock 'em dead, big guy." She kissed me. "Give me a call so I'll know when to expect you for dinner."

Inside, Dr. Schultz greeted me. "Good morning, Dave. Glad you made it!" He, Don, and Dick were waiting for me. Schultz stuck out his hand. "We've been counting the days until your arrival."

I shook his hand. The slightly built, balding veterinarian seemed genuinely pleased to see me again.

"You saw Dick yesterday. You remember Don Gordon?"

I shook hands with both Dick and Don.

"Don and I have several calls to make this morning, so I'm going to leave you with Dick. He'll show you around the place again and get you familiar with what's going on in the practice. If anybody comes in with a dog or cat, feel free to take care of it. You OK with that?"

"Sure, whatever you think is best."

I watched Don drive off, Schultz in the passenger seat writing something.

"Well, we can start here in the reception area," Dick said. "I used to own this property. Did you know that?"

"No, I did not."

"I had a boarding kennel with a pet shop and grooming business before Doc moved here. I used to vaccinate dogs and cats, castrated some tomcats, and even spayed an occasional dog. If something came in seriously sick, I put 'em to sleep. Mrs. Schultz's old man gave me a damn good price for this property, tore everything down, and built this place. As part of the deal, I got the job as office manager. The pet supplies and pet food business we do here is still mine, along with whatever dog grooming comes along. They also built a nice two-bedroom apartment attached to the building through that door behind the reception desk. My wife and I get the apartment rent-free."

"I wondered where that door went."

We walked through the combination examination and treatment room and then into the surgery.

"It's as I remembered," I observed.

We went from the exam/treatment room into the large room, now equipped as a pharmacy/clinical laboratory/X-ray room.

"Remember this?" asked Dick opening the door to the closet. It was painted black and fully equipped as a darkroom with a red blackout light in the ceiling fixture. "Since you were here, Doc brought in another desk and chair so you can share the office."

"I saw that when I made the phone calls to landlords yesterday. It's nice."

We poked heads into each of the two small animal wards. There was a dog in one of the cages. I walked over, sticking my fingers through the cage door. The black, shaggy-haired mutt inside licked them, wagging an overly long tail.

"What's the deal with this guy?"

"Tapeworms. I treated him last night. They're supposed to come and pick him up this morning."

Back in the multipurpose room, Dick continued the tour. "Doc said you sent him a list of the new equipment you thought we needed, including the X-ray machine, so he bought this new Picker 100 MA machine, nice, huh? The rep unpacked and put it together last week. He set up the new darkroom equipment as well."

I walked to the machine and turned it on, playing with the settings.

"This is really nice, Dick. Just as good as what we had at school. This will do very nicely."

"We also got all the equipment for the clinical path laboratory you wanted, including that fancy new microscope." He pointed to the microscope covered with a plastic globe, standing on one of the counters with a laboratory stool handy.

"None of us have had the time to figure out how to operate the X-ray machine or to learn to develop radiographs. Suppose that'll be up to you. Doc has done some fecal exams and red and white blood cell counts with the lab stuff, but most of the rest is still in those boxes over there in the corner."

We went quickly through the large animal wing. A milk cow lay quietly in one of the box stalls.

"She prolapsed after calving. They brought her in, and Doc fixed her up yesterday; should go home tomorrow."

Out in back, I examined the pens and holding chutes and found all the gate hinges were well oiled and in good working condition. While playing with the levers on the squeeze chute, I asked, "So, what's the story with Don?"

"Doc hired Don soon after he and his family moved here. Three generations of Don's family have been helping their neighbors— pulling calves, replacing prolapsed uteruses, castrating calves and horses, and vaccinating livestock. Don and his wife live with their boys on a 120-acre farm just west of town. He has about twenty head of beef cattle grazing on ground no good for anything but pasture and raises alfalfa hay, sugar beets, barley, and oats on the sixty, or so, irrigated acres."

"So Dr. Schultz hired you two quacks, and he didn't have to file charges for practicing veterinary medicine without a license against you. A win-win situation." I smiled to show him I was teasing.

Dick looked at me hard and then smiled his acknowledgement, or perhaps his intent to get even at first opportunity. "Doc's deal with Don is that he gets a steady-paying job as Doc's assistant but he can't do any veterinary work on his own. He drives, assists with the large animals, and keeps the truck stocked. He gives me a list of drugs and supplies as they use them so I can reorder. I'm happy enough with my deal.

"Doc's plenty smart and a good vet, but you need to know that his wife is the real boss. My office manager title doesn't mean much. Living right here only means my wife or I am here most of the time to answer the phone. I mostly schedule calls, run my pet shop business, look after the hospitalized animals, and clean the kennels. Don takes care of the barn and pens. Mrs. Schultz runs all the business aspects of the practice. She does the billing, keeps the books, and writes all the checks. Her family never allows anything to intervene between themselves and control of the money."

I stopped, turning to face Dick.

"I just thought you should be aware of the situation. Things get a little testy between Doc and the missus sometimes. He tends to spend more time here or on calls than he does at home, and she nags him about it but complains when the practice is slow and he's not bringing home the bucks. She was never much to look at. Her major attribute is that her old man owns just about everything worth owning in town, the bank, the grain elevators, the lumberyard, and lots of commercial real estate. The old man wanted her close so he built this place."

"So, are you from here, Dick? Raised here?"

"Oh yeah, born right here in Sidney. My folks had a small place just south of town. Went all through school here, graduated from the high school in thirty-seven. Worked at the drug store until the war started and then ended up in the quartermaster corps; never even got overseas, thank goodness. Doc was in France and Germany; never talks about it. When the war ended, I came back here. I knew my wife Barbara from high school. Her folks moved here from Glendive when we were both in eighth grade. During the war, her family moved back to Glendive, and when I got back, I looked her up, and things kinda progressed from there."

"You have children, any family here?"

"No kids; just never happened. My folks are both getting older, and I got a kid brother. He and his family live out in Bozeman. He's a miner. You come from a big family?"

"Not really. My mom and dad, a younger brother and sister, all of them still live in Phoenix."

"Well, you'll find the weather here a lot different from Arizona."

"Expect I will, but not that much different from Colorado. I spent six years there going to school."

"Well, it might be a lot different out working in it, compared to going to school in it."

～

On the way home after my first day, I stopped at the lumberyard and bought some two-by-fours and two sheets of three-quarter-inch plywood. That evening, I built a raised platform five by six feet. I carried the mattress from the other bedroom and placed both mattresses on the platform. The result was a high, not so elegant, but firm and sturdy bed that remained silent when we got on it. I slept with my feet and ankles hanging over the end, but we didn't roll into each other.

The next two days I spent getting the X-ray machine, clinical pathology lab, and darkroom equipment all functioning properly. I wrote down the fee schedule that Dick Mathes dictated and studied a map learning how to find the major clients. Dr. Schultz allocated his two-year-old panel truck to me after taking delivery on a new truck for himself.

CHAPTER 5:

WILD HORSES

Four weeks after Skipper was pronounced fit, I pulled into the hospital garage. The Joneses' pickup, still covered with the same dried mud but fresh dust, pulled in behind me. The whole Jones family, including Skipper, was stuffed into the cab. John jumped out, smiling, extending a callused hand.

"Hi, Doc. You doin' OK?"

"Yeah, John, you bet. How's Skipper doing?"

"Oh, she's great, hardly limps, running all over the ranch, almost as good as new. We really appreciate what you did for her. Here's the hundred we owe you." He handed me two fifties.

"Listen, our place neighbors the Simpson brothers' ranches. You've heard of 'em?

I nodded that I had.

"When they heard about Skipper, they each chipped in fifty bucks for the pick of her first litter. They're also my partners in a horse deal. We've rounded up some wild mustangs that need cutting. We'd like you to come out to the place and take care of it for us, providing, of course, you're up to it." He grinned.

I ignored the challenge and walked to the pickup.

"Hi, Kathy. Ferdie, how're you doin'? Jenny, you're more beautiful every time I see you."

The little girl scrunched down to hide behind her mother. I patted Skipper on the head, received the expected tail wag, and turned back to the rancher.

"OK, John, I'll level with you. I'm not apprehensive about castrating wild horses. The problem is restraining them."

"Not a problem, Doc. We've got plenty of experience. We'll take care of restraint; all you have to do is cut 'em."

Everyone in the community knew Ted and Ed Simpson—professional rodeo cowboys, world-champion saddle bronc, bareback bronc, and bull riders. For the past four years, they had taken turns being champion in one or more of the three riding events, and the previous year Ted had won the All-Around World Championship of the Rodeo Cowboy's Association.

The free-range public lands constituting most of the North Dakota Badlands were home to feral horses. Badlands ranchers harvested the wild horses because of their value as saddle horses, rodeo stock, or dog food. More important to the ranchers, any grass the horses didn't consume was available for their cattle. All the privately held lands were originally 160-acre homesteads, and most of the ranches were able to sustain only a hundred or so cows. The ranchers survived only if they could find extra income.

"OK, John, when is this rodeo scheduled to happen?"

"Dick and I already set it up for tomorrow morning. He thought you'd go for it. We'll expect you at our place for breakfast, about six thirty."

Dick is getting even already, I thought.

He drew a quick map on a scrap of paper and then jumped into his pickup, squeezing his family against the passenger side door. They all waved as he sped out, spraying gravel. Skipper waved her tail.

⌒

I drove east from Sidney, across the Yellowstone, and into McKensie County, North Dakota. Continuing through Cartwright, I passed a combination grocery and gas station, the school, where church services were conducted on Sundays, two frame houses, and a mobile home. Five miles later, I glanced at Jones's map taking the road indicated. After fifteen miles of washboard dirt road, I arrived at a rusted mailbox, peppered with bullet holes. The mailbox sat on top of the corner post of a three-strand barbed wire fence. There was no name or number on the box. I turned in, rattled over the cattle guard, and followed the deep tracks that served as a road. The ranch buildings came into view as I drove over a small steep hill in second gear.

Silhouetted against the clear sky was a disproportionately tall, two-story, wood-frame house, badly in need of paint. Corrals and a ramshackle barn stood on the opposite side of a large a dirt yard. The Joneses' familiar Chevy was parked in the yard; next to it was a new, black, Ford pickup.

I parked my panel truck on the other side of the Chevy as John came out of the house, a steaming mug of coffee in each hand. The two men who followed him were short and lean, with long legs and compact bodies. All three men were wearing Wranglers, wide, tooled leather belts, trophy buckles, and much-laundered, blue, Oxford, dress shirts, the collars buttoned down and long sleeves closed at the wrist. None of the three wore hats, but all had distinct lines on their foreheads separating skin rarely exposed to the elements from the remainder of their weather-beaten faces.

"Doc, this is Ted Simpson and his brother, Ed."

Ted was a scant inch or so taller than his brother. His nose was majestic, perhaps an indication of some Sioux blood. His thin lips pulled into a welcoming smile. A nasty scar ran from just above his left ear down to his cheekbone, no doubt the souvenir of an engagement with a bucking animal. His brother, Ed, had no scar to mar his face.

I shook hands with all three men, and the four of us walked to the house, John and I sipping coffee.

Kathy served us bacon, ham, sausage, fried eggs, pancakes, syrup, and crispy potatoes fried with onions. There was plenty of fresh coffee from a blue, enamel coffee pot kept on a back burner of the stove.

"Well, we've got sixteen head of horses to cut," Ted said. "They're in a corral on my place about two miles from here. I suppose we ought to get on with it."

"Is there clean water at the corral, or do we need to take some with us?" I asked.

"There's a good well," John answered.

"So, how are you guys going to restrain them?"

"Oh, don't you worry about that; we're old hands at this," Ed answered. All three conspirators smirked.

We thanked Kathy, the Simpsons giving her a quick kiss on the cheek. John embraced her in a bear hug, swung her around, and planted a wet kiss on her lips.

Blushing she said, "I'll drive over later in the morning and bring some lunch. Ferdie, you go with the men. I'll bring Jenny with me when I come."

John and Ferdie joined me in the practice truck following the dust trail left by Ted and Ed in the Ford. It took minutes for the dust to settle onto the two vehicles after we stopped at the rounded, six-rail corral. A windmill and water trough abutted the corral, half the water trough situated inside. Three saddled horses stood quietly, tied by halter ropes to the third rail of the corral. There was a black four-horse trailer parked next to the windmill. The horses inside the corral were quiet, but all were facing the trucks, watching, their ears twitching.

I opened the back of the practice truck. After half filling a stainless steel bucket with the cloudy water flowing from the windmill pipe, I added three times the recommended amount of disinfectant and dropped in a scalpel with a disposable blade, two curved forceps, and my White's emasculator.

"What's that gizmo?" Ferdie asked, pointing.

"That's an emasculator." I took it out of the bucket to show him. "I use it to cut and crush the spermatic cord in one squeeze. Do you know what the spermatic cord is?"

"Ouch," Ferdie said. "Is that what leads to the nut? I think it's what Dad scrapes with a knife until it separates when we cut calves."

"It's the same in horses, except the blood vessels are a lot bigger and bleed a lot more if you don't crush them." I put the emasculator back in the bucket and placed a package of chromic catgut in the pocket of my shirt. I filled a syringe with a half-and-half mixture of Combiotic and long-lasting benzathine penicillin. I left the hypodermic needle stuck in the rubber stopper of the bottle of penicillin. Then I put the two bottles of antibiotics and the syringe into a second bucket.

The Simpsons pulled their Resistols down tight, mounted their horses, and got ready to move into the corral, uncoiling their nylon throw ropes. John pulled his hat down and mounted his horse. He held an inch-thick, twelve-foot-long, cotton rope with a small slip loop at the end. Ferdie opened the gate, the three men rode into the corral, and Ferdie closed the gate after them. The boy then climbed to the top rail. I threw my Resistol on the driver's seat of the panel truck, rolled up my shirtsleeves until they were tight around my biceps, and hitched up my Wranglers. Taking the two buckets, I climbed up next to Ferdie.

I can't believe I agreed to do this.

John looked over. "You ready to go, Doc?"

"Whenever you are," I answered.

John nodded to the Simpsons.

"Let's do it." Ted squeezed his horse with his legs and moved toward the now milling mustangs. He held a big loop with his right hand low off the left side of his saddle horse, his throwing arm across his chest. With one motion, he stood in the stirrups, brought the loop across his body and then over his head, and flipped it, backhanded, over the head of one of the horses.

I had practiced throwing the hoolihan on foot but had never seen it done from horseback. Twirling the loop over your head frightens horses, and they are apt to do stupid things, like run through corral rails or over the person trying to rope them.

The horse Ted caught was a nice-looking dun. Dun horses range from a sandy yellow to reddish brown in color. Their legs are usually darker than their bodies, and some duns have zebra-like stripes on their legs. Duns always have a dark stripe down the middle of their back. Sometimes the stripe extends over the rump to the head of the tail. The tail is dark, and their manes can be dark as well. Many duns also have a dark face; this one did not.

Ted took a couple of turns with the rope around his saddle horn, called dallying, and then turned his horse, pulling the dun out of the herd. The dun strained against the rope, tossing his head, fighting and choking until he realized he had to go forward to be able to breathe. Ed laid his loop just in front of the dun's back hooves, jerking out the slack as the horse stepped into the loop. Both Simpsons spurred their horses off in opposite directions stretching the dun between them.

John bailed off his horse, ran up, grabbed the mustang by the tail, and jerked him hard onto his side. Leaning across from the animal's back, John slipped the loop of the cotton rope over one front hoof and flipped the slack in a half hitch around the other. He pulled both legs up to the dun's chest, put a knee on his neck, and nodded at Ted, who let up on his rope, jumped off his horse, and grabbed the dun's head, twisting his nose up. He made a second loop in the nylon rope, passed that through the loop around the neck, and placed the second loop around the dun's nose creating a crude halter. Ted then straddled the horse's neck and twisted the animal's head up to his chest. The dun started to struggle. Ed backed his horse dragging the dun by his hind legs, his brother and John holding on.

"OK, Doc," John called. "You're up!"

I jumped off the top rail with a bucket in each hand, stumbled, fell to one knee, but managed not to spill the contents of my buckets. I ran to the back of the dun, put down my buckets in the loose dirt, took out the scalpel, leaned over the animal's back, and palpated the scrotum, making certain both testicles were down. I made a bold incision through the skin over the lower testicle, pulled it out, and separated the cremaster muscle with my fingers. Ferdie was standing behind me holding up the bucket of instruments.

I smiled my thanks as I reached back, dropped the scalpel into the bucket and found the handles of the emasculator. When I applied the instrument, the dun squealed. I squeezed down and held the instrument closed. Ed's horse dragged the dun, with the three of us attached, two feet through the dirt. After counting to ten, I removed the emasculator and straightened up. I replaced the emasculator in the bucket of disinfectant, rinsed it, and fished out the scalpel, repeating the procedure for the second testicle. When finished, I replaced the instruments in the bucket of disinfectant and rinsed off my hands. I took the syringe, removed the needle from the bottle, buried the needle into the dun's thigh, attached the syringe, and injected the antibiotics. There was only a slight amount of bleeding from the castration wound.

"Come on, cowboy," I said to Ferdie. "Let's get back on the fence before they let this gelding loose."

Ferdie and I jogged back and climbed onto the top rail. John disengaged his rope from the front legs. Ted removed his rope but still held the dun's head up against his chest. When John was clear, Ted nodded at Ed, who urged his horse forward as his brother let go and scrambled back to his own horse. The dun lay on his side for a few seconds and then struggled to his feet. He stood with all four legs spread, shaking his head and trembling. Blood poured from his wound for a couple of seconds and then slowed to just a few drops. He staggered back to the herd.

We proceeded as we had with the dun. I changed water and disinfectant every other horse. Four hours later, we had roped, cast, and castrated ten of the horses. It was eleven thirty in the morning, getting hotter. All five of us, Ferdie included, were caked with a mixture of sweat and dust. The front of my shirt was splattered with blood.

"Well, Doc," said Ed Simpson, "you're a pretty good hand, but we've still got a ways to go. You gonna hold up?"

I ignored the question. "I'm more concerned about how upset the rest of these horses are getting."

"Yep," Ed said, "but this corral's the only one tall enough and strong enough to hold 'em. I reckon the four of us will be involved in a real wild horse rodeo by the time we get to the last couple." He smiled in anticipation.

"Well," I said, "let's get on with it."

We castrated two more before Kathy and Jenny drove up. Kathy spread a clean oilcloth in the bed of the Chevy and set out a platter of thick roast beef sandwiches, a Mason jar of bread-and-butter pickles, a huge bag of potato chips, and a plastic pitcher of iced tea. She also had a cooler filled with ice and a case of Coors. We all washed up at the windmill. John and the Simpsons attacked the cold beer, each downing his first can in long gulps before reaching for another.

I sipped my beer.

"This certainly tastes good, but we still have four to deal with," I observed. I finished the beer and then filled a plastic glass with iced tea.

"Hey, Doc, there's plenty of brew. You not going to drink your share?" Ted teased.

I'll be happy to match you one for one once we finish with these horses, but I'm not going to get kicked in the head because I'm buzzed, I thought. "After we're done," I said aloud.

"It's OK, Doc. We understand. Some guys just can't handle their beer," Ed needled, reaching for another while taking his third sandwich.

To my surprise, none of the three men showed any effects from the four beers each consumed. If anything, they seemed to be more efficient roping and casting the remaining horses.

The last one was a scruffy-looking black with wild, pig-like eyes. He had dodged and ducked all day, avoiding Ted's rope. At some point, the three, without saying anything, had agreed to leave "Pig-Eye" alone until the end.

John moved his horse slowly into the herd of milling horses. Pig-Eye crowded further into the herd, always keeping two or three other horses between himself and John. The mustang didn't notice that Ted had positioned himself on the opposite side of the herd. The black finally broke from the herd to make a mad dash around the edge of the corral intending to rejoin the others from the opposite side, putting the herd between himself and John. Ted's rope slicked out and Pig-Eye's head went directly through the loop. He didn't seem to notice. He hit the end of the rope at a full run and was yanked over backwards, all four hooves in the air.

"Jesus . . . surely that broke his neck or his back!" I murmured looking over at Ferdie who seemed unconcerned.

Pig-Eye rolled over on his side, jumped to his feet, bucking and kicking, squealing with indignation. He reared up on his hind legs, fighting the rope. He charged directly at Ted who spurred his horse away to keep the rope tight between them. Suddenly the black changed direction trying to snap the rope or pull Ted and his saddle off.

Ed maneuvered his horse to get a loop on Pig-Eye's hind legs. He missed with two throws at the kicking hind legs but on the third caught one leg. They stretched Pig-Eye out with the roped hind leg kicking wildly. John moved in and dropped his cotton rope, with a big loop, just behind the black's front hooves. Ed pulled him back by the one leg, his horse, Old Red, straining. Pig-Eye bucked, hopped backwards stepping with both front hooves directly into John's open loop. John immediately spurred his horse off to the side while dallying the rope on the horn of his saddle. Pig-Eye went down hard.

I put my hand on Ferdie's shoulder. "You and I are staying right here until they get him under control."

Ed got Old Red straightened out and jumped off. The well-trained horse leaned back into the rope keeping tension on the one hind leg. They now had Pig-Eye on his side, in the loose dirt, stretched in three directions.

"OK, Doc," said Ed, "when I say, you get up on Old Red. When you do, he'll give me some slack, and I'll loop both them hind legs."

Ed leaned over Pig-Eye's back and narrowly avoided being kicked by the horse's free leg. Ted added a little more tension on the neck as Ed grabbed the rope attached to the other flailing hind leg.

"OK, Doc," he shouted.

I mounted, the rope slackened, and Ed made a loop and half-hitched both hind legs.

"Back, Doc. . . . Back him up," Ed shouted.

I hauled back on Old Red's reins, but the horse was already leaning back into the rope. John threw the end of his rope to Ed, who pulled Pig-Eye's forelegs up, bracing his knees against the animal's back. John jumped to the ground, ran around to the black's head, sat on his neck, and twisted the head up when Ted gave him some slack.

"OK, Doc," Ted said. "I'm going to stay mounted so I can stretch him out if I have to. Old Red knows what to do; you can come down."

I dismounted and went for the buckets I had left at the edge of the corral. The first testicle came off cleanly, although the black grunted and struggled when I applied the emasculator. I made a second incision in the scrotum, and Pig-Eye went berserk. He threw John off his neck and almost got away from Ed, who managed to maintain his hold on the front leg rope.

When John went airborne, I retreated towards the fence, both buckets in hand. Old Red pulled Pig-Eye and Ed three feet through the dirt.

John and Ed got back in position, and I returned to the fray. I got the second testicle dissected and placed the emasculator. As I clamped down, the black again came off the ground, this time tossing both Ed and John into the dirt. I kept my hold on the emasculator, but it tore off the spermatic cord, and I joined John and Ed sitting on our butts in the dirt.

Ted and Old Red got control, and John and Ed rejoined the action. John bit down on the animal's ear while holding Pig-Eye's head up against his chest. Ed regained control of the front legs. I leaned over Pig-Eye's back to get a look. Blood was spurting out of the wound, forming a red pudding in the powdered dirt.

"Shit!" I exclaimed. "He's bleeding like a stuck pig. Hold onto him. I have to go fishing for that artery."

I found one of the hemostats in the bucket, leaned over, opened up the wound with my left hand, and reached in as far as I could. After three attempts, I found the cord, pulled it out far enough to see what I was doing, and clamped it with the hemostat. The bleeding stopped. Hunting for the second hemostat in the bucket, now full of dirty, bloody water, I cut my thumb on the scalpel blade. Dissecting with the second hemostat, I isolated the spermatic artery and clamped it.

I leaned all the way over, peering into the scrotum. *If he gets loose, I'm in deep shit,* I thought. I glanced at John.

John nodded his understanding of the situation and bit down harder on Pig-Eye's ear. The horse struggled again, and blood from his ear oozed out of the corners of John's mouth.

I shook my head in amazement, reached into my shirt pocket with my left hand, and extracted the packet of catgut. After ripping the packet open with my teeth, I tied a tight ligature around the artery and removed the hemostats. Pig-Eye struggled, but there were only a few drops of blood. After rinsing off my hands, I filled the syringe, administered the antibiotics, and returned to my perch on the corral.

They released him, and Pig-Eye jumped to his feet, kicking out with both hind hooves. Blood dripped from the injured ear, now hanging at a ninety-degree angle from his head. Only a few drops of blood fell from his scrotum.

I dumped the bloody disinfectant out of my pail filling it with fresh water and more disinfectant. I washed my hands making certain the slice into my thumb was clean and dry before bandaging it.

The Simpsons hooked up the horse trailer to their pickup and loaded the three saddle horses that, when taken to the door of the trailer, calmly walked in, all their efforts just an ordinary day. The two brothers hoisted four bales of sweet-smelling alfalfa hay out of the bed of their pickup and threw them over the fence. One of the bales broke open when it hit the ground. John went into the corral, cut the wire on the other three bales, spreading them out. He collected the wire from all four bales, twisted it into a bundle, and pitched it over the fence.

The mustangs were munching hay as everyone gathered around me. I finished cleaning my instruments and put them away. Kathy opened the beer cooler, and they each polished off two quick beers.

I took out my receipt book and wrote up a receipt for castrating sixteen horses at ten dollars a head.

"Who gets this?" I asked

Ed fished into his shirt pocket and pulled out a wad of ten-dollar bills, folded over once. "I'll take that Doc," he said.

I took the bills without looking at them, shoved them into my bloody shirt pocket, and gave Ed the receipt. I glanced at my watch as I put it back on my wrist. It was almost three thirty.

"You should hold the horses here for no more than a couple of hours. They'll do better in a pasture where they can move around without stirring up a cloud of powdered dirt and manure. They'll probably be pretty sore for a few days. If you see any with a swollen sheath or any kind of pus draining from the wound, let me know."

While the three ranchers discussed the logistics of how they would care for the horses for the next few days, I sipped at a beer and called in on the two-way radio. Dick Mathes gave me one more call to make on the way back to town.

"How did your day go?" asked Dick.

"Regular," I answered.

The cowboys smiled their approval. When I put down the microphone, Kathy was standing by the door to the truck.

"You married, Doc?" she asked.

"A little over three months. . . . Her name's Rosalie."

"Well, how about you and Rosalie come out this Sunday to share dinner with us?"

"I'll have to check with the boss, but I'm pretty sure she doesn't have anything else planned."

"We'll be in town to shop Saturday afternoon," Kathy said. "Give us a call before then so we'll know if you're coming. You can show up anytime Sunday, but I'll plan dinner for about one or two in the afternoon."

"That's great, Kathy. Thanks. I'll have Rosalie give you a call. I really appreciate the invitation."

I made the rounds, shaking hands and saying goodbye to the three men and Ferdie. I tried to give Jenny a kiss on the cheek, but she ran and hid behind her mother. I thanked Kathy for breakfast, lunch, and the invitation for Sunday dinner.

⌒

Remembering these events after fifty years, I marvel at the apparent cruelty and disregard we displayed for the horses. However, at that time, anesthetic agents available for use in horses were limited. We had local anesthetics, not an option for use in these wild animals. The tranquilizers had little or no effect on excited animals, unlike some of the agents available today. We also had succinylcholine chloride, a muscle-paralyzing agent that would immobilize a horse for a short time but could also cause paralysis of the respiratory muscles. Succinylcholine left the animal conscious, able to perceive pain but paralyzed. Finally, we had an intravenous general anesthetic combination of chloral hydrate, pentobarbital, and magnesium chloride, called Equithesin. It was difficult to dose, especially in excited animals, and potentially lethal. It left the animals anesthetized and immobilized, so in this case they would have been lying in a thick layer of dirt and manure, for a couple of hours or more.

Despite the fictionalized and romanticized tales of feral horses running free through the West, these horses led a difficult life. There are few natural predators of wild horses, so the number of animals tends to multiply rather quickly. This results in overgrazing and the threat of starvation. Because about half of the foals born are males, competition and fighting amongst the adult males results in a high rate of injuries. These injuries go untreated and can lead to death or permanent lameness. In addition, these wild horses were exposed to bad weather, drought, starvation, high parasite loads, and other dangers that made life unpleasant. Compare this to a life of good care provided by humans who have a stake in keeping the animals healthy and working productively or just functioning as pets.

CHAPTER 6:

THE JONESES' RANCH

ROSALIE BALANCED A WICKER BASKET on the floor of the passenger seat between her feet, safe from Mister. The basket was full of chocolate cupcakes slathered with a thick layer of chocolate frosting.

The sun hung directly overhead, fierce in the cloudless sky. We crossed the Yellowstone River ascending out of the valley onto the plateau. Hot wind blew in through open windows. The North Dakota Badlands, sparsely covered with prairie grasses, buffeted by winds, and slashed by deep coulees, presented grotesque, twisted formations of sandstone and clay, carved by wind and water. The whole was a monotonous gray-brown, occasionally interrupted by bands of dirty yellow and vermilion. In early spring, the Badlands are briefly green, but it was summer, and those bits of prairie grass that managed to find a plot of soil sufficiently fertile to support life were brown and brittle.

I glanced in the rearview mirror and spotted a chicken hawk circling close to the life-giving water of the Yellowstone. The Ford was kicking up a thick rooster tail of dust. The air in the car was thick, but it was too hot to roll up the windows.

We arrived at the Joneses' mailbox.

"How do they manage to live in this much isolation?" Rosalie asked. "We haven't seen a sign of humans for the last fifteen minutes."

I didn't answer. Concentrating on driving, I kept the right-side wheels of the low-slung Ford precariously balanced on the mound between the two deep ruts constituting the road into the ranch. The left-side wheels made a new path. If I let the car fall into the deep ruts, I would loose an oil pan or worse.

Rosalie let out a gasp, and I slammed on the brakes. We were on the crest of the hill, the Joneses' place spread out before us.

"What?"

"Oh, Dave," she sighed, "it's so poor looking."

The track ended in an acre of dirt yard. To the right, the dilapidated barn struggled to maintain an upright position, a sturdy-looking corral on the north wall of the barn seeming to hold it up. A windmill and stock tank were north of the corral. To the west, insolently weather-beaten but standing proud and stark against the massive horizon, was the two-story frame house. Small sections of tenacious white paint clung to petrified siding. There were no trees. Brown prairie grass spread west and north. Parked in front of the open barn door, the driver's side door ajar, was John's Chevy pickup.

"Well, they don't have much in the way of material things, but I think you'll find them pretty rich otherwise," I said.

I eased the car down the hill into the yard. Kathy and Jenny came down the steps from the house, their blond hair pulled back in identical ponytails. Ferdie raced around the corner of the house. Skipper, eyes focused, herded him.

"Look at Skipper running. Looks like she's doing very well after her ordeal," I observed.

Rosalie patted me on the arm. "Don't get the big head; you got lucky."

Bent over in the doorway to the barn, John held the left hind leg of his bay gelding between his knees. He had a mouth full of horseshoe nails and held a horseshoe hammer in his right hand. He smiled around the nails and waved the hammer as I got out of the car and went around to open the door for Rosalie.

Kathy, the kids, and Skipper all came to the passenger side of the car. When I opened the door, Mister forced his way out before Rosalie could move.

The two dogs performed the requisite sniffing of each other's sites of identification, Mister circling stiffly, ears pointed forward, Skipper making quick, jerky movements. They circled each other three times, noses buried, then Skipper rushed off with Mister following, determined to keep her close.

"Honey, this is Kathy, and these two are Ferdie and Jenny. Kathy, this is Rosalie."

John finished with the horseshoe, dropped the horse's leg, and came over to the car.

"And this is John," I said.

Rosalie extended her hand. The rancher took it, pulled her in close, and gave her a hug.

"Welcome," he said. "Please feel you are with family here. That's quite the dog you folks have. Biggest shepherd I've seen. Looks like he and Skipper have hit it off. How's he act around cows? Maybe we've found a sire for Skipper's first litter," John said.

"Don't know, John. He doesn't chase livestock, and he listens to commands, but I've never tried to work cattle or sheep with him. He's got the genes for it, though," I answered.

"Here, Kathy, the basket is a present for you to keep; the goodies are dessert," Rosalie interrupted.

"Oh, that's very nice Rosalie; you didn't have to do that. We just wanted to get to know you. Let's go up to the house. I best rescue my green beans; they should be boiling by now. Come along, Jenny."

Ferdie and I joined John in the open doorway of the barn. He finished rasping the nails on the hoof he was working on and then reset the shoe on the right hind hoof.

"I haven't heard anything about a break in the weather or rain," I said.

"Haven't had a drop out here for four weeks now," John replied.

"I have heard of a couple of people in the market for good saddle horses."

"Now that's good news," John said. "We plan to break and train the whole bunch, then sell them. By the way, does Rosalie ride?"

"We went riding once. She managed."

"We've got an old mare; she's rock-solid gentle. Ferdie and Jenny both learned to ride on her. I need to go by the Simpsons' this afternoon; they're off rodeoing. We moved all the mustangs to a pasture on Ed's place. Thought you might want to see how they're doing. If Rosalie is up to it, we could all ride over," John said.

Before going to the house, we stopped at the water tank. John yanked the rope releasing the rudder on the windmill, allowing it to swing into the breeze. The windmill turned, and after a few moments, water ran out of the galvanized pipe into the stock tank. John rinsed off his hands drying them on the back of his shirt.

I played with the ropes controlling the rudder of the windmill.

"Here, Doc. You disconnect the rudder with this one."

The windmill swung free, luffing, and stopped turning. Water stopped running out of the pipe.

"Ingenious," I said.

"Yeah . . . technology from the eighteen hundreds," John replied.

The three of us crossed the hundred yards to the house and entered the enclosed back porch. Winter coats and coveralls hung on nails pounded into the rough-cut, full-thickness two-by-fours framing the house. Against the inside wall, there was a bench, three feet tall and two feet wide, running the length of the room. It held two plastic dishpans, an enamel wash pan, and two galvanized buckets, the later full of dusty water. Three limp but clean towels hung from wood pegs over the bench.

An assortment of boots sprawled under the bench, Rosalie's new boots amongst them. John sat on the bench, removed his boots, kicking them in with the others. When he got up, I did the same, thankful my socks didn't have holes. Ferdie pried off his boots with his feet while still standing, then kicked them to the side, aimed in the general vicinity of the bench.

A square, pine wood table standing on worn, flower-patterned linoleum occupied the center of the kitchen. Kathy stood at the stove stirring something. Rosalie sat on a wood kitchen chair, Jenny on her lap, her chin resting on the top of the little girl's head, her arms wrapped around her. All three talked, simultaneously.

"Three women, everybody talking, nobody listening, it's déjà vu." I turned to John. "Whenever Rosalie, her mom, and grandma get together, it's the same scene."

John walked over, lifted Kathy's ponytail, kissed the back of her neck, and went to the propane refrigerator. "You ready for a beer?"

I glanced at my watch. "It's barely past noon, but yeah, why not?"

"Miss Rosalie, how 'bout you? Kath?"

Rosalie raised a class of iced tea. "I'm good. Thanks anyhow, John."

Kathy raised her glass. "I'm set too, hon."

Ferdie squatted, checking out the cupcakes inside the wicker basket sitting on the floor next to the table.

"Come on Doc," said John. "We'll let the ladies be."

We walked through a windowless dining room, filled by a battered but lovingly polished mahogany table and six matching chairs. A pot-bellied stove with a scuttle of coal next to it was tucked into the opposite corner of the adjoining living room. A worn, leather sofa sat under a window, a matching chair next to it. Floor-to-ceiling bookshelves, sagging with books, lined all available wall space.

John plopped into the chair. One section of books drew my attention. I noticed DeVoto's *Across the Wide Missouri* and a battered edition of Larpenteur's *Forty Years a Fur Trader on the Upper Missouri*. I picked up a book I didn't recognize, Donald Jackson's *Voyages of the Steamboat Yellow Stone* and then replaced it when I spotted a set of leather-covered books in a wood-and-glass case.

I shook my head. "John, I can't believe you've got the Biddle-Coues journals. Are these a first edition?"

"Yeah, they are, Doc. You are welcome to borrow the Jackson book, but if you want to read any of the Biddle-Coues, you'll have to take the time to visit them here."

"How did you manage to accumulate this library?" I asked.

"We all do a lot of reading, especially in the winter, and the Simpson brothers carry a list for me. They haunt used bookstores when they're rodeoing. Ted says it keeps them out of the bars."

"John, this is fantastic! How did you get interested in mountain man history?"

"I'm related to Reuben Field on my mother's side. He was my great-great-great-," he counted them off on his fingers, "grandfather. I'm the sixth generation.

"After they returned with Lewis and Clark, Reuben and his brother each collected five dollars a month in back pay and received land warrants for 320 acres. The brothers cashed in the land warrants in 1822 and settled adjoining plots of land in Missouri. My grandfather married a Field girl and moved his family to this homestead in 1897. I'm the third generation on this place."

❧

In the kitchen, the women continued their conversation with Jenny mostly just listening.

"So, were you raised on a ranch?" Rosalie asked.

"Oh no, I'm a town girl, but John and I started dating in high school. Got married the week after we graduated, kind of a rush job." She winked at Rosalie.

"John's been working this place pretty much by himself since he was sixteen. His dad was sick for a long time before he died from cancer five years ago. His mom died when he was still in grade school. How about you and Doc? It appears to me you haven't been married very long—he still opens the car door for you."

Jenny squirmed, turning to look up at Rosalie.

"I'm an only child too. We've been married a little over three months," Rosalie answered.

"Did you have a big wedding? John and I got married by a JP with just his dad, my folks, and a few friends."

"Ours was small too. Dave flew home to Phoenix from Denver on a Friday. We got married that Saturday night. It was just both of our parents, Dave's brother and sister, his grandfather, his grandfather's brother and his wife," Rosalie answered. "Dave's parents have a little

Chihuahua, and his grandfather has a Chihuahua mix. We locked them in the kitchen, and those two little dogs barked the whole time trying to get into the living room with us. We flew back to Denver the next day, and Dave was back in the teaching hospital Monday.

"A rabbi married us. That's an interesting story. He insisted that we come in for counseling before he would marry us. We did that when Dave was home over the winter break. The only thing I remember that he said that was worthwhile was that we should never go to bed angry. We should talk things out before going to sleep. Well, we recently found out he left his wife and ran off with his secretary. Not something you expect from a rabbi."

At that point, John, Ferdie, and I came into the kitchen to see how things were progressing.

Rosalie pulled me close and whispered into my ear.

I smiled, nodded, and in a stage whisper, replied, "It's out back."

Rosalie's mouth dropped open.

I took her hand. "I'll show you," I said.

I took Rosalie around the house and showed her a shaky-looking shed with a crescent-shaped hole cut into the door. She put on her determined face.

When we returned, Kathy was covering the dining room table with a white tablecloth. Next, she put down an eclectic assortment of dish patterns and silverware and then tested Rosalie.

"This is Henrietta," she announced. She was holding a roasted chicken on a platter. "She stopped laying. I rubbed a mixture of fresh butter with wild sage, tarragon, and salt under and onto her skin."

"OK," Rosalie smiled, "I'm anxious to taste Henrietta. Do you grow your own herbs?"

Kathy laughed, put down the platter, and patted my bride on the arm. "Rosalie, you are going to fit in just fine with this outfit. I was just trying to find out how much of a city girl you are. I'll show you my garden after dinner."

There was a huge bowl of mashed potatoes, plus a casserole made with sweet potatoes, brown sugar, and black walnuts. Kathy had also prepared fresh green beans, lightly sautéed in butter, herbs, and wild onion. Her dessert was a fantastic black walnut pie. Ferdie and Jenny opted for the chocolate cupcakes.

～

John picked up a dented galvanized bucket, put a scoop of grain in it, and stood at the open corral gate shaking the bucket. Three horses picked up their heads and trotted towards the corral. Five others walked in, the dun mustang at the end of the line. Once all the horses were in the corral, John emptied the bucket into a long feed trough, spreading the grain out. While the horses munched the grain, I closed the gate.

John walked up to an old mare that didn't move as he slipped a rope over her head. "Sally here will do for Rosalie. You can use that saddle and bridle," he pointed, "on my bay in the stall. I'll be taking the dun outside the corral for the first time. We'll see how he does."

Ferdie put a halter on one of the other horses and then looped the halter rope around the neck of his sister's pony leading them both into the barn. Kathy caught her sorrel gelding.

I saddled the bay and stood in the open doorway between the corral and the barn watching John shake out his throw rope, build a loop, and flip a hoolihan. When the loop settled around the dun's neck, he froze and then turned to face John. The rancher worked his way up the rope talking softly. He then walked all around the horse rubbing him with the rope, petting him with both hands, and talking in a soothing voice. John led him into the barn and groomed him with a stiff brush. When he put on the saddle blanket, the dun flinched, but when he cinched the heavy saddle, the horse stood still. Finally, John slipped a hackamore over the dun's ears. He checked on everyone and took a final tug on Sally's cinch.

"OK, group, we're ready to go," John announced. "Rosalie, hold onto the saddle horn with your left hand and the pommel of the saddle, here, with your right hand. Now raise your left foot back. I'm going to lift on your left instep while you pull yourself up with both hands and throw your right leg over. Good!"

Sally stood as still as a courthouse statue, understanding that her job was to make certain Rosalie stayed on her back.

Rosalie patted the mare on the neck. "She's beautiful, John."

Sally turned her head and looked at Rosalie, acknowledging the compliment.

I mounted the bay, and John, Kathy, and both children mounted their horses. The dun pranced, threw his head from side to side, and gave a couple of half-hearted bucks. The six of us were off, Skipper and Mister trailing as we rode through two pastures and then down into a tree-clogged ravine.

"Those evergreens are junipers. This is where I harvest juniper berries and the black walnuts," Kathy explained. "We're now on government land. Those are the black walnuts," she said pointing to a tree loaded with nuts still wrapped in their thick green covering.

"Is that what's in all those mayonnaise jars full of nutmeats in your kitchen?" Rosalie asked.

"Yep, I keep a lot of them around for cooking; the price is right."

Twenty minutes later, I spotted a group of ranch buildings off to the north as John led us in that direction. We entered a pasture surrounded by a five-strand barbed-wire fence. Inside was the wild horse herd. The castrated horses mingled with mares and young foals. The dun whinnied, and several of the horses raised their heads responding in kind.

"How many horses are here?" Rosalie asked.

"Should be forty odd, but some of Ed's saddle horses are mixed in," explained John. "There are thirty-five wild ones."

The influence of rodeo purses was obvious. The house was red brick. The corral and barn were situated like those at the Joneses' ranch, but they were in good repair and constructed of superior materials. There was no sign of an outhouse.

"That little shed there off to the side is a well house with their Delco generator and batteries," John explained.

We rode into the corral. Ferdie dismounted and went into the barn, returning with two buckets of grain. The horses in the pasture moved toward the corral, watching. Seeing the grain buckets, they started moving in.

Pig-Eye was the last to enter. Keeping a wary eye on me, he moved to one of the feed troughs and found some grain. Every few moments, he raised his head to keep track of me. There was no sign of swelling, and his chewed ear was again erect.

I dismounted to turn on the windmill and top off the water tank, my back turned to the horses in the corral. Pig-Eye broke from the feed trough, charging at me with his teeth bared. Mister streaked into the corral leaping at the black's head, teeth snapping. Pig-Eye slid to a stop. Mister circled, growling, snarling, making short fake charges at Pig-Eye, drawing the horse away from me.

John, on the dun, loped in to herd Pig-Eye out of the corral. "Damn, Doc, I think Mister just saved you from a world of hurt."

"Yeah, well, that's his job; he figures these things out," I agreed.

We finished the chores at Ed's place and rode to Ted's. From the top of the hill separating the two ranches, I observed that they were mirror images.

After finishing the chores at Ted's, we started back. When we arrived at the Joneses' ranch, our shadows were reaching out to the east.

Mister and Skipper, after trailing the whole trip, sought out the shade of the stock tank. Mister lay down leaning against the cool tank, eyes closed and allowed a sigh to escape. Skipper came over, flopped down, resting her head on Mister's flank. Both dozed.

"Well, gang, I'm ready for something cold to drink," John announced.

"I'll take care of the horses, Dad," Ferdie said.

"Thanks, son."

Kathy convinced us to stay and eat leftovers for dinner. We talked until it was dark and then crowded around the kitchen table, eating supper by the light of a Coleman lantern hung from a hook in the ceiling.

"No thanks. I'm going to pass on two desserts in one day," I said, patting my stomach. "But I will take a cup of coffee. I'm going to need some help staying awake after all this good food."

~

The night was dark, the stars masked by high clouds. The headlights of the Ford searched out the dirt road in front of us. Rosalie sat close, her head against my shoulder, common behavior in those days before seat belts. No light defined the horizon. We drove through the black void in the glow of the dashboard, isolated from the rest of the world.

"I really like them," she announced, "but they live so poorly. No electricity or indoor plumbing. And the water they used for washing and cooking, shouldn't they filter it or something?"

"Not having indoor plumbing is inconvenient, but they seem happy. Jenny and Ferdie are super kids. They probably should filter the water."

We drove down off the plateau into the Yellowstone River valley. The glow from the lights of Sidney cast a dome of light into the black sky. Mister stood up in the back seat, stretched, and reached out with his tongue to lick Rosalie's ear.

CHAPTER 7:
THE L-BAR-J

SALLY AND JOE LUFKIN'S PLACE, the L-Bar-J Quarter Horse Ranch, occupied forty acres of pasture and woods on a bluff overlooking the Yellowstone River.

Sally's short blond hair and blue eyes testified to her Danish background. Her short legs and round face and body made her look soft and cuddly, but she was no-nonsense tough and very fit. I never found her anything but warm and pleasant. When we met, both she and her husband were in their early thirties.

Her husband, Joe, was a full inch taller than I am. He was rail thin, his graying hair cut into a crew cut. He had dark-brown eyes and large hands with very long fingers. After we got to know them, I found out he had played shooting guard on the basketball team at Northwestern and graduated from Northwestern University medical school.

I first met the Lufkins when they brought their calico cat, Patches, in for a general exam. Patches was twenty-three years old but in remarkably good health. After completing a physical exam, I recommended cleaning the accumulation of tartar from her teeth. Other than the needed dental work, she seemed perfectly happy and content, purring constantly from the time Joe took her out of her carrying case—purring so loudly, in fact, that I was unable to auscultate her lungs and barely able to discern her heartbeat.

"Do you mind if we stay with her while you work on her?" Sally asked. "She's been with me since she was a kitten. I'm a nurse in charge of the emergency room at the hospital, and Joe is an orthopedic and trauma surgeon."

"That's great," I said. "You can monitor her breathing and depth of anesthesia while I work on her. I'm going to anesthetize her with Pentothal, which should give me ten to fifteen minutes to get the tartar scraped off."

Everything went smoothly. I was able to anesthetize Patches without having to restrain her. I held her right foreleg with my left hand, clipped the hair over her cephalic vein with a scissors, occluded the vein with my thumb, and injected the anesthetic. After putting in an endotracheal tube, I scraped the accumulated tartar from her teeth and then whitened them with cotton balls dipped in hydrogen peroxide. Patches started to wake up as I finished whitening her teeth.

"Well, Doctor Gross, that was slick. I'm impressed," Dr. Lufkin said.

"Please, call me Dave. We haven't been here long and are trying to make friends."

"In that case, Dave," Sally responded, "I think we need to invite you and your wife over for dinner. How does a week from this Saturday night sound? Neither of us is on call."

"Sounds great to me. I'm not on call either, and I'm sure Rosalie will be very pleased to get to know you both."

❧

Sally served an appetizer of smoked salmon on rounds of garlic toast while we sipped a chilled California Chardonnay.

"A number of vineyards in California are putting in this variety of grape," Joe explained. "It's going to be hugely popular."

Rosalie and I murmured appropriate compliments.

"So, don't you want to see the horses?" Joe pleaded.

"Why don't we give them the guided tour of the house first?" said Sally. "I think Rosalie is more interested in the house than she is in the horses."

"Not more interested," Rosalie replied, "but I would love to see the house."

Their home was log built with an open floor plan and a hunting lodge atmosphere. A log barn matched the house. The front porch overlooked the river and ran the length of the house. The door from the porch opened directly into the great room, the kitchen area to the left. A powder room was around the corner from a walk-in pantry next to the kitchen space. An oversized laundry and mudroom was located next to the pantry and served as a passage to the garage. A side door from the garage opened onto a small porch feeding onto a covered raised board walkway to the barn. Opposite the kitchen, a stairway led upstairs to two bedrooms and a bath. Under the stairs was a door that opened into the master suite. In the great room, a massive stone fireplace dominated the back wall with a leather sofa and two leather easy chairs facing the fireplace.

After touring the house, we took the boardwalk to the barn. Behind the barn were four paddocks that stretched out, long and narrow. The horses were better than I had expected.

"We've got eight well-bred brood mares, but Hickory Joe is special. He's a direct descendent of Old Sorrel. Do you know about Old Sorrel?" Joe asked.

"Sure," I answered. "He was the foundation sire for the King Ranch herd, the origin of quarter horses. He bred mares until he was about thirty years old. They enhanced his bloodline by breeding him to thoroughbred mares with early speed."

"So, you know quarter horses," said Joe. "Did you know that both of the Simpson brothers rope off of geldings that we bred?"

"That I did not know," I replied.

We each rested a booted foot on the bottom rail of the wood fence, observing four mares, one of them heavy with foal.

"John Jones just spoke for that foal. It should be dropped within the next few weeks," Joe explained.

"Yeah, I heard last week that they found oil on his place. He and Kathy are very excited. We're happy for them. I guess that oil money is burning a hole in their pockets." I smiled. "I think Rosalie and I would have put indoor plumbing in their place first."

"That would be our choice too. He said the foal was a birthday gift for Ferdie."

I nodded my head. "Figures."

We watched the mares for some time and then went into the barn. I was anxious to see Hickory Joe, and the stallion was impressive. I watched him for some minutes from outside the stall. He was deep chestnut in color, a white star on his forehead, only fourteen and a half hands high at the withers, but thick across the chest. His back was straight but sloped from high hips down to the withers. His manner exuded royalty.

"Well, he's a little mutton withered for my taste," I teased, "but he's well muscled and passably well cared for."

I opened the stall door stepping into eight inches of wood shavings. As I approached the stallion, I talked to him quietly. The horse stood still enjoying the attention as I rubbed and slapped him.

"Looks as though you are feeding him plenty well," I said. "He's a little mushy. Maybe a little less sweet feed and a little more exercise would be in order."

Joe Lufkin smiled. "Yeah, yeah, less food, more exercise. I do need to turn him out in the pasture more often. He's a little much for Sally to ride, and I don't seem to find the time."

Sally and Rosalie had trailed us but now returned to the house. Joe and I continued talking about the stallion.

"I bought him as a yearling, a lark. Because of his breeding, I decided to turn him over to a trainer and race him. He did pretty well at Riudosa Downs as a three-year-old but cost us more in training, boarding, and veterinary fees than he won. He did win a couple of allowance races and then bowed his left tendon. The trainer brought him back too early, and he fractured the opposite leg lateral sesamoid. After he broke the sesamoid, I decided to get out of racing and into breeding."

I palpated the stallion's left fetlock and the enlarged tendon sheath and then pinched both sesamoid bones on the right leg hard. "He doesn't seem to have any pain or tenderness now."

"It's been three years. He is sound enough, but I don't push him. He breeds just fine," Joe smiled.

We returned to the house where Joe put on a blue denim apron to help Sally cook. Rosalie and I sat on stools on the other side of the island counter separating the kitchen from the great room.

Roasted new potatoes smothered in onions were keeping warm in the oven. Sally combined lightly steamed, fresh green beans with shallots sautéed in butter and a squeeze of fresh lime. Joe took out four beautiful fresh trout from the refrigerator, breaded them very lightly, and sautéed them in butter, adding a handful of almonds into the skillet after removing the fish and then put in a splash of the Chardonnay and stirred until it was reduced. He poured the almond and wine sauce over the fish and put the platter on the table. Sally finished dressing a huge fresh green salad with olive oil and balsamic vinegar. Joe opened another bottle of the Chardonnay, and we all sat at the dining room table to enjoy a great evening of good food and conversation.

~

Nine o'clock in the evening, three weeks later, Rosalie and I were just finishing dinner when the phone rang. Dr. Schultz was on call so I was not expecting any interruptions. Rosalie answered the phone.

"Hello? . . . Oh, hi, Joe. . . . Yes, he's right here." She held out the phone to me.

"Hi, Joe. What's up?" I listened for a moment. "How long has she been at it? . . . OK. No, that's too long. Something's wrong, I'll be there as soon as I can. Try to get her up and walking around. I don't want her down and straining if we can avoid it. . . . OK, I'll ask her. Hang tough. We'll be there soon."

I set the receiver back. "It's the mare with Ferdie's foal. Joe suggested you might want to ride along. He said Sally would be glad to see you."

Rosalie nodded. "Yeah, OK. I'll put on some fresh jeans and a shirt." She was already combing her hair into a ponytail with her fingers.

When we arrived, all the lights were on in the barn. I parked and took my bucket, OB chains, disinfectant, and soap out of the truck. I also grabbed the case containing syringes and needles and a bottle of Procaine. Inside the barn, Holiday Joe was stomping back and forth in his stall, whinnying, creating a disturbance. Joe shook my hand.

"Thanks for coming out, Dave. We appreciate it."

Sally and Rosalie hugged.

"You probably ought to put Hickory Joe out. Him being excited and disturbed isn't going to help," I said.

"Yeah, should have done that already. Sorry. The mare's in that stall," Joe indicated with his chin. "I'll turn Joe out."

I looked over the half door and saw the mare lying on her side in the deep wood shavings, straining. I looked at Sally and raised my eyebrows.

"I know. We were supposed to keep her up. She just now went down again. Every time we get her up, she stays on her feet walking for five or ten minutes; then she flops on her side and starts straining."

I nodded, opened the door, and went into the stall. The mare lifted her head and watched me, wondering if this was finally someone who could help. I knelt down to check the sclera, the whites of her eyes, and gave her a pat on the head.

"She's not toxic," I said. I took off my shirt and hung it over the half door, exited the stall, and filled my bucket with warm water from the laundry room sink in the alleyway and then added some Nolvasan disinfectant to the water.

"I'll need you to sit on her neck and hold her head up," I told Sally. "Held like that, she won't be able to get up. Here, I'll show you how."

Sally came into the stall with me, and I demonstrated how she should sit on the mare's neck, with one leg on each side, pulling the head up to her chest. I got up, and she took my place. "This OK?" she asked.

"Perfect," I said. "Just hang with her if she tries to get up. As long as you control her head like that, she'll stay down."

I soaped up my hands and arms and reached inside the mare's uterus with my left hand. Only the foal's neck, bent around with the head facing back into the uterus, was in the birth canal. I tried to push the foal back in, but the mare strained, catching my wrist between the bones of her pelvis and the foal's neck. After extricating my arm, I rinsed off. Then I gave the mare an epidural and, while waiting for it to take full effect, wrapped her tail with gauze to keep it clean and out of the way.

Joe returned and took over sitting on the mare's neck.

"Here, Sally." I handed her the wrapped, now limp, tail. "You can hold her tail out of the way."

Again, I soaped up and this time was able to push the foal back into the uterus. I reached in far enough to grab the foal by the nostrils and pull its head around into the proper position. Even with the epidural, the mare was straining but with less force. I bent the foal's left leg at the knee and, cupping the small hoof in my left hand to protect the uterus, pushed the foal back with my right hand and brought the foal's left hoof forward; then I repeated the procedure bringing the right hoof in place. I straightened out both forelimbs with the foal's head positioned between them, placed an OB chain around each fetlock and another underneath the foal's ears, around the sides of the head, and into its mouth. The next time the mare strained, I gently pulled on all three chains simultaneously. The legs and head all came forward until the foal hung up at the shoulders. I pulled one leg at a time gradually walking the shoulders out. The mare strained again, and the foal delivered in a rush. I quickly removed the OB chains. Sally provided some clean towels, and we rubbed the foal down, wiping out his mouth and nose. It was a sorrel colt with a white blaze starting on his forehead and running down to a point between his nostrils.

I put gentle traction on the placenta, and it came away easily. Then I got up and bent over the bucket to wash off.

"Just stay on her head a while longer, Joe. I need to go to the truck for some drugs for her and the foal. I'll be back in a minute; then we can let her up."

I returned, double clamped and cut the umbilicus and then doused it liberally with iodine. I gave the foal a dose of penicillin and another to the mare.

"OK, Joe, you can let her up."

The mare got immediately to her feet, went over to the foal, and started nuzzling it.

"Please hold her by the halter and move her away from the foal while I put some sulfa boluses into her uterus. . . . Thanks. Now we're done. OK, folks, let's leave her alone and see if she can get this foal up."

Joe unhooked the lead rope from her halter, and the mare went to the foal, licking and nudging him until he got himself into a sitting position, his front legs splayed out. He stayed in that position for almost two minutes, wobbling from side to side. Finally, he steadied himself and, with a heave, got his back legs under and stood, all four legs splayed. A couple of minutes later, he found his balance and took a few hesitant steps. All the while, the mare had been nuzzling and encouraging him with soft, guttural noises. She moved away and then turned to look at him, calling softly. He took one step, then another, then a little prance, and he was at her side, his nose buried in her flank, searching for a teat.

I smiled at Rosalie, and she smiled back. I washed up again, using one of Sally's clean towels to dry off, and then put my shirt back on.

"Come on up to the house," Dr. Joe ordered. "I've got a bottle of 1948 Cabernet that will be perfect to celebrate this event." He grabbed his wife around the waist and propelled her towards the house. Looking back over his shoulder, he called out, "Come on, you two, or we'll polish it off ourselves."

I took hold of Rosalie's arm. "Being able to do this sort of thing is really important to me. Can you understand that?"

Her eyes were shining—with tears of pride, I hoped. She nodded and lifted her head to kiss me, standing on her toes. "I understand, and I love you. Wouldn't you like a glass of wine? I would."

"Yeah, you go ahead. I'll put everything back in the truck and be there in a minute."

PART II:
FALL 1960

Chapter 8:
The Labor Day Barbeque

IT WAS EARLY IN SEPTEMBER, a Friday evening, only seven forty-five, and I had already showered. We were eating a new recipe Rosalie was trying out, chicken tetrazzini. She had also baked me an apple pie, my favorite. Before digging into the pie, I loosened my belt a notch.

"Are you aware that the Simpsons and John are famous all over western North Dakota and eastern Montana for their barbeques?" Rosalie inquired.

"I've heard that."

"Did you know they are putting one on for Labor Day at Ted's ranch?"

"Yeah, I heard about that too. Did you want to go?"

"Well, I happen to know they start preparing the night before, and we've been invited to join them tomorrow evening. My understanding is that very few people are ever invited to help with the preparation."

"Really? . . . Well, we better go then."

⌐

The previous Wednesday, Dick had said Mrs. Schultz wanted me to come to their home to pick up my check. Previously, she had left it with Dick at the hospital.

When I arrived and rang the doorbell, Mrs. Schultz opened the door and instructed me to follow her to her office. She took me to the first room on the left off the large entry hall. The old Victorian house could have served as the set for a horror movie, but it was extensively refurbished and updated. Dr. Schultz complained to me about the cost. It was huge, six bedrooms and four bathrooms—too big and too expensive he told me—but his wife insisted they buy it, and they spent a fortune on it.

I sat across from her at a large oak dining room table that served as her desk. She got straight to the point.

"I have no idea why Marcus made the deal you and he have, but I told Dick to keep track of the time you are actually working. Your accounting appears to match his, so you are honest, but you are averaging over sixty-five hours a week and then getting 40 percent of what you bill after you work two hundred hours each month. That is exorbitant!"

"It's what Dr. Schultz agreed to. I've been working every weekend since I got here. Dr. Schultz said he needed some rest, and I can understand why. It's a very busy practice."

"I see you have also doubled his fee schedule, so you are earning even more than anticipated."

"That's true, and the fee adjustment was overdue. We're both charging the new fees so the practice is grossing significantly more than before I arrived, and we haven't lost any clients that I am aware of."

The edges of her mouth turned down. I was fascinated. I didn't think it possible for anyone to have that intense a frown.

"Well, I have instructed Marcus to alternate weekends with you from now on. You don't need that much extra time. In any case, 40 percent is too much. We need to renegotiate."

"I don't think so," I answered. "If the practice is not netting 60 percent of the gross, it is not being managed efficiently. I'm not prepared to renegotiate, and I have had no indication from Dr. Schultz that he wants to. In fact he seems quite pleased with the job I am doing."

"We'll see about that. Here's your check."

I took the time and examined the amount. "Thank you; it's the same total I calculated."

I left as quickly as possible.

—

The next morning, I left the house at five thirty, getting an early start on an assortment of routine calls. Dr. Schultz was on call for all emergencies until Monday morning.

Don and I finished the farm calls a little after two in the afternoon; then I performed an ovariohistorectomy on a dog brought in while we were out. Don helped me clean up and restocked my truck. I went home after telling Dick that Rosalie and I would be at Ted Simpson's ranch if he needed me.

"You got invited for the prelims?" He sounded envious.

"I don't know about me, but Rosalie did. She's become quite friendly with Kathy Jones and Linda and Sue Simpson."

At home, after I showered and changed clothes, Rosalie and I loaded Mister into the practice truck just in case Dr. Schultz was occupied with an emergency and someone else called. We set out for Ted and Sue Simpson's ranch and arrived about eight in the evening. John Jones showed us the barbeque pit.

"It's four feet wide, ten feet long, and six feet deep. Yesterday, we hauled black walnut logs from a dead tree in that grove over yonder. This morning, early, we started the fire, and we've been adding logs all day. We added the last batch of wood a coupla hours ago; now we just wait until the fire's burnt down to coals."

Ted and Ed came out of the house and joined us. They shook hands with me and gave Rosalie a hug.

Stacked on the ground next to the pit were two large grates, each six feet square.

"They weigh close to two hundred pounds each," Ed commented.

I helped them place six large cement blocks on end on either side of the pit. Each of us lifted a corner, and we placed the grates side by side on the blocks, leaving the grates positioned sixteen inches above ground level. The fire in the pit was so hot that within minutes the steel grates were red.

"Sterilizes 'em," John remarked.

I noticed two wood picnic tables, end-to-end on the lawn, about twenty-five feet from the pit. Each table was covered with an oilcloth and, on top of that, half a steer carcass.

"Ed and I have a little feedlot just outside of Sidney," Ted explained. "Our sister, Natalie, lives there and takes care of things for us. We cut out the best of our steers, feed them out to prime, and custom slaughter. We hang the halves and age them for at least four weeks. George, who owns the Stockyards Café, buys some hindquarters for his restaurant, and we have other customers in town. After they're aged, we wrap the halves we're going to use for barbeques in plastic and keep them in the freezer."

"He neglected to tell you they are half-owners of the meat locker," John contributed, smiling.

John reached under one of the picnic tables into an ice chest and pulled out four cans of Coors, throwing one to each of us. We all caught them in the air, one-handed. He held up a beer and raised his eyebrows at Rosalie. "Miss Rosalie?" he asked.

She smiled and shook her head. "No thanks, John; I think I'll pass. Where are the ladies?"

"Up in the house," said Ed. "They're working on potato salad."

"Well, I'll go see if I can help. You boys have fun."

At that moment, Ferdie came running around the corner of the house with Mister and Skipper herding him.

"Hey, Dad," he shouted, "watch what Mister does if I run off in another direction."

He took off at a right angle, away from the four of us. Mister ducked, intercepted him, and using his right shoulder, turned him back towards the picnic tables. Skipper trailed, barking, enjoying the game. Ferdie laughed so hard he tripped and fell face first. Both Mister and Skipper were on him immediately, licking his face and nuzzling him, their tails wagging in wide circles while Ferdie covered his head with his arms, laughing and screaming at both dogs to leave him alone.

John paused for an instant to make certain his son wasn't hurt. He took a church key off one of the picnic tables, opened his beer, and tossed the key to me.

I checked the beef on the table closest to where I was standing. There was green mold on portions of the fat, well-marbled carcass.

"We moved it from the freezer to the cooler early yesterday and brought it out from town early this morning so it's still cold," Ed explained.

John stirred the fire in the pit with a steel pole. "I think by the time we get the beef seasoned, the coals will be ready."

Ted went to his pickup, lifted the hinged wood top to a large wood box that filled the bed, and removed a rolled-up length of greasy leather. He unrolled the leather exposing four sharp butcher knives and four even sharper boning knives, each in a separate leather pocket.

Ed selected one of the knives and removed the tenderloin and a large amount of kidney fat from each of the half carcasses. Ted, John, and Ferdie went to the house and returned, each carrying a cardboard box containing boxes of kosher salt and large cans of black pepper.

John emptied two boxes of the salt and a can of pepper on the inside surface of each carcass. The men mixed the seasonings together with their hands and then started rubbing the mixture into the meat. After the inside of both halves was well coated, they each took a thin boning knife and made numerous puncture wounds into the meat filling the holes with the salt-and-pepper mixture. They turned the carcasses over and repeated the procedure on the outside surface.

John took a butcher's bone saw from the box in the pickup and cut two eight-inch-long lengths from the end of each leg.

By the time, the men had completed their tasks, the coals had settled below the lip of the pit. They laid the carcasses on the grates. The meat sizzled, and fat dripped into the coals sending flares of flame to within inches of the meat.

John walked over to Ted's pickup and from the same box extracted three long steel rods with sharpened hooks on one end and wood ax handles on the opposite end. They used these pikes to position the halves over the center of the pit.

I wandered over to have a look at the box in the pickup. It was divided into several compartments, one of which contained two twenty-gallon, stainless steel cooking pots.

"Hey, Doc," hollered Ted, "bring those pots over, and we'll get the beans going."

Ted placed the pots on the end of one of the grates. Before long, they began to smoke. He divided bones and fat between the two pots. Ed returned from the house carrying a plastic dishpan filled with onions cut into quarters. He split the onions between the two pots, stirring with a canoe paddle until everything browned. John came from the house with a five-gallon jug of water on his shoulder. He divided the water between the pots, ducking to avoid the clouds of steam.

"OK, let's get the beans," said Ed.

We found the four wives and Jenny working around a large table centered in the kitchen. Rosalie was chopping celery. Jenny stood on a chair next to her providing instruction on size and technique. Kathy was chopping onions. Sue, Ted's wife, was chopping green peppers. I counted ten large stainless bowls filled with boiled potatoes and two others filled with hard-boiled eggs.

Rosalie looked up as we entered the kitchen. "There you are." She smiled at me. "Isn't this an amazing kitchen?"

She put down the knife, and Jenny picked it up continuing to chop with Kathy watching her closely.

Rosalie showed me a six-burner stove, a huge mixer, a walk-in pantry, and a walk-in refrigerator that extended out from the side of the house.

"Well," I said, "I guess if you feed five hundred people at a time, you have to be set up to do it."

On the floor of the refrigerator were two huge pots filled with soaking pinto beans.

John and Ted each took a pot of beans over to a large stainless steel sink where they poured off most of the water. Ed grabbed a bowl filled with quartered onions from a shelf in the walk-in refrigerator. Next, he took two huge bottles of ketchup and a can of cayenne pepper from a cupboard that was standing against the wall next to the stove.

We returned to the barbeque pit in fading light. Ed and Ted added the beans to the boiling pots, then the onions, a bottle of ketchup, and a handful of the cayenne pepper to each.

"The cayenne," John explained, "and the beef kidney fat are our secret ingredients." He added more water until the pots were three-fourths full, stirring with the canoe paddle.

"I assume the paddle is kept for only that purpose," I said.

John gave me a fake glare. "You ready for another beer, Doc, or are you just going to question our integrity?"

The ladies came to join us, each carrying an aluminum lawn chair. John sent Ferdie to bring chairs for the men.

"Ferdie," Kathy called out, "make two trips; don't try to carry all five chairs at once." Then she muttered, "That was wasted breath."

"Sue and Linda, I don't think you've ever met Dave," Rosalie said. "Kathy and I had lunch with Linda and Sue a couple of times when they were in town, but you've always been off doing your veterinary thing."

Sue Simpson was younger than her husband Ted, who was then in his early thirties. Ed, I remembered, was two years younger. Sue looked like a teenager, long chestnut hair, green eyes, very well endowed, dressed in very tight Wranglers and an even tighter blouse that emphasized her attributes.

She must be at least in her mid-twenties, but she sure doesn't look it.

"Doc, I'm happy to finally meet you." Her hand was rough, her hand shake as firm as any man's.

I wonder why I'm always so aware of people's hands and the manner in which they shake hands. I suppose it tells me a lot about them.

"Hi, Sue. It's a pleasure to meet you. Rosalie has told me how much fun she has when the four of you get together."

"And this is Linda," Rosalie continued.

Linda stood a full two inches taller than her husband. Two long thick braids held her jet-black hair out of the way. Her eyes were deep blue, but her complexion and facial features hinted of some Native American blood. She ignored my proffered hand and gave me a quick hug.

"We've heard a lot about you Doc. I'm happy you could join us."

"The potato salad is in the refrigerator melding," said Sue. "Everything is cleaned up and put away. The only thing left is to make the barbeque sauce. All your ingredients are ready for you, Ed."

"He's the sauce guy," Linda explained.

Nobody mentioned anything about dinner. We all sat in our chairs, silently staring at the coals in the pit as they flared from the dripping fat. My stomach growled, and everyone laughed.

"Laugh all you want, but I haven't eaten anything since breakfast, and I put in a full day's work before we got here," I said.

"Well, Hoss," said Ted, "I guess we better do something about feeding you then. What about you, Miss Rosalie? Are you hungry too?"

"I could eat."

"Me too," Ferdie said, and everyone laughed again.

The three partners skillfully flipped the two halves of beef to sear the outside, while the fire was still hot. Sue and Linda went into the house and returned with clean oilcloths for the tables and a Coleman lantern.

Ted went to the pickup and removed a long steel pole with a hook on one end, along with a length of galvanized pipe with a sharp point welded to one end and a sledgehammer. He pounded the pipe into the ground between the two picnic tables, slid the pole into the pipe, fired up the lantern, and hung it from the hook.

The four ladies went back to the house returning with a pot containing baked potatoes wrapped in aluminum foil, heavy plastic plates, plastic glasses, two pitchers of iced tea, a pitcher of lemonade, a large brick of cheddar cheese, two boxes of Ritz crackers, and a red wax-sealed bottle of Maker's Mark Kentucky Bourbon.

They placed the pot of potatoes on an outside corner of one of the grates to keep warm. After holding his hand over a portion of the other grate, Ed declared the fire had cooled down enough for the tenderloins.

"Okay, people," said Ted, "as the most senior person here and official master of ceremonies, I declare it time to get serious." He used his pocket knife to cut the wax seal on the bottle of Maker's Mark, opened it, and poured an inch into a glass for each of the adults.

Kathy, with the same seriousness of purpose, poured an equal amount of lemonade into glasses for Jenny and Ferdie.

Once everyone had a glass, Ted raised his. "We are gathered here tonight and tomorrow to welcome into our midst Dave and Rosalie Gross who, by virtue of their skills, smarts, attitude, moral fiber, toughness, determination, athletic ability, and only in Miss Rosalie's case, exceedingly good looks, have demonstrated their worthiness to join this family of kindred spirits. We are also celebrating the Jones family's good fortune. We hope that we will all be blessed with the discovery of black gold as well!"

"HEAR! HEAR!" we all shouted.

"The initiation to this group is simple—down the hatch!" With that, Ted downed his drink in a gulp.

Everyone, including Ferdie and Jenny, shouted, "DOWN THE HATCH," and emptied their glasses.

"Now," said Ted, filling glasses again, "this is the finest sippin' Bourbon whiskey distilled. This stuff is supposed to be savored, not tossed down like rotgut. I expect everyone to behave like civilized folk from here on out." He took an appreciative sip of the amber fluid and sat back. "Now, brother Ed, I want you to explain exactly how that bull managed to land you on your butt in the finals down there in Mesquite."

The brothers kept everyone laughing with their tales of rodeo mishaps. While the tenderloins roasted over the coals, we helped ourselves to cheese and crackers.

When the meat was done, Linda and Sue went back to the house returning with a bowl of salad, two fresh loaves of bread, and a tub of sweet butter. Ed removed one of the tenderloins from the grate and sliced it into thick steaks. At ten o'clock, we were eating, talking, sipping whiskey, tending the slowly roasting halves of beef, and stirring the gently simmering beans with the canoe paddle.

After the second round of drinks, the four wives filled their glasses with tea.

Jenny and Ferdie fell asleep, Jenny on Kathy's lap, Ferdie curled up on the lawn with Mister and Skipper lying on either side of him. John carried Jenny and then Ferdie into the house. By two-thirty in the morning, the two children and four ladies were all in the house, stretched out on couches and beds. We four men swapped stories, sipped whiskey, nibbled tenderloin, turned the roasting beef, and stirred the beans.

A little, after five in the morning, the sky lightened, and the sun gradually peeked over the eastern horizon to find all four of us asleep in our chairs.

Sue came out of the house carrying four cups and a big pot of coffee. She found us with our legs out straight, boot toes pointed toward the sky, hats pulled over our faces, arms crossed over our chests. She kicked Ted's right foot, and he jerked up, snorting.

"Up and at 'em, cowboy. I thought you four were minding the meat."

Ted checked his watch and frowned, getting to his feet. "We're only a half-hour off; no harm."

At the sound of voices, Ed, John, and I simultaneously pushed our hats up, looking around.

Ted went over to check the pit. "It's time to lower the grates again," he said.

During the night, we had turned the cement blocks on their sides, lowering the grates eight inches. Now we kicked the blocks aside allowing the grates to rest on the ground. The meat was still dripping small amounts of fat resulting in muted flares as each drop hit the ashes covering the hot coals.

"We've got to be careful turning the meat now," John told me. "It's tender enough to tear off the bone."

The four of us were standing around the pit drinking black coffee when Sue called out from the kitchen door. "Come in and wash up, you all; breakfast is ready."

Soon we were all seated at the long kitchen worktable eating sausage and fried eggs, pancakes, and hash browns.

After breakfast, we rearranged the two picnic tables and set up six aluminum folding tables.

"Most folks know to bring their own picnic tables and chairs and something to drink," explained Linda. "We also arranged for delivery of fifty folding chairs from the Methodist church in town. Jimmy, who owns the bakery, is delivering fresh rolls and bringing the chairs. Those folks that can't find a place at a table will have to eat off their laps."

Two folding tables were set up next to the picnic tables and then loaded with World War II surplus Melamine dishes.

"These dishes are indestructible," Sue explained. "The flatware is also army surplus."

They set up so four lines could be served at the same time. Sue explained they would carve and serve the meat from both ends of the wood picnic tables. Two folding tables were set up to hold potato salad, barbeque sauce, rolls, and beans.

A few minutes after eleven-thirty, the first pickup arrived, and a steady line of trucks and cars discharged passengers from then on. Everyone seemed to arrive with ice chests, and almost all brought chairs and folding picnic tables. Some also brought tarps, setting them up for shade.

The baker arrived with the extra chairs and rolls. A net was set up, and a chaotic volleyball game was soon underway with twenty or more people on each side. A softball game was organized, again with too many players but less confusing than the volleyball. Dogs were chasing through the crowd. Several car and truck radios played music.

John came over and pressed a cold Coors into my hand. "Don't want your throat to dry out. It's way past noon."

Sally and Joe Lufkin found us and joined our table.

At one thirty, Linda handed me a knife and steel. "Reckon you can figure out how to carve, Doc?" she asked.

"I suppose I can manage."

Sue rang the huge triangle hanging just outside the kitchen door. Within minutes, four lines formed. Everyone loaded his or her plate and found a place to sit and eat.

The two halves of beef were reduced to bones. Most people sat quietly, chatting in groups. All the dogs present were working on large bones, glancing furtively around to make certain none of their mates coveted what they had. Another softball game was in progress, this time only ten young people to a side, but co-ed. The volleyball court was unoccupied, the ball resting under the net.

It was after four in the afternoon when people started gathering their stuff and loading vehicles. Rosalie and I were helping to clean up, although most everyone had been good about putting their trash in the fifty-five gallon drums the Simpsons provided for the purpose.

"What do you do with all the trash?" Rosalie asked Ted.

"We have our own dump in a gully about a quarter mile from here. When it gets rank, I go out with a tractor and blade and cover it over with dirt; works pretty well. We compost most everything we can for the garden."

Sue came out of the house. "Dick Mathes is on the phone for you, Dave. He and Barbara just got back to the hospital from here and there's an emergency of some kind."

"OK, thanks, Sue. I'll go find out what it's about."

I returned from the house and signaled Rosalie that we had to go by whistling for Mister.

"Got a colic case, and Dr. Schultz has a dystocia he's working on," I explained. "Thanks for everything, guys. It was a great party, and we really appreciate the invitation to participate. We're ready to do it again any time you call. Sorry to leave you with more clean-up to do, but duty calls."

CHAPTER 9:

SKUNKED

I CLIMBED THE STAIRS FROM OUR BASEMENT APARTMENT, went outside, and let the door to the stairway slam shut behind me. The chilled morning air was redolent with fall. I climbed into the truck and turned the ignition key. The truck sputtered, coughed, and started. Three minutes later, mine was the only vehicle on the county road. Flood-lights illuminated scattered farmyards, their influence receding in the gathering light of an overcast dawn.

Here I am out and about healing the sick, easing pain and suffering, responding to the needs of our four-legged brethren. I wish I were still in bed with Rosalie!

The lane into the farm circled around the house and ended in the yard separating house and barn. All farmyards in this part of the world seemed to be the same—barren with a large floodlight on the side of the barn closest to the house.

Fred Homer farmed five hundred acres of river bottom. He had recently purchased adjacent pasture on the bluff and was now in the process of getting into the dairy business. His milk parlor, a gleaming new Butler, prefabricated metal building, sat behind an old livestock barn. Since his was an affluent farm, the yard was paved with a thick layer of river gravel. Most yards were dirt, which turned to mud when it rained.

I opened the truck door, and the screen door from the back porch banged open. The floodlight went off as Homer, average height, medium build, sporting three days' growth of graying whiskers, clumped down the two wood stairs, pulling on a plaid-lined Levi jacket. A "gimme cap" advertising Yellowstone Livestock Company was pulled down low over his forehead.

"Mr. Homer, good morning."

We shook hands. The farmer's were short fingered, callused, cracked, weathered.

"Doc, I've never seen the like. She's in the calving shed out behind the new barn. Just came fresh three days ago. Damnest thing I ever seen; paralyzed she is."

I took one of the black leather cases from the truck. "She's lying on her chest with her head twisted round to her side in an S?"

Homer stopped and turned. "Damn, Doc. I heard you was good, but how'd you know that afore you ever seen her?"

I smiled. "Lead on, and we'll have a look."

The black and white Holstein was lying half out of a three-sided shed in a soggy mixture of dirt and manure. As foretold, she was on her sternum, her head twisted to the left.

"You tried to get her up, and she wouldn't, or couldn't, right?"

"Yeah, even used the cattle prod on her. She just bellowed and stayed down."

I conducted a quick exam finding what I expected. I pulled her head out straight, released it, and her neck returned to the same telltale S-shape.

"Well, Mr. Homer, she's got what we call eclampsia, or milk fever."

I loved these cases. I would be a hero in short order. I opened the case and pulled out a bottle of calcium gluconate, an intravenous drip set, and a sixteen-gauge hypodermic needle.

"It's a metabolic disease. We don't know exactly what causes it, but usually only high-producing cows get it three or four days after calving. It's associated with low levels of calcium in their blood. Because of the low calcium, they can't control their muscles, and they end up like this, sort of paralyzed. I'm going to give her this bottle of calcium solution in the vein."

I slipped the needle into the jugular vein, hooked up the bottle, and held it high while the fluid gurgled in. Every few minutes I lowered the bottle and checked the cow's heart rate. When half the bottle was gone, the cow started to focus her expressive dark eyes on me. When the last of the liquid ran out of the brown bottle, the cow brought her head out from her side, moving it back and forth, rediscovering her surroundings.

"I'm going to put everything away in the truck," I said.

I returned in a few minutes, my stethoscope draped around my neck. I listened again and found her heartbeat much slower, significantly stronger.

"Well, Mr. Homer, I think we're ready."

"Ready for what, Doc?"

"Ready for this," I smiled. I stood and gave the cow a quick kick with the side of my boot. She immediately rose up on her hind legs, her front legs still curled under. She paused, in the praying position, released a magnificent burp, and then scrambled to her feet. She walked over to a nearby feed trough and started munching on some fresh-smelling alfalfa hay.

"Well, I'll be damned," Homer, mumbled.

"Yeah," I said, "one of the miracles of veterinary medicine. She'll be fine."

Back at the truck, I finished writing up the bill. When I joined the practice, Dr. Schultz was charging three dollars a call, plus ten cents a mile, plus drugs and extra for some specific procedures. After working in the practice three weeks, I convinced him to double the call and mileage charges and significantly increase the procedures fees. The changes in fee structure were more than making up for my salary. I handed Mr. Homer the bill.

"Doc Schultz finally upped his fees, uh? 'Bout time, I expect. A man ought to know what his skills are really worth. Don't expect that's a problem with you, eh, Doc?"

"Hope not, Mr. Homer. A man ought to be paid for hard-earned knowledge."

"Looks as though this is about double old Doc's rates, but I'll give you credit. I thought that cow was a goner, and I give 'most four hundred for her. I'll stop by and settle up with Dick next time I'm in town. That suit?"

"That'll be fine. Let me know if she has any more problems."

I checked with Dick Mathes on the two-way radio and wrote down the directions for three additional calls. Two hours later, I pulled into the garage of the animal hospital and parked next to Dr. Schultz's truck. There was a car already spotted with leaves under the ancient oak in the parking lot.

In the reception area, I found Dr. Schultz, a middle-aged couple, and a boy, about six years old. The boy was holding a burlap sack with something moving inside.

"Ah, Dr. Gross, here you are," Schultz said. "I want you to meet Bill and Jennifer Jansen."

The man stood straighter, trying to match my height but lacking two inches. He was clean-shaved with thinning reddish-brown hair, nice smile, even teeth. His handshake was firm.

Mrs. Jansen stayed seated, smiled, and murmured, "Hello."

I smiled and nodded. "Mrs. Jansen. Pleased to meet you both."

Schultz put a hand on the boy's shoulder. "This is Billy."

I extended my hand, and the boy took it, shaking once, hard, up and down. The boy had red hair, a wide grin, no front teeth, and lots of freckles.

"Pleased to meet you, Doctor Gross," he said politely.

"What's in the sack, Billy?" I asked.

The boy held the top of the sack open and showed me a small, shiny black animal. A stark white stripe ran the length of its back and down a feather-duster tail.

Mrs. Jansen got to her feet. She was a foot shorter than her husband and matronly. Her curly, reddish hair was cut short. "Some neighbors claim skunks make good pets. I'm not so sure. Billy found this baby, and he wants to keep him. What do you think? If we de-scent him will he make a good pet?" she asked.

"I told them I don't do that kind of surgery, but I was pretty sure you could handle it," Schultz smiled.

I was certain I remembered the description of the procedure from a surgery class. The skunk was still too young to have learned to spray, but there was bound to be musk in the sacs.

"Sure," I said. "I can descent him, but we won't be able to give him anesthesia in the vein as we do dogs and cats. We'll have to put him in a closed container with ether. There's a possibility he'll die from the anesthesia."

"I guess the more important question for us is will a skunk will make a good pet," Bill Jansen repeated.

Billy fixed his eyes on me, his face full of apprehension. "What will happen if I don't take care of him? I've been feeding him milk with a doll bottle. He'll die!" Billy exclaimed.

I held out my hand and Billy handed me the sack.

"OK, Billy, I'll do my very best to take good care of him. However," I squatted directly in front of the boy, "a de-scented skunk is still a wild creature, not like a dog or cat. Do you understand? You will have to be careful around him when he grows up, or he will bite you."

Dick Mathes walked into the room.

"Oh, I've known several young people with pet skunks. They're lots of fun."

He is anxious to watch me struggle getting those scent glands out.

"I'm going to do this out in the barn. If I nick one of his scent glands, it will stink up the whole hospital. Dick, have we got an old ice chest we can use for an anesthetic chamber?"

Dr. Schultz and Dick Mathes followed me to the barn.

"You ever even seen one of these done, Dave?" asked Schultz.

"Nope."

I carried the sack with the skunk in one hand, a hard-used ice chest in the other. I left both in the barn while Dick and I carried the small animal surgery table out. I poured ether onto a wad of cotton, dropped it into the ice chest, opened the sack, dropped the skunk into the chest, and closed the lid. I listened carefully until the skunk stopped moving around, lifted the lid, and gave the animal a poke.

"Well, he's anesthetized and still breathing; so far, so good," I announced.

"Dick, do you suppose you can find some plastic sandwich bags?"

"I expect so. What do you need them for?"

"We'll need something to put the scent glands in."

"Gotcha."

I took the skunk out of the ice chest and arranged him on the surgical table, on his belly with his tail tied up over his back. I added ether to a cone designed for a cat and placed it over the skunk's muzzle, then clipped the entire area around the anus, and prepared the skin for surgery.

Dick returned with a box of sandwich bags.

"Well, the glands are where they're supposed to be at five and seven o'clock," I said. "Except it's a she, not a he. Guess we need to tell the Jensen family that before they take her home. Dick, please monitor her breathing and remove the cone periodically. We need to keep her anesthetized just enough so she doesn't move."

I found the right side papilla, clamped it with a mosquito forceps, and slowly dissected the gland. To my surprise it peeled out whole, the duct held closed by the forceps.

"As soon as I remove the clamp you need to close up the baggie," I told Dick.

I deposited the sac in the plastic sandwich bag that Dick held open for me.

Only a faint scent escaped before Dick sealed the bag. The left side sac also came out whole. When I tried to drop the gland into a second plastic sandwich bag, the duct stuck to one of the jaws of the forceps. I gave a shake to flip it off, but the gland missed the bag and landed directly on top of my right foot. Stink filled the barn. Dr. Schultz and Dick beat a laughing retreat into the clinic slamming the door behind them. The sac was firmly stuck to the instep top of my new rough-out boot.

The skunk started to wake up. Breathing through my mouth, I sprayed the open wounds on both sides of her anus with antiseptic and put her back in the burlap sack.

The fragrance from my boot brought tears to my eyes. I picked the half-empty sac off my boot with the forceps and deposited it into the sandwich bag Dick had dropped on the floor while making his escape. Washing off my boots with the high-pressure hose used to clean the barn did very little to abate the odor, but both of my feet now made squishy noises with every step. I took off the boots and my soaked socks, put them outside the barn door, and slipped into the rubber boots I should have been wearing from the onset.

The Jansens paid ten dollars and left with newly named Petunia.

"So, Dr. Gross, what happened to your boots?" Dick could barely get it out for laughing. "If you wash them in tomato juice, it will take the smell away . . . or so I've heard."

Mumbling under my breath, I put my wet boots and socks in a plastic garbage bag and went home for lunch.

~

"You're joking?" Rosalie giggled when I described what had happened. "You dropped the scent gland on your boot? I think I can smell it. Aren't those the boots you bought last week?"

"Nonsense, you can't smell the boots. I left them outside in a plastic bag. Do we have any tomato juice? Dick claims if I soak them in tomato juice it will take away the smell."

I left the boots soaking in tomato juice while Rosalie and I ate tuna salad sandwiches. After lunch, I washed the boots again and left them outside to dry.

~

That evening I was home early, a little after seven. After dinner, I washed the dishes; Rosalie dried.

"I met Mrs. Rosenstein today," she said.

"Who is Mrs. Rosenstein?"

"She and her husband own the jewelry store on Main."

"Really, are you in the market for jewelry?"

"No, silly." Rosalie punched my left arm. "Kathy told me she thought the Rosensteins are Jewish."

"Really? So did you have a nice visit?"

"Yes, she was very nice, about our parents' age. She told me they go to Billings for the High Holy Days."

"Is that something you think we need to do? Is that the closest? Billings is about 275 miles from here."

"I know. I looked it up on the map. I feel we ought to attend services, and apparently, that's the closest. It wouldn't feel right to me not to go at least for evening services on Rosh Hashanah and Yom Kippur. Didn't you always go?"

"Yeah, I did, even when I was in school. I usually drove from Fort Collins to Denver. My family went for both evening and morning services on Rosh Hashanah and pretty much all day on Yom Kippur."

"Well then, don't you think you'll feel weird if we don't go?"

"Probably. Did you find out when services are?"

"Yes, the eve of Rosh Hashanah is September 22; that's a Thursday night. Yom Kippur eve is the thirtieth, Friday night."

"OK, I'll talk to Dr. Schultz and see if he has a problem with my being gone. It will take about six hours to drive there. I suppose services start at sundown, about six-thirty or seven, so if we left here before noon, we could get there in time. We could get a motel room for that night, change clothes, then go to services again in the morning, and drive back in the afternoon. For Yom Kippur, we could do the same thing, but we won't get back here until very late if we stay for closing services. Will we need tickets?"

"I didn't know if you would be willing to ask for time off, so I didn't ask."

"OK, I'll talk to Dr. Schultz tomorrow and find out."

The next day I asked Dr. Schultz if I could take the necessary time off explaining the importance of the Jewish New Year and Day of Atonement.

"I've heard of your 'Row Shashana' and 'Yom Keeper' but never really knew what they were all about. We had a coupla Jews in my outfit during the war, and I know it was a big deal to them. Some

Jewish baseball players refuse to play on those days, like Sandy Koufax. What days will you be gone?"

"We'll leave before noon on Thursday the twenty-second and return late the next night and then again at noon on Friday the thirtieth and come back the next day, very late."

"OK, sure, not a problem."

~

We spotted Congregation Beth Aaron on the eleven hundred block of North Broadway, across the street from St. Vincent Hospital. The building looked like a residence. There were no signs of any kind to identify it as a synagogue.

"Mrs. Rosenstein told me that until a few years ago there was quite a bit of anti-Semitism, even some Ku Klux Klan stuff in the 1920s, so when the temple was finished in 1940, they didn't want it to attract any attention."

I nodded and frowned, not happy with that information. We found a motel, checked in, showered and changed clothes, ate a light dinner at a small café next to the motel, and parked around the corner from the synagogue at 6:45, services to start at 7:00 p.m. There was a small gathering of folks standing outside talking in front of the building. Rosalie introduced me to Mr. and Mrs. Rosenstein, who both seemed very nice. They introduced us to some other very friendly folks who were all happy to welcome a young Jewish couple into their community.

After the service, we introduced ourselves to Rabbi Samuel Horowitz and his wife, Minna, who also made us feel welcome. They understood that Sidney was too far away for them to expect to see us more than a few times a year, but they seemed happy we had made the effort for these High Holy Days.

When we showed up again for Yom Kippur, almost every Jew in eastern Montana and northern Wyoming welcomed us, but it was a small congregation.

~

The "skunk boots," stained and ugly after repeated tomato juice soakings, were scentless when I wore them outside. When I was in the heated truck, I could smell skunk. When I stopped for coffee or for lunch in a heated restaurant, everyone within ten feet started sniffing and looking around. Two weeks after Yom Kippur, I threw the boots in the trash.

CHAPTER 10:

BLACK CATTLE, BLACK NIGHT

I INCORPORATED THE RINGING OF THE PHONE into my dream. After the third ring, I roused, fumbled for the light, knocked the receiver off the cradle, and retrieved it from the floor.

"Yes, this is Dr. Gross," I mumbled.

Dick Mathes's too-happy voice brought me only half-awake. "Doc, you awake? You drop the phone?" He didn't wait for me to respond. "The Simpson boys just pulled in with some waterbelly steers. You need to get over here."

"What the hell time is it?" I croaked.

"It's already four thirty, time to get up and going," Dick responded.

"How the hell did the Simpsons find the steers in the middle of the night?"

"They found 'em late yesterday afternoon." Dick laughed. "They brought 'em in from the pasture and loaded 'em into their stock trailer last night. They were just being nice, letting you sleep in."

"I'll thank them when I get there," I grumbled.

Summer was gone. Every morning now brought a hard frost.

The Simpson brothers seemed extraordinarily happy to have gotten me out of my warm bed and gave me a big "Good morning, sunshine" when I came through the barn to the outside pens. I refrained from showing them my middle finger.

The pens and chutes behind the hospital were brightly lit. Unfortunately, the lights did not create any warmth. Five steers occupied one of the holding pens. Another four were lined up, head to tail, in the chute leading to the squeeze.

"The ones in the pen aren't completely blocked," Don Gordon said, handing me a steaming cup. I sipped the coffee as we observed the five in the corral. The steers were stamping their feet straining to urinate. All five were dribbling a little urine, their tails flicking in all directions, indicating pain.

The four steers in the chute were in bad shape, their urethras probably blocked with calculi. They were depressed, smelled of ammonia, their eyes bloodshot. One had a distended abdomen. He was still on his feet but looked moribund.

"Don, will you get me a bottle of Depropanex and one of Combiotic, please?"

Don indicated, with his chin, a cart placed in the lane. There were five filled 10 cc syringes and the bottle of Depropanex standing next to them. Depropanex relieved smooth muscle spasm. I hoped it would allow the steers to urinate with enough force to flush out the calculi. Five additional syringes were filled with the white antibiotic. The Simpson brothers helped Don and me crowd the five steers in the pen into one of the other chutes, and I gave each of them an intramuscular injection of Depropanex and another of the Combiotic.

I removed my coat but kept on my down vest. Rolling up my shirtsleeves as high as possible, I pulled a plastic rectal sleeve over my left hand and arm and then lubricated the sleeve with mineral oil from a squeeze bottle. I climbed up and over the chute containing the sicker of the steers and down behind the last one in the line. I lifted the steer's tail with my right hand and pushed my left hand into the warm rectum. The steer pressed forward into his cohorts bellowing his indignation. His bladder was distended, ready to burst. I removed my hand, inverting the rectal sleeve as I pulled it off.

"Don, if you Ted and Ed will move these steers, please," I said. "Put the one I just examined in the squeeze chute first. His bladder is just about ready to rupture."

Don and the Simpsons moved the animals while I did rectal exams on the other steers. Don plugged in clippers and removed the hair over the tail head and from the area under the anus on the steer restrained in the squeeze chute.

I opened up one of five "heifer" packs of surgical instruments that Don put on a cart next to the squeeze chute, along with a bottle of procaine and syringes and needles. I washed both of the shaved areas with soap and water and then applied some tincture of iodine.

I injected procaine into the epidural space, and the steer's tail went limp. He didn't respond to needle pricks of the skin around and under the anus. After washing and drying my hands, I put on a pair of sterile surgical gloves.

Don held the steer's tail up, out of the way, while I made a bold incision, almost four inches long, directly on the midline about three inches below the anus. The skin and underlying tissues fell to the side as the scalpel blade slid down. It took only a moment for me to dissect between the muscles down to the penis. I pushed the retractor penis muscle to one side using my fingers to free the penis. I pulled on it with my left hand and severed it as far down as I could reach with the scalpel. I pulled the stump out, stepping to the side to avoid the stream of urine.

When the bladder was empty, I sutured the bottom of the penis stump to the bottom of the skin incision and then split the urethra about an inch up from the bottom of the stump with a scissors, spread the sides apart, and sutured each edge of the urethra to the skin wound margins on that side. Last, I closed the remaining skin over the top of the penis. The whole procedure, including the epidural anesthesia, took just over fifteen minutes. The steer was now a heifer, life saved until he could be sold for slaughter. I injected 10 cc of the Combiotic, and we turned him into one of the empty pens.

I performed the same procedure on the other steers. The poor animal with the distended abdomen and probable ruptured bladder was strictly a salvage procedure. I completed the heifer procedure on him and then inserted a trocar into his lower abdomen, draining off urine from the abdominal cavity. Next, I flushed the abdomen with three liters of saline mixed with antibiotic.

"If the tear is small and the bladder stays collapsed, it might heal. I could do a laparotomy and try to repair the tear in the bladder, but this steer is so sick he probably couldn't withstand the shock of the surgery. Even if he lives, the surgery would cost you about the same as what you'll get for him if he makes it to the sale barn," I explained.

I then turned my attention to the other five steers. Two of them had only partially emptied their bladders; the other three had evacuated and no longer showed signs of pain. I passed a small-diameter urinary catheter as far as I could up the penis in each of the two that were still partially blocked and then back-flushed saline and antibiotics into the penis, hoping to clear the obstruction.

"We should keep these two here and continue to treat them. I hope they'll flush out. The other three seem to have passed most of their stones. We need to keep them up and watch them close until you get them sold; they're likely to block up again."

"I expect we won't get much for any of the new-made heifers," Ed said. "The buyers will spot them immediately and knock down the price. The packing houses will make money off them, but we're hosed."

"Yeah, but we'll get more for 'em now than if they'd died," Ted responded.

"I need to keep and treat all of them for at least 24 hours," I said. "That will take us to sale day. If he lives, the steer with the ruptured bladder will probably need to be with us until next week."

While I started cleaning up, the Simpsons went into the clinic to settle the bill with Dick. When they returned, Ted unhooked their stock trailer. "We'll pick it up on the way home. Will you and Don join us for some breakfast?"

"No thanks, guys. Looks like we have a full day ahead. We best get on with it. Thanks anyhow. We'll take a rain check."

The brothers waved as they drove off.

I checked the steers again before going inside to clean and re-sterilize the instrument packs. The two un-operated steers were passing urine in intermittent streams. All the steers, except the one with the ruptured bladder, were at the hayrack working at a bale of alfalfa hay. None of those happily eating indicated any displeasure about their recent ordeal.

"That's a good sign," I said to Don. "Have you ever seen an animal die with its head in a feed rack?"

"Nope," Don replied.

"Let's put the one with the ruptured bladder in a stall inside the barn," I said.

The temperature never got above freezing all day. I did two more steer-to-heifer operations at two different ranches, treated a milk-fever case, three cases of foot rot, two mastitis cases, and an assortment of injuries to both horses and cattle. When I returned to the hospital, it was almost seven in the evening. I checked on the Simpsons' steers while Don cleaned and refilled the truck. They all seemed to be doing well.

The phone rang, and I heard Dick's voice: "I don't know of any rabies in cattle round here."

I went to the office door and gave Dick a questioning look. He made a face and shrugged.

"OK, Mrs. Greene. . . . Yes, I know how to get to your place. . . . Yes, I know. The mister just told you to call. I'll send out the new young doc. . . . Yes, I'm certain he can handle the problem for you, probably twenty minutes or less."

I called Rosalie. "Hi, honey, it's me. I just got another call, and it sounds as if it's going to take a while. You should go ahead and eat dinner; don't wait for me. I don't know when I'll get home. . . . OK, see you after a bit. Love you!"

I told Don I could handle things, and he went home.

The Greenes' farm was on the east edge of town, directly off the highway. I drove past their place many times each day. That morning,

I'd seem twenty or thirty head of Black Angus cattle turned out in the sugar beet field that morning and already had a good idea of what the problem was.

I turned off the highway into the Greenes' drive. Thick, low-hanging clouds hid both moon and stars. The headlights of the truck struggled to penetrate the gloom. I drove to the yard back of the house where a single light showed from the kitchen window. The yard was frozen mud. I parked twenty feet from the back porch door. As I turned off the ignition, the porch light came on, and Mr. Greene stepped out, pulling on his coat while sticking a three-battery flashlight into the back pocket of his coveralls. He waved for me to stay in the truck and walked around to the passenger door. I leaned over and opened it for him.

"She's out in the beet field, Doc."

Great . . . he has a black cow out in a field, either dead or dying, on a black night. I wonder if he actually knows where she is and if there are more than just the one.

"The last time I saw her," Greene responded to my unasked question, "she was in the northeast corner of the field. There might a bin two or three others just standin' around droolin' too. I turned 'em out into the beet tops afore light of the mornin' and saw 'em lookin' sick when I come in for lunch. I had another field of beets to finish harvestin' and hadn't thought to tell the missus to call 'til I come in for dinner. It was mostly dark, and I didn't see the cows on the way in."

Wonderful . . . we're going to drive out into a forty-acre field to look for an unknown number of black cattle, dead or dying, on a dark night. "Well," I said aloud, "since we don't know where the sick cows are, we need to do a systematic search."

Greene got out and opened the field gate. After I drove through, he closed it and got back into the truck.

"Go left from here. Th' east-west fence is 'bout forty yards out. We can come off that."

We slowly weaved our way back and forth across the field.

I hope these cattle aren't moving around.

The beet farmers harvested sugar beets with a machine that digs up the beets and chops off the tops. The beets then ride a conveyer that dumps them into a truck or trailer. The discarded tops, with a small portion of the beet, end up back on the field. It was common practice to turn cattle into the field after harvesting the beets since the beet tops provide highly nutritious feed.

"As you know, cattle don't normally chew their food much," I said. "They swallow what they bite off and then eructate it up and chew at their leisure. When the beet top is large and frozen, it sometimes lodges in the esophagus. We call that choke. If the obstruction is complete, the animal can't eructate."

The glow from the dash barely outlined his face. A glance told me that Greene understood nothing of what I had just told him.

"What I mean is they can't burp. The methane gas produced in their rumen builds up. When the rumen fills up with gas, it puts pressure on the diaphragm, and the animal can't breathe. Eventually the cow suffocates." Another glance told me Greene was nodding without comprehension.

"I think the cows have beet tops caught in their gullets. If we don't find them and push the tops down into their belly, they will bloat and die."

The beet farmer finally demonstrated understanding and an eager interest in finding the animals. He peered intently out into the darkness, leaning out through the open window of the truck, scanning with his flashlight.

I managed to stop the truck just before hitting a large black hump on the ground. I backed the truck up ten feet. The headlights illuminated a cow lying on her right side, her abdomen distended, her legs thrust out straight from her body. I jumped out of the truck and ran to her. She was still breathing but with extreme difficulty. Greene was directly behind me.

"You gonna stick her, Doc?" he asked.

"No, I'm going to try something else first," I said.

An emergency rumenotomy, sticking a knife or trocar into the rumen, could save an animal's life but almost inevitably results in infection and gastrointestinal problems. I trotted back to the truck, grabbed a large, stiff, rubber tube called a probang, about twice the diameter of a garden hose. I also took a mouth gag, a block of wood with a hole drilled in the center and straps to affix the device to the head.

"Mr. Greene, would you please turn off the truck but leave the headlights on? . . . Thanks."

I put the mouth gag in place, buckling the straps behind her head. The cow struggled weakly. I pushed the probang down her throat advancing the tube until it met resistance. Taking the free end of the tube in my mouth I blew in it as hard as I could, dilating her esophagus while continuing to push the tube forward. The obstruction moved. A sudden "whoosh" of methane gas filled the immediate area. I jerked my head to the side. Greene stepped back three steps.

"Whew," he said. "Stinks pretty rotten, Doc."

"You got that right," I responded.

The cow's abdomen gradually collapsed to normal, and she struggled, rolling onto her sternum. I held her head, moving the tube around to let off more gas. The cow looked at me stupidly. When no more gas escaped, I removed the tube and the mouth gag. The cow stayed on her sternum for a short time and then struggled to her feet.

"Well, I think she'll make it," I said. "Let's get back in the truck and try to find any others."

After ten minutes of searching, we spotted another cow. This one was standing with her head down, salivating profusely. I stopped the truck, and we got out. When we got within a few feet, the cow trotted off a few yards and stopped. We went back to the truck and searched for her with the headlights. When we found her again, I got out my nylon throw rope and roped her from twenty-five feet away. She dragged me for two steps and then stopped, breathing hard. I snubbed her to the front bumper of the truck, put in the mouth gag, and relieved the choke.

After covering the rest of the field, we returned to the north fence and completed a basket-weave search at right angles to the first pattern. I thought I spotted two more cows having trouble, although it might have been the same cow. Each time the animal wandered off into the darkness before we could get out of the truck.

I finally lost patience.

"This is pretty hopeless. If there are any others here, we're going to have a devil of a time finding them. It's pointless to chase around in the dark. I don't think it's wise to leave these cattle out in the field."

Greene seemed confused.

"When the beet tops are frozen, the cattle don't chew them; they swallow them whole and they get stuck," I repeated impatiently. "That's what's causing the problem. I suggest you ask your neighbors to help you. If you get enough people out here with flashlights, you can probably herd all the cattle out of the field and into a dry lot, preferably one with lights. If you find any more choked animals, they'll be where I can get to them. If you do that, I'll be happy to come out again and take care of them."

"Well, I reckon gettin' the neighbors together and bringin' in the cattle would be considerable trouble," Greene said. "Besides, I bin turnin' cows into these beet fields as long as I bin farmin', and my Daddy afore that."

"That's your decision. I don't think we can accomplish anything looking for them in the dark." I was fighting a losing battle to keep exasperation out of my voice. I dropped Greene off at the house and made out a bill for my services.

"Have a good evening, Doc. I'll stop by to pay this next week, after I get the check for my beets. Thanks for comin' out. I think you saved them two."

"You're welcome, Mr. Greene. Check the field at first light and call if you find any animals in trouble."

CHAPTER 11:
THE STOCKYARDS CAFÉ

AFTER LEAVING MR. GREENE and his Black Angus cattle, I drove home and clumped down the stairs to our apartment, grumbling.

Mister was sitting at the door. Rosalie came out of the kitchen, drying her hands, a big welcoming smile on her face.

"Hi," I said and held out my arms.

"Hi," Rosalie responded, slipping into my embrace.

I was cold, dirty, tired, and hungry. She was soft and warm in my arms. The top of her head reached just to my chin, and her hair smelled of wildflowers.

She leaned back. "Whew, you don't smell so good. I have an idea. Why don't you grab a quick shower and change your clothes? I'll get our dinner into the oven."

"You won't believe what I've been doing, but you're right. That's rumen gas you smell. I'll take a shower and change. Tell you all about it while we eat. You shouldn't have waited for me, though." I glanced at my watch. "Jesus, it's after nine!"

Mister whined and went to the door. He had been busy protecting Rosalie all day, and now that I was home, he was ready to go out. I followed him up the stairs, patted him on the back, and opened the door. The dog turned, looked at me, wagged his tail, and ran through the opened door.

My turn for relief, I headed for the shower. After washing off, I gradually reduced the cold water keeping the hot water faucet wide open. I stood in the steaming torrent, muscles relaxing, until I heard a soft knock at the door.

"You planning to stay in there all night?" asked Rosalie. "I'm hungry."

"Be right out."

I toweled off padding, barefoot, towards the bedroom. Mister was back in the apartment. He chased after me, pushing his cold nose under the towel. Rosalie, laughing, encouraged the dog to do his best.

⌁

The alarm went off at 6:00 a.m. I let Mister out into the dark. A light dusting of snow covered the ground. I went back down the stairs as quietly as possible trying not to awaken Rosalie.

I started some coffee and then placed six strips of thick-sliced bacon into our cast iron skillet. Rosalie and I were not Jewish enough to forego bacon. When it was crisp, I walked to the bedroom, leaned over, and kissed Rosalie's forehead. She smiled, stretched both arms, then her legs, pointing fingers and toes, finally opening her eyes.

"Hi," she said.

"Good morning. Are you planning on joining me for breakfast?"

Rosalie sniffed, "Smells good. Since you've gone to all that trouble, guess I will."

I tickled her ribs.

She shrieked and called out for Mister to protect her.

"Mister's out," I told her. "You'll have to protect yourself." I pretended to tickle her again. "This can easily lead to something," I murmured, "but the damn phone is bound to ring soon."

We sat at the table eating, chatting about our respective plans for the day.

"Sue and Linda Simpson and I are meeting for lunch. They're bringing along Natalie Simpson, the sister, so we can get acquainted."

A shadow flicked past the window. I looked up and saw a creature on its side, sliding by.

"What the hell!" I jumped up to peer out the window. "It's a deer, actually a deer carcass. Mister is dragging it towards the door."

I bounded up the stairs and out the door as Mister came around the corner of the house. His trophy was a field-dressed, spike-antlered mule deer.

"Mister, drop it! Get downstairs," I pointed down the steps to the apartment.

Dejected, he obeyed.

I went over to inspect the carcass, covered in dirt, leaves, and twigs and then went back down for my coat.

"Mister stole some hunter's deer, probably off an open back porch," I explained. "I've got to find out where he got it."

The carcass was heavy enough to leave clear drag marks. I followed them down the street and around to the back of the house five doors down. There was an open back porch with an empty steel hook attached to a rafter. I went around to the front of the house and knocked on the door.

A thin, scowling man answered. He was balding, gray at the temples, holding a mug of very aromatic coffee.

"Hi, sorry to disturb you. I'm your neighbor, Dave Gross. I live in the basement apartment down the block. I'm afraid my dog stole your deer from the back porch."

"No way. That spike was over a hundred pounds before I gutted him."

"Sorry, I'm afraid he did."

"Let's go see," said the man. "Come on through."

I stamped my feet on the porch and followed him through the cluttered but clean house.

"Well, it's gone for sure, and I see something dragged it off." He laughed and held out his hand. "You're the new vet, aren't you?"

"Yes, sir."

"I'm George Kemper. I own the Stockyards Café. I heard about you from the Simpson brothers."

He was dressed only in pants, an undershirt and house shoes, but he insisted we go have a look at the deer.

"I need to meet the dog capable of hauling that carcass off."

I apologized all the way back to the apartment about the condition of the carcass.

"Ah, no problem," said Kemper. "Some judicious use of the garden hose will clean it up."

I opened the outside door to the stairs and called down. "Rosalie, please let Mister out."

Mister ran up the stairs to reclaim his trophy but responded immediately to my command to sit.

Kemper patted the dog on the head. "He is beautiful. Best looking shepherd I've seen. It never occurred to me that there might be a dog strong enough to cart off that deer. I was going to take it in to have it cut up this morning."

I helped Kemper carry the deer back, Mister trailing. We carried the carcass into his kitchen and put it on the table.

"You want a cup of coffee?" asked Kemper. "It's a special blend I get for the restaurant."

"No thanks, but I feel real bad about this. I'm happy to pay you whatever the deer is worth."

Kemper laughed. "No harm done, I'll just wash everything off; it'll be fine. I'm going to have it ground up for sausage anyhow. However, I do expect you and your wife to visit my restaurant soon. Best steaks in this part of the country."

"That sounds like a good deal to me," I said. "Maybe this Saturday night?"

"I'll expect you."

⌐

Saturday was a busy day. It was almost 8:00 p.m. when I held open the door of the Stockyards Café for Rosalie. George Kemper was standing behind the bar.

"There they are! I almost gave up on you, Doc." He came out from behind the bar and approached us. "Who's this beautiful lady?"

"Honey, this is Mr. Kemper. This is my wife, Rosalie."

"George, please. Christ, Doc, how did someone as ugly as you get such a handsome woman? Miss Rosalie, have a seat at my bar. What do you drink?"

George fixed Rosalie a Cuba libre and me, a Chivas Regal on the rocks. After we had our drinks in hand, he escorted us through the restaurant, introducing us to the diners, all of whom he knew by name. There were patrons in all but two of the twenty leather-upholstered booths. He led us to one of the empty booths and then leaned over to talk to the two couples in the adjacent booth.

"So, their dog, the biggest, strongest half-wolf I've ever seen, picked up and carried off a hundred-and-fifty-pound, eight-point buck from my back porch. He ate half of it on the way back to their place."

He gave us a wink as we sat down. "How about you two let me bring you the best meal you've had in Montana?"

"Do we have a choice?" I laughed. "We're in your hands."

"Good." As Kemper made his way back to the kitchen, he stopped at each table in his path to exchange a few words, pick up an empty plate, or fill a glass. Within a few minutes, he returned carrying a large plate filled with pickles, olives, and an assortment of raw vegetables and a basket of fresh bread. A waitress trailed him with a water pitcher, a small tub of butter, and a second bowl.

"This little bowl is a dip we make for the vegetables," explained George. "Now, how do you two want your steaks cooked?"

"Well-done for me," responded Rosalie.

"No, no, no, how about just a little pink inside?" begged George. Rosalie smiled and acquiesced.

"No blood," I said. "She won't touch it if she sees any red juice coming out, but I'll take mine medium."

George made his way back to the kitchen, again stopping at several tables along the way.

The waitress returned with a bottle of red wine. "Mr. Kemper says this will go well with your steaks."

"Well, we don't know anything about wines, so whatever he says. I'm sure it will be great."

She showed me the label on a bottle of Coast Ridge, California Zinfandel, estate bottled in 1952. I nodded not knowing what I was supposed to do. The waitress removed the cork, gave it to me, and stood waiting. I looked at the cork and shrugged at Rosalie.

Rosalie leaned over and whispered, "You're supposed to smell it; then tell her it's OK to pour some for a taste."

I frowned and whispered back. "What am I supposed to smell for?"

Rosalie shrugged.

I looked up at the waitress for guidance.

"Beat's me." She smiled and said, "Let me go get Mr. Kemper."

A moment later, George appeared at my side, "Doc, it's time you got educated. Mind if I sit down and join you for a minute or two?"

"Please," I said.

"OK, you inspect the cork to make certain it's not dried out and that there are no indications the bottle has been leaking around it. See, the cork is wet partway up, but the line between the wet part and the dry is clear. The cork should also be nice and pliant, not dry or crumbling. You smell it to make sure there is no vinegar smell. Do it."

I did as instructed.

"OK, now you just nod at the server. He or she will pour a little into your glass. We do this for two reasons. First, if there are any bits of cork on top of the wine, you will get them, not your guests. Second, you get a chance to judge the wine and make certain it is acceptable. The server should show you the label prior to uncorking. That is to make certain it is what you ordered. It also gives you the opportunity to make a mental note so you will recognize the wine again if you like it. You should, in fact, start keeping a diary of both label names and vintage years that you enjoy.

"With a red wine, you want to let it breathe for a while in your glass. Swirl it around. A wine with full body will stick to the glass."

He swirled the wine in my glass and then tipped it to the side and back upright. I could see the wine adhere to the glass.

"See? That means the wine has 'legs.' This is a good thing for a wine to have."

He handed back the glass. "Now, take a sip. Notice if there is any vinegar taste. If there is, you can reject it. Otherwise, you're stuck with it, even if you don't like the taste, unless it is very bitter or off in some other way. If you think it's really bad tasting, most places will just take it away and not charge you. Keeping the customer happy is important."

I took a sip.

"So, what do you think?" asked Kemper.

"I like it," I said. "It's very nice."

"Bullshit," Kemper snorted and then added, "Sorry," directed at Rosalie. "You have to be able to tell me something about it. Can you taste grapes? Does it remind you of some other fruit, plums maybe, strawberries, cherries, or blackberries? Is it smooth, or does it have a bite? Would you describe it as full flavored, watery, tannic, fruity, or musky? Does it leave an aftertaste? Is the aftertaste pleasant or unpleasant?"

"OK," I said frowning with concentration, "I can sort of taste grapes, maybe plums, but it's not sweet. I taste something that is kind of smoky, and there is a bite to it. I also smell something that reminds me of tannic acid, but it is not nearly as unpleasant as a true tannic acid smell."

George smiled broadly. "Good," he said. "You're a quick student. Folks don't appreciate these California Zinfandels yet, but they will. You don't just sit around and drink this wine though. You must have something to eat with it. A strong cheese is good, but it is best with red meat." He poured half a glass of wine for each of us, taking a taste in the bottom of a third glass for him.

"A toast," he said, raising his glass, waiting for us to do likewise. "To the most beautiful Mrs. Gross," he gave Rosalie a slight bow of the head, "and to Doctor Gross. I predict you will both experience much in this life, most of it good. You will come to appreciate fine wines and fine food, and I hope you will remember George Kemper who started you on this journey of discovery. As you become more sophisticated and knowledgeable, you will find people who denigrate the American kitchen. Tonight you will experience the best of that kitchen—the most flavorful beef produced anywhere in the world, fine potatoes properly prepared, fresh bread, and good wine. If you have room afterwards, I even have some homemade apple pie with homemade ice cream for dessert. Now, you two enjoy yourselves. I have other guests to attend to."

It was as he had promised. There was a fresh green salad of Romaine lettuce, crisp and crunchy, with a hint of onion, and the whole smothered in blue cheese dressing. The large hunks of the pungent cheese in the dressing made the wine smoother. The steaks were huge T-bones, well-aged and prime. Each was still well over an inch thick after broiling over George's mesquite fire. They were tender enough to cut with the table knife. Rosalie was appalled at the size of it.

George leaned over her shoulder. "Just eat the tenderloin part of it," he told her quietly, pointing to the inside of the T-bone. "That's the most tender and flavorful. We'll pack up anything you don't eat, and you can make a stew from it or feed it to Mister." Then he was gone again.

"Aren't you surprised to find a plush place like this here, with the smell of the stockyards just outside the door?" Rosalie asked me.

"It is unique, isn't it?"

During the meal, we chatted about Sidney and about what I had been doing all week. Rosalie filled me in on what the Jones family was doing. After our visit to the ranch for Sunday dinner, she and Kathy talked almost daily. I finished my steak and most of the potato. Rosalie ate just the tenderloin portion of her steak and maybe a fourth of the potato. There was still an inch of wine left in the bottle when we pushed our plates away and leaned back, satiated. Only one other booth still housed customers.

George appeared at my shoulder. "You guys done?"

"Stuffed, George," I answered.

"You spoke the truth. That was the best meal ever," added Rosalie.

"Molly," George spoke to the waitress, "please clear their plates and bring back Mrs. Gross's steak in a doggie bag." He split the remaining wine between our glasses.

"You ready for dessert?"

"Mr. Kemper, I can't possibly eat another bite," Rosalie said.

"George, please," he insisted. "You'll make me feel ancient if you don't call me George. How 'bout you, Doc?"

"I think I have barely enough room for a cup of coffee, but not much else," I replied.

We invited George to sit down for conversation, and Rosalie effortlessly proceeded to extract his story.

"I was raised on a ranch in the Badlands but left home before the Simpson brothers started school. I served in the infantry in World War II and fought in France and Germany. While in France, I met and fell in love with a French girl. After I mustered out of the army, I returned to France and married her. Her family is the third generation to own and operate the same *maison* in Reims. We lived in France for six years while I learned the restaurant and hotel business. I finally convinced Marie to come back to Sidney with me in 1952, and we opened this place, but she couldn't, or wouldn't, get used to living away from her family. She returned to France last year. I stayed here. We aren't divorced, but I suppose that will happen eventually. She doesn't want to live here, and I don't want to live in France. Luckily, we don't have any children to complicate things."

"So, does Doctor Schultz bring his family here?" I asked. "He's never mentioned the place to me."

"Rarely. When they do, it's usually with the whole Watts clan, Mrs. Schultz's family. When that outfit is here, the place becomes somber. They're the most disliked family in the county. I don't know of anyone who has had business dealings with them who thought it was a pleasurable experience. How are you getting along with Mrs. Schultz?"

"Well, about the only time I have contact with her is when I get my check at the end of the month. She's not overly warm and makes no attempt to be friendly, but the checks all clear," I said.

"Well, Doc Schultz is a good guy, but if you have to do business with the Watts clan, you'd best be careful. I just bought some land, about a hundred acres, from the lawyer brother, and he did his best to screw me, but unsuccessfully." George smiled.

"Oh? Whereabouts is the property?" I asked.

"It's just this side of the bridge, on the south side of the road. There's been a 'for sale' sign on it for some time. You've probably seen it."

"Oh, yeah, that's a nice spot; has some river frontage too, doesn't it?"

"Yeah, I'm in the process of fixing up the house. I think I'll keep my house in town as a rental property once the farmhouse is finished."

"Well, George, we might be interested in renting your place if we can afford it. We're getting pretty tired of living underground," I told him.

"If you don't mind my asking, what are you paying to rent that basement?" he asked.

"Seventy-five a month," answered Rosalie.

"Well, my house only has two bedrooms and one bath, but the rooms are all pretty good size, including the kitchen. The basement is unfinished, but it's dry and good for storage. I could let you have it for a hundred a month."

"That sounds wonderful," said Rosalie, looking at me for confirmation.

I nodded. "Let us know when you're ready to move. We'll need to buy some furniture, but in a few months we can probably manage."

"I'm buying all new kitchen appliances for the new place, so I can leave you the stove and refrigerator," said George.

The bill for our meal was $14.50 including the wine. Last of the big spenders, I left a $3.50 tip for Molly.

CHAPTER 12:

CHICKEN SOUP

Dr. Schultz, raised on a pig farm sixty miles west of Des Moines, Iowa, was a veteran of World War II. When the war ended, he returned to Iowa and took advantage of the GI Bill. He attended Iowa State University and graduated from the veterinary school there in 1951. During his second year of vet school, he married Cheryl Watts, who was majoring in home economics until she found a husband. Their first son was born six months after their wedding. They lived in Veterans Village in a Quonset hut, as did many other veterans and their families. Since her hometown did not have a veterinarian, her wealthy father convinced the couple to make their home in Sidney where he set Schultz up in practice.

Dr. Schultz was a good mentor for me. He was unassuming and competent and encouraged me to attempt whatever I felt comfortable doing. He was always willing to offer help and advice but only if I asked for it. He probably knew everything worthwhile there was to know about doctoring pigs and cattle and was happy to let me do most of the work on horses and small animals.

Dr. Schultz and I were sitting in the office chatting when the phone rang. Dick answered it.

"Sidney Animal Hospital. . . . What? . . . Well, cook it. . . . Oh, OK, I'm sorry. I'll ask one of the doctors."

He stood in the doorway to the office. "What do you do for a chicken with a broken leg?"

We answered in unison: "Make chicken soup!"

"Tried that. She was irritated with me and let me know it. It's a pet rooster."

Dr. Schultz turned to me. "You're the small animal expert. I don't want any part of this deal. In fact I'm going out to feed my pigs."

Unable to escape his Iowa pig farmer genes, Dr. Schultz kept a boar and half a dozen sows around at all times, selling weaned piglets to farmers with feed to spare. He kept his animals in the hospital barn in the winter and in some outside pens when the weather was warm.

"Well," I said, "tell her I can probably set the leg and it should heal but it will cost the same as for a cat or dog. I'll have to anesthetize it, set the leg, and put it in a splint. Then I'll have to take radiographs to make certain it is properly aligned. It will probably cost her at least twenty-five, maybe thirty dollars."

"That ought to bring her to her senses," Dick muttered returning to the reception desk.

"Doc says he can fix it, but it will cost you twenty-five or thirty dollars, needs X-rays, and he'll have to set it and splint it. . . . Yeah, well OK. He's here now. If you bring it in right away, he'll take care of it."

Even in 1961, exotic pets were becoming a part of the practice.

Janice Freeman was not the person I was expecting. She was almost as tall as I. A luxuriant mass of light-brown, curly hair with a few streaks of gray sprang in multiple directions from her head. Her eyes were widespread, child-like, pale blue. Her fingers were long, the nails painted bright red. Her handshake was as firm as any man's, but her hand was soft, feminine. She wore no wedding ring. She was dressed in very tight new jeans, pressed, with sharp creases front and back. Her white oxford blouse was tucked into her jeans emphasizing her attributes.

"Dr. Gross, thank you for agreeing to take care of Banty. He's my baby."

The bantam rooster tucked under her left arm was pressing into her bosom. Considering the obviously fractured left tibia, he was seemingly content to be held, at least in that position.

"I'm always happy for a new experience," I said, "and treating a chicken with a broken leg will be an entirely new experience for me."

"Well," she said, "Banty is not an ordinary chicken. He's my buddy, and I want him whole and healthy."

"OK," I said. "Let's take him into the treatment room and see what can be done. How did this happen?"

"I haven't a clue," she said. "He was out in the back yard. I have a chicken-wire protected area with a converted doghouse for shelter for him. The pen is strong enough to keep out hawks, as well as ground predators. When I went out to feed him this morning the pen was intact, but I found him like this."

"Is he always this calm?" I asked.

"When I hold him he is," she said.

"Well, that's good. The biggest problem I thought we would have is anesthetizing him so I could set the leg. Giving him an anesthetic could be fatal. If he remains as calm as he is now, we might be able to do what we need to do without anesthesia."

Miss Freeman continued to hold the rooster under her arm while I constructed and fit yet another Thomas splint. I was getting quite adept at fashioning these devices. The rooster didn't respond to the manipulation of his broken leg the whole time I was fitting the splint. Once I had the splint constructed, I taped his foot to the end of it, easily manipulated the fracture to align the ends, and taped the leg in place.

"Now let's get some radiographs to make certain the fracture is aligned properly," I said.

Taking the radiographs proved to be more difficult than setting the leg. Miss Freeman and I put on lead aprons, and she held Banty with a hand on either side of his body, With one cumbersome lead-lined glove, I tried to hold the end of the Thomas splint in position for a slightly oblique anterior-posterior view of the fracture and the X-ray cassette under his leg with the other gloved hand. Banty managed to free both wings and commenced to twist and turn while beating his wings, squawking all the while. Miss Freeman let go, and I was holding the bird by the splint, with the impossible-to-manipulate glove. I shook off the opposite glove and managed to grab him before he escaped the table.

"I'm sorry, Doctor. I didn't expect him to struggle like that. We were hurting him, I think."

"I don't think so," I answered. "I think we put him in an abnormal position, and he was responding to that."

I held the bird with both hands, the glove still on my right hand. Banty started pecking with enthusiasm and evil intent on the glove.

"Can you try to hold him again, Miss Freeman? Maybe pick him up and put him under your arm again. He seems comfortable with that."

She did, and Banty calmed immediately. I took a clean towel from a drawer and, with her help, wrapped the bird with the towel, leaving just the splinted leg free. Once his head was covered, Banty became still.

"I'm sorry," I said. "I should have wrapped him like this from the onset. It would have made things easier."

With Miss Freeman holding him, still wrapped in the towel, I was able to get the two radiographic views I needed. I exited the darkroom with the still dripping films in their holders. Banty was unwrapped and again content under his mistress's left arm. I held the films up to the viewer and pointed out the site of the fracture.

"The alignment is very good," I said.

"Would it be possible for me to have a copy of those X-rays?" she asked.

I was puzzled. "I really don't have any way to copy them," I said, "and I'm supposed to keep all radiographs as part of the patient's records."

"OK, I understand. What if I come back with my camera and take a photo of the X-rays here? Would that be OK?"

Now I was really puzzled. "Sure, I guess. Do you think that would work? Why do you want them?"

"Just like to have them." She smiled.

Miss Freeman returned that same afternoon setting up a very expensive-looking thirty-five millimeter, single-lens reflex camera on a tripod. She took several photos of the X-rays on the view box, changing settings each time.

When I arrived at the hospital the next morning, that day's edition of the *Sidney Herald* was on my desk. On the front page was a photo of Banty walking on his splint and another photo of his radiographs. The headline proclaimed: "New Vet Does His Thing."

I looked at the masthead of the paper and found Janice Freeman listed as the special features editor.

PART III:
WINTER 1960–61

PART II
WINTER 1960–61

CHAPTER 13:

SIAM

WINTER TOOK A FIRM GRASP on the practice. Outside, the incessant wind pushed the cold through any amount of clothing and outer garments. Dr. Schultz and Don were out on calls. I was in the office, warm, cozy, dozing with my feet up on the desk. I heard a car drive up and someone getting out and then screaming, the sound tomcats make while fighting over a female in heat.

I walked into the waiting room as Mrs. Neilsen came through the door. The head of a Siamese cat poked out from its baby blanket wrapping, the source of the awful racket. Mrs. Neilsen was white haired, trim. She changed arms holding the constantly wailing cat while removing a long overcoat. She was dressed neatly in a wool suit.

"Mr. Mathes," she addressed Dick, "is one of the vets here to take care of Siam? She has been carrying on like this since early this morning. I don't understand it. She was fine yesterday, playful, ate her dinner. I just don't understand what's going on. She's in terrible pain."

"Yes, Mrs. Neilsen. This is Dr. Gross. He'll take care of Siam."

I walked over and held out my hands. "Hello, Mrs. Neilsen. Let me take her, and we'll see what we can figure out. Something is certainly making her terribly unhappy."

The caterwauling continued as I took Siam into the exam room and put her on the stainless steel exam table. I removed the hand-knitted, powder-blue baby blanket from around her and just managed to catch her as she tried to jump off the table, holding her by the scruff of the neck. Her back arched, her abdomen tucked in pain. The scleras of both eyes were rife with bulging blood vessels and were a brownish color, rather than their normal white. The mucous membranes of her mouth were also off-color, and her perfusion time, the time it takes for the membranes to turn pink again after pressing a finger and blanching them, was slower than normal. Her heart rate was fast, but her heart sounds were normal, as were her breath sounds. Her rectal temperature was a little lower than normal. Her hair coat was shiny, well cared for, but her screaming intensified when I gently palpated her abdomen.

"Well, Mrs. Nielsen, Siam has some serious abdominal problems, but I'm not certain what they are. I need to do some blood work on her and take some radiographs, X-rays. I'm going to give her a tranquilizer to make her more comfortable and make it easier for me to position her for the radiographs. You can leave her, or if you prefer, you can wait in the waiting room. It shouldn't take more than an hour or so, and I should have some answers for you."

"That's fine, Doctor. I'll just wait until you can tell me what is wrong. Her screaming is awful, is it not?"

I gave the cat an intramuscular injection of Acepromazine. Dick came into the kennel room as I put her in a cage and handed me a folder containing the cat's records. I looked through the file as I walked to the waiting room.

"Let me get a little more history while the tranquilizer is taking effect," I said to Mrs. Neilsen. "You say the signs of pain started just this morning?"

"Yes, she ate her dinner last night, finished it right off. Generally, she is a little fussy, but last night she seemed very hungry, almost wolfed it down. Then, after I finished doing the dishes from dinner, the mister and I were in the living room. I was darning some socks and had my mending basket on my lap. I dropped a spool of thread on the floor, and she was playing with it, batting it around the room, and chasing it."

I looked up. "A spool of thread. Did she unravel it?"

"Now that you mention it, she did unravel it. It was just some ordinary black mending thread, and I have several spools of it, so I didn't care. She was having such fun with it. Before I went to bed, I picked up the spool from the floor. It was empty. I didn't think anything of it, just assumed I would find the thread the next time I vacuumed the carpet."

"You know, my mom has a habit of sticking the needle she's using into the spool of thread when she's done mending. Do you do that?" I asked.

"Yes, as a matter of fact I sometimes do. I usually stick it through the paper on the end of the spool. Is that what you mean?"

"Yes, was there a needle on the spool when you picked it up?"

"No, now that you mention it, I don't remember that there was, but I didn't think anything about it. I don't always attach the needle to the spool. You don't suppose she ate a needle. Oh my word!"

"It's a possibility and would explain her symptoms. If she did swallow a needle, it should show up on the radiographs. It sounds as though the tranquilizer has taken effect. I'll get started."

Cats with sore abdomens are difficult. I had to rule out pyometria, an infection of the uterus, an abdominal tumor, kidney problems, a host of GI problems, and a long list of other things. First, I got a blood sample and took the time to do red and white blood cell counts and a differential blood cell count. The white blood cell count was a little high, but the differential count was within normal limits. I asked Dick to help me by holding Siam in position to take radiographs of the thorax and abdomen, both lateral and dorso-ventral. I took the plates into the dark room and developed the film. When I put up the films in the viewer, the problem was obvious. I called Mrs. Neilsen into the treatment room and showed her the radiographs.

"You see right here? That's her stomach." I outlined it for her. "And here, poking into the wall of the stomach, is the needle. I suspect it is wrapped up in a ball of thread. That's probably how she swallowed it."

"Oh, Doctor, what can you do? She can't pass that, can she?"

"Well it's possible, but it could also perforate the gut someplace along the way, and that would cause really serious problems. The best thing we can do is operate and remove it."

"Have you done that before?" she asked.

"No, but when I was in vet school, I assisted one of our surgeons on a couple of stomach surgeries on dogs. The surgery is straightforward. I'm certain I can do it."

She looked at me critically. "How much?"

"How much what?" I asked.

"How much will it cost? And can you save her?"

"Well, I can't guarantee a good result, but I'm pretty certain she'll do fine. The surgery will be . . .," I tried to calculate quickly in my head. *We charge twenty dollars for an ovariohistorectomy. This is trickier than that . . .* "Thirty-five dollars, plus the radiographs, the blood work, drugs, and three or four days of hospitalization. The total bill shouldn't be more than sixty to seventy dollars."

"That's a lot of money, sonny," she said, "a lot more than the cat cost."

"Yes, but do you really think you can replace Siam with another cat, Mrs. Neilsen? It wouldn't be the same, would it?"

"No, I suppose you're right. The mister and I are quite attached to her. The mister will have a fit about the cost, though. You don't suppose you can do it for less?"

"No, I don't think so. You know if you needed this kind of surgery it would cost hundreds, maybe thousands for the same procedure."

"So you think I'll be eating sewing needles?"

I looked for but didn't see any indication of humor. She was serious, as near as I could tell. "No, that's not what I meant," I said. "I meant veterinarians perform the same services as medical doctors with equal amounts of training and skill needed and get paid a fraction of what the medical profession receives. We're a bargain."

"I suppose you should have gone to medical school then." She still wasn't smiling.

"Well," I decided to meet her bluntness with my own, "we have to do something for her. Siam's in a great deal of pain, we either have to give her a bulk laxative and hope, without much reason to, that she'll pass the needle and thread without puncturing something along the way or operate or euthanize her. The choice is yours. Do you want to call and consult your husband?"

"No, that's not necessary, young man. I can make the decision." She finally smiled at me. "I like your grit. Most folks back down from me. Go ahead. We do love her, maybe the mister more than I. Is it all right if I wait here until you finish so I know how everything turns out?"

"Yes, of course. You may even be able to convince Dick to make you a cup of coffee while you wait."

"Do you suppose Dick Mathes could really do that?" she responded. "When I allowed him to graduate from high school, I never thought he'd amount to as much as he has." She gave Dick a withering stare.

Dick looked at me and shrugged.

"You think she's tough now, you should have met her before she retired as principal of the high school ten years ago, was it Mrs. Neilsen?"

"Seven," she responded, "and you still haven't learned to hold your tongue."

"Yes'm," he said. "I'll go start a fresh pot of coffee. Do you take cream and sugar?"

"Just a teaspoon of sugar, no cream, and in a real cup, please, not one of those paper things."

"Yes'm."

I had never seen Dick so cowed.

"I'll get Siam ready for surgery," I said. "I'll let you know when I'm done, and you can see her then."

Siam was still relaxed from the tranquilizer so I decided to mask her down using the gas anesthesia machine Dr. Schultz had purchased at my insistence. After I anesthetized her, I put in an endotracheal tube and hooked it to the anesthetic machine at a low setting. I placed a needle in her cephalic vein and hooked up an intravenous drip of saline. Next, I clipped all the hair from her abdomen and washed and prepared the skin with antiseptic.

I opened a general surgery pack on the instrument tray and dropped sterile towels, drapes, and gloves onto the tray, along with some chromic catgut and skin suture material. I decided to rescue Dick and called him in to the OR to monitor anesthesia and act as a gofer for any other supplies I might need.

"Did you get her situated OK?" I asked.

"Yeah, what a tough old bitch she still is. Always did bust my balls. You see how stiff and straight her back is. She's got to be at least seventy-five years old and still made of steel."

"If you talk a little louder, she'll probably hear you. That should make her smile," I said. Behind the surgical mask, I smiled at his discomfort.

After a surgical scrub of hands and arms, I put on a surgical gown and gloves. Dick tied the gown in back, and I placed the towels and drapes and then made the skin incision. When I opened the cat's abdomen, there was a most unwelcome smell. I manipulated the stomach into view and saw the sewing needle sticking out through the wall along with an accumulation of greenish fluid oozing from the puncture.

I packed off the stomach with gauze sponges and made an incision adjacent to the needle. I removed the needle entwined in a ball of black thread and closed the stomach incision with catgut.

"Dick, I need you to empty a five hundred ml bottle of saline into this stainless bowl and then add twenty cc of benzathine penicillin to it. I need to flush and clean up her abdominal cavity. She's getting a case of peritonitis started. Also, add two cc of aqueous penicillin from the bottle of potassium penicillin in the fridge into the IV. Thanks."

I poured some of the penicillin-laced saline into her abdomen and then sucked it out with the sterile turkey baster I had propitiously dumped on the instrument tray as an afterthought. After repeating that procedure three times, I instructed Dick to shoot two more cc of the long-acting penicillin directly into the abdominal cavity. I closed the incision in three separate layers of catgut and then closed the skin.

"Let's turn off the anesthetic and let her wake up," I instructed, peeling off the surgical gloves.

I removed the mask and cap as I walked into the waiting room. Mrs. Neilsen looked up from an issue of *Life* magazine she was reading.

"It went pretty well." I held out a stainless bowl with the needle and thread for her to see.

"This is what we removed. Unfortunately, the needle pierced the wall of her stomach, and she has some peritonitis, which we are treating. The antibiotic we're using should take care of the infection, but we'll have to wait and see. We may have to switch to another antibiotic if the penicillin doesn't work."

"Peritonitis is serious business," she said. "My father died of peritonitis after a hunting accident."

"Yes, but that was probably before the advent of antibiotics. There's a lot more we can do now."

"How will you monitor her condition and make certain the antibiotic you use is having a beneficial effect?"

This was one sharp retired school principal.

"Well," I said, "we'll keep a close watch on her rectal temperature looking for persistent fever. I expect her temperature to spike after the surgery, but it should go down again by tomorrow morning. I'll also follow her white blood cell count. We'll keep close tabs on her."

"Good." She finally favored me with another smile. "You sound as if you know what you are doing, young man. May I see Siam now?"

"Certainly. You can help me put her in a cage and stay with her as long as you like."

"Thank you, Dr. Gross. I appreciate everything you have done for her. As I told you before, she is dear to us."

❧

The next morning, Siam's temperature was three degrees above normal, and she was not eating or drinking. Her white blood cell count had almost doubled from the day before. I decided to switch antibiotics and loaded her up with intramuscular injections of gentamicin every six hours.

Gentamicin is no longer used extensively, too many adverse side effects, but in those days, it was considered a very effective broad-spectrum antibiotic. It worked exceedingly well in this case.

Mrs. Neilsen visited every morning promptly at nine, always dressed in a different suit, clean and pressed, hemline well below her knees. She returned each afternoon at four, still immaculately turned out. On the fourth postoperative day, Siam accepted the teaspoonful of canned tuna Mrs. Neilsen offered. She reported the event to me beaming with pleasure.

"That's great, Mrs. Neilsen. Her temperature was back to normal last evening, and her white count was also normal, but I wasn't able to get her to eat anything. She has been drinking water since yesterday, though, and as you saw, we don't have to give her fluids under the skin any more. Please come back to the ward with me. I want to see for myself how she's eating."

We walked back to the ward, and Siam came immediately to the cage door, purring and rubbing against the bars. I opened the door, and she immediately leaped into Mrs. Neilsen's arms, snuggling. Her purring was almost a roar.

Mrs. Neilsen's laugh filled the room with joy and hope. The two dogs in cages below joined in, barking their good wishes.

"Let's take her out to the treatment room," I said. "We'll put some of that tuna in a bowl for her and see how she does."

Mrs. Neilsen put Siam gently on the table, petting her to keep her in place. I put the remainder from the opened can of tuna into a bowl and set it in front of the cat. She immediately wolfed it down. After she emptied the bowl, she meticulously cleaned her face, alternating front paws after licking them.

"Well, I think we can send her home. She will do much better with you taking care of her than she will here in the hospital. Bring her back in six days, and I'll remove the skin sutures. Call if she stops eating, gets depressed, or acts sick in any way."

CHAPTER 14:

PENELOPE

REBECCA SMYTHE, DICK INFORMED ME, taught the fourth grade. One of the two turtles she kept in her classroom was acting strange. She was bringing it in after school.

She arrived with three girls and two boys in tow. Placing a hand on each child's head in turn, she introduced them. "Dr. Gross, this is Carly . . . Jennifer . . . Susan . . . Tom . . . and Jack. Children, Dr. Gross is a recent graduate of the veterinary school at Colorado State University. He's going to diagnose what is wrong with Penelope."

She turned to me. "We have divided the class into groups of five. We have twenty-five students, and each group is responsible for the care of the turtles for a week. This group is responsible this week. Can one of you tell Dr. Gross what kind of turtle Penelope is and how we take care of her?"

All five raised their hands.

"Good. Carly, why don't you tell us what kind of turtle she is," Miss Smythe said.

Carly was a very bright-looking girl, the tallest child in the group. Her weight hadn't yet caught up with a recent growth spurt, judging by how short her pants were. Her dark hair was in a ponytail that reached just above her shoulders. Her brown eyes, magnified by round, metal-rimmed eyeglasses, stared at me without blinking.

"She's a water turtle, *Clemmys* species. We keep her and her mate in a small stock tank in our classroom."

"Her mate?" I asked.

"Yeah, he's bigger than her and has a bigger head; that's how we know."

"So, how did you get them, and how do you take care of them?" I asked.

The other four children raised their hands.

I looked to Miss Smythe, a petite, young woman who couldn't have been teaching for more than a couple of years. She was wearing gray slacks and a royal-blue blouse, her almost jet-black hair falling loose below her shoulders.

"Jack, you found them and brought them in," she said. "Why don't you tell Dr. Gross where you found them, how we take care of them, and what we plan to do with them at the end of the school year," Miss Smythe instructed.

Jack was dressed in worn but clean Wrangler jeans, scuffed cowboy boots, a T-shirt, and a flannel-lined Levi jacket. He had pushed back the cowboy hat on his head exposing a shock of thick dark-brown hair.

"My family has a ranch on the Missouri about five miles upstream of where the Yellowstone joins it," said Jack. "Before school started, I was helping my dad move some cattle to another pasture, and we found two turtles on the riverbank, sunning. Dad said I could take them and see if Miss Smythe might want to keep them in our classroom for a science project. She thought it was a good idea. The whole class did research to learn how to take care of them properly. At the end of the school year, we are going to put them back where we found them."

"That sounds like a great science project," I said smiling at Miss Smythe. "It also sounds to me as if you have a very good teacher. What did you find out about taking care of turtles?"

I looked at Jennifer, a slightly overweight blond girl with the promise of real beauty. "Jennifer, isn't it?"

"Yes sir. The man that owns Livestock Supply gave us a small, galvanized water tank for them. We learned they need to have about six or seven inches of water to swim in. Sometimes they just walk on the bottom or stay still on the bottom. We have some pieces of wood floating in the water that they climb up on, but sometimes they hide under the wood. We blocked off one end of the tank and filled that end with rocks and sand. They get out of the water and just lie out and get dry. That's called basking.

"We have both a regular light and a fluorescent light over the tank and keep a thermometer in the water. We have to keep the water temperature about eighty degrees. We do that by adding hot water and stirring it around when we need to. We learned that the most important thing is to keep the tank clean. Each week we empty it with a pump, scrub it out, and disinfect it with chlorine bleach. Then we rinse out the chlorine and refill the water. We have a pump and filter in the water and have to change the filter every other week."

"That sounds like a lot of work," I said. "Do you make sure you wash your hands thoroughly every time you do anything with the turtles or their tank?"

"Oh yes," they answered in unison. "Miss Smythe told us they can have bacteria in their digestive tract that can make humans sick."

"Do you know the name of the bacteria?" I asked.

Jack answered, "Sal something . . . salmonica?"

"That's very close. How about salmonella?" I suggested.

"Yeah, salmonella," they all agreed.

"OK, that all sounds pretty good," I responded. "What do you feed these creatures . . . Susan?"

"Oh, they eat lots of different stuff. Mr. Mathes gets us some special turtle food that has all the vitamins and stuff they need. It comes as small pellets and floats in their water. Then we give them lettuce leaves to chew, and sometimes we thaw out some frozen pieces of fish or beef. They like beef heart the best. Sometimes we put a couple of earthworms in the water, and they'll eat those."

"Well, it sounds to me that you guys are taking very good care of your turtles, but it's a lot of work, isn't it? What makes you think Penelope is ill?"

"Well, Doctor," it was Carly again, "about two days ago, Penelope made a nest in the sand, right under the light, where it's warmest. She laid two eggs and covered them up. Since then we've seen her kind of squatting and digging in the nest with her hind feet, but no more eggs. She won't eat and acts kind of depressed, we think." She looked at her classmates and Miss Smythe, who all nodded their agreement.

"Well, OK," I said. "Let's have a look at Penelope and see what we can find."

The turtle was about ten and a half inches long. Her eyes were not sunken, so I assumed she was not dehydrated. She seemed to be breathing a little abnormally, but I hadn't consciously observed turtles breathing, so I couldn't be certain. I turned her over to examine the cloaca. I thought it appeared swollen. I washed my hands carefully, trying to set a good example for the children. I put on a pair of surgical gloves and some K-Y jelly on the little finger of my right hand. I lubricated the cloaca and then advanced the finger until I encountered an egg. I pushed against the soft shell, but the egg did not move. After lubricating the cloaca again and placing a small amount of the K-Y jelly as far around the egg as I could reach I removed the gloves.

"OK," I said, "I think Penelope is egg-bound. She has at least one more egg in her, and it seems to be stuck. I'm going to take an X-ray and see how many more eggs she has. Then I'm going to give her a shot. We'll see if that allows the egg to come out. After I'm done, you can take her back and put her in her nest. If she hasn't laid the eggs by tomorrow morning, you'll have to bring her back, and we'll see what else we can try."

I took the X-ray and then showed the group three eggs in Penelope's reproductive tract.

"Can you all see the three eggs? This one at the end of the line is larger than the others, and that's probably the reason it got stuck. I can also see that she's not constipated and doesn't seem to have any stones in her urinary bladder, a couple of other things that could cause the same symptoms. So, I'm pretty certain the correct diagnosis is that Penelope is egg-bound. Anybody have any questions?"

They all shook their heads that they did not.

"OK then, this shot is oxytocin. It's a hormone that should help her push out the rest of the eggs. Mammals are animals that give birth to live babies and nurse their young. Mammals produce this particular hormone. You've studied about mammals, haven't you?"

They all indicated that they had.

"Reptiles like Penelope lay eggs and produce something very similar to oxytocin. It's called arginine vasotocin, but I don't have any of that, and I don't have a clue where I could even find it. So we'll give her the oxytocin and hope for the best.

"Miss Smythe, will you give me a call tomorrow and let me know if we've helped Penelope through this? I would really like to know if this works so I can know what to do the next time I'm called on to treat a turtle for being egg-bound."

"Absolutely, Dr. Gross. I thank you, and I'm sure the children thank you, don't you, children?"

Again, there was unanimous agreement.

"What do we owe you?" Miss Smythe asked.

"Well, this has been a learning experience for me too, so I'll just charge you for the oxytocin and the X-ray. How about five dollars?"

She looked at me and grinned, reaching into her purse. "All the children in the class agreed to each pay a dime a week to purchase food and supplies for the turtles," she said. "So I think we can cover that. Thank you, Doctor."

━

The next day, while I was out on farm calls, Dick took a message from Miss Smythe: "Penelope delivered all three eggs, and both she and Daddy Turtle are doing well."

━

Two evenings later was the first night of Chanukah. At home before seven, I showered, shaved, changed clothes, and was ready to enjoy our first Chanukah dinner together. Rosalie had been on the phone with her mother several times over the past few days and had been cooking all day in preparation.

One of the dishes she prepared was a roast brisket. She told me about her brisket shopping experience. "I got a four-pound brisket at Safeway this morning, but I had to explain to the butcher that I wanted it whole, with the fat left on it. He kept asking if I was certain about trying to roast it. Apparently, they only use it for stew meat here. Guess what I had to pay for it."

"No idea."

"Thirty-nine cents a pound!"

Along with the brisket, Rosalie prepared potato latkes—shredded potatoes, shredded onion, egg, and a bit of flour mixed and then fried in butter and a little corn oil. She also made a Jell-O salad—lemon Jell-O with shredded cabbage and carrots. For dessert, she made a cherry pie. With so much time alone, she was becoming a very good cook, and my waistline was expanding in response.

After dinner, we lit two candles, the shamus and the candle for the first night of Chanukah, and exchanged gifts. I got her a warm pair of gloves, sheepskin with the wool inside. Rosalie gave me a new down vest. The one I had was decorated with a variety of animal-origin stains. She had also brought home from Safeway the proximal half of a bovine femur and had kept it wrapped in the refrigerator. Now, she presented it to Mister.

"Did you think we forgot about you, Mister?"

He took the ball end of the bone that fits into the hip joint in his mouth and squirmed under the table where he proceeded to work on his treasure.

Rosalie looked at me sadly. "Are you even a little sad to be so far away from family during Chanukah?"

"Yeah, I am, but we have each other. It's harder for you, I think. This is your first away from home, isn't it? Unless Chanukah came within a few days of Christmas, I was usually away at school. You're right. Even if I wasn't home for the whole thing, I was usually around for at least a couple of days, so we celebrated some of it as a family. But I didn't always get a Chanukah dinner like that one."

I took Rosalie in my arms. We stood in our basement living room, amongst the shabby rented furnishings, hugging and thinking about family.

Chapter 15:
Freddy's Bar

A MAN WEIGHING WELL OVER THREE HUNDRED POUNDS seemed to fill the waiting room, lapping over the edges of the chair in which he was wedged. The legs of the chair were vibrating with the strain, doing their best to bear the burden, the outcome yet to be determined. A green parrot with a bright red blaze extending over its beak and forehead filled the songbird-sized cage on his lap.

"Doc," said Dick, "this is Alex Washburn. He owns and runs Freddy's next to the implement dealer's. You know the place."

Freddy's was a local bar, infamous to the more solid citizens of the county. It seemed to be always crowded from late afternoon to closing time on Friday and Saturday nights. I had yet to set foot in the place, but in the summer, the smell of stale beer whiffed through the truck whenever I drove past with the windows open.

The man hoisted himself to his feet, accompanied by an explosive grunt from him and a grateful sigh from the chair.

"Yeah, hi, Doc. I got this bird about a year ago when I was in Mexico. He was only about a year old they told me. He's been pretty good up to about three weeks ago when he turned mean and vicious. He used to take food from my hand and act kind of comical and playful. Now he squawks at me whenever I'm close, and he flaps his wings and bites my hand when I offer him anything. He's become a real pain in the ass. Too mean to give away."

"Well, Mr. Washburn, I see his beak is a little overgrown, and his flight feathers look as if they need to be trimmed. Is this the cage you keep him in?"

"Naah, I've got one ten times bigger at the bar. It's right by a window. He stays in that."

"Well, I can't say I know much about bird behavior. What kind of parrot is he, do you know?"

"They told me he's a green-cheeked Amazon. I dunno if that's right or not. He's quite a hit at the bar; the customers seem to like him, and he'll speak some words now and then, mostly cuss words. That's the kind of customers I got, but now he's got so aggressive folks are scared to get too close to his cage. Not good for business."

"Well, let's take him into the exam room. I'll have a look at him. I'm pretty sure I have a reference book about pet birds. I'll look for it and see if I can find anything in it about this kind of behavior. Hopefully, it's something common, maybe a sign of some kind of disease we can do something about. Can you get him out of the cage and hold him?" I asked.

Immediately after he got the bird free of the cage, the beast grabbed Washburn's forefinger in his beak and clamped down. This elicited the longest string of non-repeating cuss words I had ever heard.

I grabbed a towel, wrapped the bird in it, and holding on to the folded towel in back, out of reach of his beak, I used a closed-bandage scissors to pry the bird from his owner's finger. Washburn shook his injured hand several times, spraying blood onto the floor, wall, and ceiling of the exam room.

"Damn, that hurts!" he exclaimed.

"Dick," I yelled, "can you come hold this bird while we get Mr. Washburn's injuries under control?"

Dick took the bird, cooing to it, with no apparent effect. The bird gnawed with evil intent on the towel and spread a mixture of feces and urine everywhere his rear end was pointed.

"Jeez, Dick, hold him still. He's spreading feces all over the room," I complained.

I took Mr. Washburn's elbow and led him to the sink. We ran water on the finger and determined, since he could move it, that it was just lacerated, probably not broken. I bandaged it for him and excused myself to find my reference book.

I came back into the exam room reading the book. "Here we are, green-cheeked Amazon parrots. Says they are great family pets that interact well with their humans. Comical, good-natured, ah . . . here we go. It says that when the males go through adolescence the testosterone levels increase sharply and they can turn aggressive. He is trying to establish a dominant position in the 'flock.' In this case, the flock is you, and I suppose your customers. It says the owner must establish a dominant position, but it doesn't say how."

I continued to read; "Oh, oh . . . it says this adolescent aggressive stage can last up to two years. Also says you shouldn't keep him caged all the time. The birds need a minimum of three to four hours outside their cage every day, or they'll get fat and lazy. Apparently, being out of the cage also stimulates them mentally, and they are easier to teach to talk. It says they need one-on-one time with the owner on a daily basis.

"Oh, here's something else you need to know. You've made a serious commitment getting this guy. These birds can live over seventy years. Got any kids to leave him to?"

My lame attempt at a joke fell flat.

While Dick held the parrot, I gave the bird a cursory examination, not really knowing what to look for. His eyes were clear, his feathers were not ruffled, and they appeared glossy. There were no abnormal discharges aside from the copious excrement from his cloaca, which as far as I could tell, was normal bird guano. He was apparently healthy. While reading about the species in my book, I noted the procedure for trimming his beak. I accomplished that feat without too much fuss using the toenail clippers I normally used for dogs.

"What do you feed him?" I asked.

"Almost any kind of fruit and vegetables, bird seed, and some mixed nuts with the shells on."

"That sounds about right. You might have Dick get you a stone to hang in his cage so he can rub his beak on it. You won't have to get his beak trimmed as often," I said.

"Dick, if you'll grab the towel on either side of his head and try to hold him still, I'll take out one wing at a time and clip four or five of his flight feathers."

My book also provided the necessary information about how to avoid "blood feathers," feathers with blood vessels supplying them. I carefully cut one flight feather at a time, four feathers from the bird's right wing, taking care to make certain the feathers I cut didn't have any visible blood vessels. After finishing the right wing, I took a deep breath and we did the same with the left wing.

"Now," I said, "he can't fly very far."

"What about letting him lose in the bar?" asked Washburn.

"If I were you," I suggested, "I would check with the health department and make certain you don't run afoul of some law. Besides, your customers might not like getting hit with parrot poop."

"Hell, most of that lot wouldn't notice." Washburn smiled broadly.

"Well if you want to turn him loose in the bar, that's up to you," I said. "I don't want or need to know about it. As long as you have someone guarding the door so he doesn't escape, you should be able to let him lose so he can exercise. If you can convince him you're the boss of the flock and if you're patient with him, you should have a good pet for a long time."

"Him getting outside shouldn't be a problem. The entry into the place is big, and the outside door closes before you get to the inside door; that keeps the heat in during winter. All the windows have screens. The regulars will make sure he doesn't get out."

"Well, that should do it for him. Good luck," I said.

"Thanks, Doc. I really do kinda like him, even when he attacks. He's a comical SOB."

"Not so comical when he crunches your finger," I said. "I never did ask. What do you call him? What's his name?"

"Shit Bird."

"Shit Bird?"

"Yeah, fit's, don't you think?"

Chapter 16:

Troubles of the Heart

THE WHOLE CHASEN FAMILY was present for Bancroft's four o'clock appointment. Dick Mathes had groomed Bancroft, an eighteen-month-old miniature schnauzer, every few months since the dog was twelve weeks old. Dick told me the dog was calm to the point of being lethargic but in recent months had been progressively losing weight. He said that Mrs. Chasen told him the dog slept most of the day and wasn't interested in playing with the children anymore; he just wanted to be held.

Richard Chasen managed the local Safeway. He was in his mid-forties, bald on top with a graying fringe. He gave me his store-manager smile and extended his right hand. Unlike the hands of the farmers and ranchers I encountered daily, his hands were soft and clean. Even his fingernails were clean, but his grip was firm.

"I'm happy to meet you, Dr. Gross. Dick told us you're interested in taking care of pets as well as the large animals. Most of the vets in this part of the country just do livestock and horses. How did that brisket your wife got from us turn out?"

"The brisket was great, Mr. Chasen. My wife used her mother's recipe, braised with lots of onions, and then slow roasted it. I like the challenge of working on both large and small animals, any animal, actually."

"This is my wife, Karen," he said, "and this is our daughter, Jennifer, and son, Frankie."

"Yes," I said, "I think I've met Jennifer before. You're in Miss Smythe's class, aren't you, Jennifer? You were in the group that brought in your class science project. How's the turtle doing?"

"Oh, she's fine. Only three of her eggs hatched, but all the babies are doing well. We feed them separately twice a day."

"Good, good," I said. "Frankie, I know your sister's in the fourth grade. What grade are you in?"

"Third," answered the boy.

I was surprised. He was thin, small, wane; I figured him for only six or seven years old.

"So," I said, "That means you are what, eight years old?"

"Uh huh, I'll be nine in three months."

I extended my hand to the boy. "Well, I'm pleased to meet you, Frankie."

"Me too," said the boy, taking my hand. His grip was limp.

I turned to Mrs. Chasen. She was holding Bancroft in her arms. The dog was dozing.

"May I take him?" I asked.

She extended the dog, and I placed him on the exam table.

"Dick told me Bancroft's been losing weight and acting more and more lethargic. Anything else?" I looked at Mrs. Chasen.

"He just wants Frankie or me to hold him all the time," she said. "He's so sweet and loving, but whenever he tries to play with the children, he seems to get tired very quickly. When that happens, he comes to either Frankie or me and wants to be picked up and held."

"Well, that certainly doesn't sound normal for a miniature schnauzer. They're usually live wires. Let's see what we can find."

I put a thermometer in the dog's rectum, and then, starting at his head, I checked his mucous membranes and conjunctiva; looked at his teeth, throat, and tonsils; palpated around his ears and the lymph nodes in his neck and shoulders and under his front legs. Working back, I checked hind leg lymph nodes and palpated over his back and hips. All my prodding and poking failed to elicit any sign of pain or discomfort, and I could find nothing abnormal. Bancroft was stoic, looking up at me with sorrowful eyes. His rectal temperature was one hundred and two, normal. I could find nothing amiss. I took his femoral arterial pulse, and bells started ringing in my head. His heart rate was more rapid than normal, and his pulse felt like a water hammer. I shook my head, saddened by what I found.

"What . . . what is it?" Mrs. Chasen asked. "What's wrong?"

"His pulse is abnormal," I said. "Let me finish my exam, and then we'll discuss what I think is wrong."

I lifted Bancroft's head and observed that both of his jugular veins were distended.

I took the stethoscope from around my neck and auscultated his lungs and then his heart. What I heard was exactly what I feared, an unmistakable continuous murmur over the base of the heart. This was not good.

One of the most helpful things I learned after graduating from veterinary school was that most people wouldn't talk to me when I had a stethoscope in my ears. It was a perfect time to think about what I had observed and how to communicate with the client. I thought back, trying to remember what Dr. Smith had lectured to us about heart murmurs, especially continuous murmurs. I remembered him standing at the lectern making a very particular noise, mimicking the murmur I had just listened to, "whoosh, whoosh, whoosh, whoosh." I had never heard the murmur in an animal, but Bancroft's heart sounded exactly like the noise Dr. Smith had made while leaning into the microphone in the lecture hall.

I had to think about how I was going to break this news to the now obviously concerned Chasen family. I listened again, more intently, to the lungs and could hear moist rales, indicating congestion of the lungs. That would explain the shortness of breath. I continued to auscultate the lungs on both sides of Bancroft's chest. I wanted to go back and review the notes I had taken from Dr. Smith's lecture, but I couldn't remember when the lecture took place or where I might find it in my small animal medicine notes. I knew the prognosis was dismal, and it appeared to me that Bancroft was already in heart failure.

I straightened up and removed the stethoscope from my ears.

"When he plays and gets tired, he starts to wheeze and has trouble getting his breath. Is that right?" I asked.

Mrs. Chasen's brow squeezed tight over her nose; two distinct ridges ran from the top of her nose towards her hairline. "Yes," she nodded.

I shook my head and sucked air in-between clenched teeth. "Not good," I said. "I think Bancroft has a congenital heart defect, called a patent ductus arteriosus."

I looked up and saw Dick Mathes standing in the doorway, a quizzical look on his face.

"Dick, will you bring me a pad of paper, something I can draw a diagram on to explain what this is? Thanks."

I took the pad Dick proffered and drew a rough outline of the heart with the aorta coming off the left ventricle and the pulmonary artery coming off the right ventricle. I was concentrating hard trying to duplicate the diagram Dr. Smith had given our class.

"When puppies are growing in the mother, before they're born," I was trying to explain things so the children could understand too, "the lungs haven't inflated yet. The blood that's pumped out of the right side of the heart here," I pointed to the diagram, "doesn't need to go the lungs, so there's an opening about here where the blood crosses over into the aorta. The aorta is the artery coming out of the left side of the heart, and it supplies the whole body. The opening between the aorta and the pulmonary artery, the one going to the lungs, is called the ductus arteriosus."

I drew two sharply angled parallel lines on my diagram connecting the aorta and the pulmonary artery and pushed the pad with the diagram towards the center of the exam table so all four human Chasens could see it. Bancroft wasn't interested.

"As soon as the puppy is born and takes a couple of breaths, the lungs open up. When the alveoli, the little air sacs in the lungs open, the blood vessels in the lungs also open, and the blood pressure in the lungs drops way below the blood pressure in the arteries in the rest of the body. That causes the blood pressure in the pulmonary artery, here, to drop below the blood pressure in the aorta. This causes the aortic side of the ductus arteriosus to close since the ductus is more of a slit than a tube. Anyhow," I continued, "normally the ductus closes shortly after the animal starts breathing. Unfortunately, sometimes, we don't know why, the ductus stays open. When that happens, it's called a patent ductus arteriosus. Since the pressure in the aorta is much higher than the pressure in the pulmonary artery, the blood leaks continuously through the opening into the pulmonary artery. With each heartbeat, the pressure increases in the aorta, and that causes the leak to be greater. That's why we hear the sound that we do; it's called a continuous murmur."

"When we listen to the heart of a normal animal, it makes a noise that sounds like lub DUB . . . lub DUB . . . lub DUB." I tried to mimic Dr. Smith. "A continuous murmur makes a whoosh, whoosh, whoosh sound. Do you want to hear it?" I asked Frankie.

He nodded that he did. I wiped off the ear pieces of my stethoscope with an alcohol-soaked cotton swab and placed them carefully in the boy's ears. I then placed the head of the stethoscope over the left base of Bancroft's heart.

"Did you hear it?" I asked when Frankie removed the earpieces from his ears.

He nodded but didn't say anything.

"Jennifer, do you want to listen?" I asked, as I wiped off the earpieces again.

She listened for about fifteen seconds and then took off the stethoscope and handed it to me. "Just like you said, whoosh, whoosh, whoosh."

The two adults took their turns, listening carefully.

"This is the only thing I'm aware of that can cause this kind of heart murmur," I explained. "Unfortunately, there is nothing I can do to fix it. This defect causes both the left and right sides of the heart to work harder and harder. The heart enlarges, and finally it fails. Bancroft is already in the early stages of heart failure, and I'm afraid, he's going to continue to get worse."

~

Since those days, veterinary medicine has made enormous advances. We have board-certified veterinary surgeons who perform the relatively simple surgery and tie off the patent ductus. We also have board-certified veterinary cardiologists who, if they make the diagnosis early enough, can use a catheter system to deliver a plug to the ductus and correct the problem. I was doing well just to make the diagnosis.

～

Frankie reached up taking Bancroft off the table and into his arms. He patted the dog lightly on the head and then kissed him. The dog reached up and licked the boy's face.

I looked over Frankie's head and saw that Mrs. Chasen was silently weeping, tears carrying mascara down her cheeks.

Mr. Chasen cleared his throat, choking back emotion.

"This is very unhappy news, Dr. Gross. Is there nothing you can do?" he asked. "I should tell you that Frankie has a heart problem too. The cardiologist we took him to in Bismarck told us there is a surgeon in Salt Lake City who has developed some techniques and special instruments. The cardiologist thought he might be able to help Frankie. The Mormon Church is helping us contact the surgeon, Dr. Rumel, and hopefully we'll get an appointment for him to see Frankie soon. With God's help, Dr. Rumel will be able to correct the problem. Meanwhile Frankie's on medication, and the cardiologist says the medication will slow the progression. We're quite lucky that my company offers a very good health insurance plan to employees, and Frankie is getting the best care available. As you can see, he is very attached to the dog. There must be something you can do to at least slow down his disease."

"Maybe," I said. "But it will just delay the inevitable. I can put him on digitalis, and that should slow down his heart rate and possibly slow the progression. We can try that."

"Digitalis, I think that's one of the medicines they're giving Frankie. Isn't that right, Mother?"

Mrs. Chasen wiped her eyes with a wadded Kleenex and nodded. Jennifer was now stroking the dog with her right hand and her brother with her left.

"OK," I said. "I'm pretty certain we have a bottle of digitalis in the pharmacy. I'll get some for you to take with you, and I'll show you how to give the pill to Bancroft. Are you going to be in charge of making sure he gets his pill every day, Frankie?"

"Yes, sir," said the boy. "I can do that. After I take my pills, I'll give him his. I'll take good care of him."

I nodded and gave Bancroft a pat on his rump, no room on his head. He twisted in Frankie's arms to give my hand a lick.

"Good," I said. "I'll go get the pills."

I showed Frankie how, with Bancroft sitting on the floor, to push the dog's top lips over his upper teeth and then, with his other hand, to place the pill past the base of the tongue and hold the dog's mouth closed until he swallowed.

"You see, Frankie; he sticks his tongue out through his front teeth when he swallows. When you see that, you know he has swallowed the pill, and you can let go of his mouth, but not until you see his tongue. Now here's a vitamin pill. You try it with that."

With serious concentration, Frankie did exactly as instructed, and Bancroft happily swallowed the vitamin. After Frankie released his muzzle, the dog immediately crawled into his arms.

❧

The Chasens brought Bancroft back every two weeks. I gradually increased the dosage of digitalis, and the drug did slow his heart rate and seemed to improve his stamina.

Six weeks after the first time I saw them, Mr. Chasen told me the whole family, including Bancroft, were leaving the next day for Salt Lake City and Frankie's appointment with Dr. Rumel.

"What did Frankie's cardiologist tell you is wrong with his heart?" I asked.

Mrs. Chasen answered, "Frankie got rheumatic fever after having his tonsils out when he was four. The doctor told us that because of that his mitral valve was diseased. Apparently Dr. Rumel is one of very few surgeons in the world who has been successful at repairing that valve, so we are hopeful."

"He actually repairs the mitral valve. That's amazing," I said. "Please try to get Dr. Rumel to explain everything he is going to do so you can tell me. I would love to learn how he does surgeries like that. If you get a chance, if he's not too busy, ask him if he repairs children with PDA. I'll bet he does. It should be a lot easier than repairing a heart valve."

"What's a PDA?" asked Frankie.

"Sorry, Frankie; we use a lot of initials instead of saying the whole disease. PDA stands for patent ductus arteriosus. Remember that's what Bancroft has."

"What's my heart disease called?" he asked.

"Probably mitral insufficiency, sometimes we just call it by the initials, MI. I don't know for sure, Frankie. You should ask Dr. Rumel when you see him."

~

I next saw the family four weeks later. The LDS church had taken good care of them and arranged for them to stay in the Salt Lake City house of a church officer and his wife, who were gone for a month checking on the progress of missionaries in Peru.

After he examined Frankie, Dr. Rumel rearranged his surgery schedule. He repaired Frankie's mitral valve just four days after his initial examination and subsequent work-up.

Now, only three weeks post-op, Frankie's color was markedly improved, his eyes were brighter, and he seemed more animated, more bright, and alert.

"Well, Frankie," I observed, "you look as though you are feeling much better than the last time I saw you."

"Yes, sir," he responded. "Dr. Rumel told me he fixed my valve and I should be able to do everything the boys in my grade at school do, except it might take me a while to catch up."

He was holding Bancroft in his arms. The dog was trying to lick his face.

"Stop it, Bancroft," he scolded.

The dog quieted, looking at me from under half-closed eyelids. Both Mr. and Mrs. Chasen were beaming.

Mrs. Chasen spoke first. "When we told Dr. Rumel that Bancroft had a heart murmur and your diagnosis, he was impressed. He told us he didn't know that dogs could have that problem. He told us that he had corrected dozens of them in children, and it was a simple operation. He even gave us a card to give you. He said if you called him he would let you know the next time he had a PDA scheduled. If you can go to Salt Lake, he said he would show you how to do the surgery. He said you wouldn't need a heart-lung machine to do it."

"That's good," I said, "because I haven't the faintest idea what a heart-lung machine is, what it does, or how to use it."

In the early 1960s, open-heart surgery was just starting to become routine. This came about with the advent of commercially available, disposable bubble oxygenators. Even more efficient and safe membrane oxygenators quickly followed that advance. The availability of these devices, as well as technical advances in the design of roller pumps, used to pump blood through the oxygenators and into the patient, created a new profession, men and women who run the pumps and monitor the blood going through them, perfusionists. They make adjustments in anesthetic agents, blood gases, and the rate at which the machines pump the blood. They can also cool and warm the blood and thus the patient. These advances in technology enabled thoracic surgeons to develop innovative techniques and special instrumentation for repairing a host of abnormalities of the heart. By cooling the patient with the heart-lung machine, metabolism is slowed putting the patient into a state resembling suspended animation. The surgeon can stop the heart and repair the problem while the perfusionists and the heart-lung machine take over for the heart and lungs. When the repair is complete, the patient is re-warmed, the heart restarted, and the patient gradually weaned from the heart-lung devices.

"Anyhow," said Mr. Chasen, "here is Dr. Rumel's card."

"Thanks," I said. "I'll give him a call. I hope I can get away to see that operation. I would love to be able to do it. Maybe we can do something to help Bancroft after all."

It didn't happen. I called Dr. Rumel's office but wasn't able to actually talk to him. His secretary gave him the message that I had called and was interested. She was very nice and called me back to say they didn't have a PDA scheduled in the coming two weeks, but she would call me when they had one. Then when the veterinary practice got very busy, Dr. Rumel's secretary called to say they had a PDA scheduled, but I wasn't able to get away. The notice was too short for me to free up the three or four days I would need to drive to Salt Lake City, observe the surgery, and get back.

Shortly after I missed the opportunity to witness the PDA operation, the Chasen family brought Bancroft in. He was in bad shape. I had increased the dose of digitalis again at his last visit, and now he had a severe arrhythmia, his heartbeat very irregular. He was showing more advanced signs of heart failure. We didn't have an ECG machine in the practice, and even if we had, I probably would have missed the diagnosis of digitalis toxicity. I sent Bancroft home on an even higher dose of digitalis. That night he died.

I like to think that my treatment, as bad as it was, given today's understanding and knowledge, prolonged Bancroft's life long enough for him to help Frankie through his ordeal. There was certainly a strong bond between the two heart patients.

I recommended that the Chasens get a new puppy as soon as possible. A month later, they brought in another miniature schnauzer puppy for his shots. They named him "Bancroft Too." Frankie formed a new bond, without forgetting the first.

Shortly after Bancroft's demise, I read an article about digitals toxicity and realized that my treatment had, more than likely hastened his death. With experience, I was gaining some hard-won knowledge.

Rose Seglund was in the waiting room when I returned at noon to clean and refill the truck. There was an obese black and white cocker spaniel sitting comfortably in her lap. Checkers was a new patient. Mrs. Seglund and her husband had recently moved to Sidney from Billings after purchasing a partnership in the John Deere dealership. Mrs. Seglund was a slim, attractive woman in her early fifties with short-cut gray hair. Her eyes were an amazing sparkling blue, and her smile was huge.

"Well, it's nice to meet you, Mrs. Seglund. What can I do for Checkers?"

"I don't know, Doctor. He's ten years old now, and he seems to tire more and more easily. I thought I had best get him in and have him checked over just in case something was wrong."

"OK," I said. "Let me put him up on the exam table, and we'll see what, if anything we can find."

The dog easily weighed forty-five or fifty pounds and was soft and flabby.

"Well, one thing he needs is less to eat and some exercise," I said.

"I know, Doctor, but he's such a beggar, and my husband, James, will not stop feeding him from the table."

"Tell him he's killing the dog with kindness," I replied.

I gave the dog a complete physical. When I finally got around to auscultating the heart, I heard it. The sound was, "lub, whoosh, dub . . . lub, whoosh, dub," a systolic murmur that I was able to hear loudest over the left base of the heart. That murmur I had heard before. I hoped this one would be easier to treat than the last heart case. Since my experience with Bancroft, I had been reading every article in the veterinary journals I could find about heart disease in dogs and cats. This was essentially the same heart problem as Frankie Chasen's. It was not uncommon in older dogs, and usually the leaky valve didn't leak enough to require surgery. I hoped this was one of those cases.

"Has your previous vet said anything about a heart problem with Checkers?"

Mrs. Seglund was immediately concerned. "No, he never said anything about a heart problem, but I don't remember him ever listening to his heart with a stethoscope either."

"Well," I said, "he has a systolic murmur, but it's not very loud. The murmur is caused by a leak in the valve between the left atrium, the heart chamber that collects blood coming from the lungs, and the left ventricle, the big, strong part of the heart that pumps blood out into the body through the aorta, the large artery coming out of the heart. The left atrium beats first and sends blood into the ventricle. Then the left ventricle contracts, and when it does, the valve between the two, called the mitral valve, closes so all the blood goes out into the aorta instead of back into the atrium. If there is a hole in the valve or a malformation of the valve or some lesions on the valve leaflets, it doesn't close all the way. Some blood leaks back through the valve during systole, when the heart is contracting, and that causes the murmur.

"These murmurs are graded by loudness from one to four. I would say that Checkers's is maybe a two. Loudness isn't everything, though. Sometimes a big leak is quiet because so much blood is leaking back it doesn't make much noise. But an animal with that problem goes into heart failure fast, and Checkers isn't showing any signs of heart failure. Sometimes a very tiny hole will cause a very high velocity jet of blood. That can cause a loud murmur, but very little blood is leaking back, so that's usually not a problem.

"I'm going to take some blood and run some tests to make sure his kidneys are working properly. If his heart is not pumping effectively, the kidneys do not function as well as they should. I'll run that test this evening and let you know the results tomorrow sometime."

Checkers was very calm. It wasn't necessary to restrain him as I lifted his left foreleg, clipped the hair over his cephalic vein, held the vein off with my left thumb, and removed five cc of blood into the syringe I coated with heparin.

"It's going to be very important for him to lose this weight," I instructed as I rubbed the skin over the puncture wound I had just made." Checkers reached over to lick the hand rubbing his leg. "You should be able to feel his ribs when he's in proper shape, and he needs to be walked a couple of times a day. You must make sure he gets exercise. Will he retrieve a ball?"

"Yes," she said. "He fetches but gets to be a pest about it."

"That's good," I said. "Throw the ball for him for at least ten or fifteen minutes a day; that will be very good for him. The exercise will be very beneficial, but watch him. If he seems to tire, he'll stop bringing the ball back; let him rest.

"His heart rate is a little faster than normal, so I'm going to put him on some heart medicine called digitalis. He'll only need a half a pill a day to start with. We'll have to check him every couple of weeks initially to make sure we get the dosage correct. After that, he should do just fine. Cocker spaniels typically live to be twelve to fourteen years old, so I would expect him to live about that long, providing we get him in shape. You must not allow him food from the table. How much dog kibble have you been feeding him?"

"He gets two cups in the morning and two more in the evening."

"Well, that's at least twice as much as he needs. Dick sells some very good dog food with high protein levels. A cup of that twice a day will be plenty for him. Any other questions?" I asked as I lifted Checkers from the table to the floor.

"No, I understand. Thank you, Dr. Gross. James and I will get him in shape. He's the only baby we've ever had."

"I understand," I said. "If he seems lethargic or loses interest in eating or has any shortness of breath, call and bring him in right away. Otherwise, let's see him again in two weeks, and we'll have a better idea how he will progress. It is diet time for Checkers, though. He'll feel better, act better, and it will be a lot easier on his heart. I'll let you know if his kidney function tests are abnormal. If you don't hear from me tomorrow, you'll know he's OK."

Chapter 17:
Mangy Taco

Over the years, I have known many Chihuahua dogs. They come in three flavors—fearful and aggressive, protective and aggressive, mean and aggressive. That's not really fair. They are often very loving and faithful and tend to bond to one person. Rarely, I have encountered individual Chihuahuas who were good with all members of a family. However, when these little dogs find themselves in a strange or even mildly threatening environment, say a veterinary clinic, the unwary veterinarian is apt to sustain a bite wound.

Taco was of the protective and aggressive ilk. He was light tan in color with bulging, wide-spaced, eyes, three pounds of pure aggression. I knew what havoc his needle-sharp canines could cause, but because he was so tiny, his demeanor was actually comical. If I was willing to accept him biting me, I could strangle him into submission. The idea appealed to me, but it was not an acceptable way to build a strong client/clinician relationship.

Louise Baldwin carried him into the clinic and sat holding him close while waiting for me to finish vaccinating the most recent batch of kittens brought in by Ike Williams and his partner Jon Wilkins. When I finished with the kittens, I picked up the new patient record that Dick laid on the counter and looked up.

"Taco Baldwin," I read off the record. "What can I do for Taco today, Mrs. Baldwin?" I gestured toward the open door to the exam room.

Mrs. Baldwin stood and walked toward the exam room passing within a few feet of me. Taco did his thing, snarling, snapping at the air in my direction while growling, all the while shaking.

"I'm sorry, Doctor. He's very protective of me. Whenever a man comes close to me, he acts like this. He's really very sweet." She was all but shouting so I could hear her over the commotion her protector was creating.

"I understand," I said. "Chihuahuas are very protective of their people. I assume you've brought him in because of the skin condition around his eyes, muzzle, and ...," I peered at the top of the dog's head, "head?"

"Yes. He started losing the hair around his eyes when he was only six months old, and it has been gradually getting worse and worse. For the last month, I've been busy moving here, and I just haven't had the time to get him in to a vet. My husband's a marine sergeant, and three months ago he was posted overseas. He'll be gone at least a year and a half, we think. He bought Taco for me after I had a miscarriage. He knew he was going to have to leave for overseas duty, and he thought Taco would be company for me, and he is, but this skin thing keeps getting worse. He's losing hair around his mouth, and this morning I found this crusty spot on top of his head. That's how it seems to start."

She held the dog out towards me with her finger pointing to the spot on top of the head that I had already noticed. Taco took advantage of the opportunity to lunge at me, teeth snapping. She quickly brought him in close again.

"Taco, stop that. I'm sorry, Doctor. He seems to be getting more and more peevish."

"It's OK," I said. "If you'll just put him down on the exam table I'll cover him with this towel, and we should be able to control him. Usually once we get them away from their mistress and into a non-familiar environment, they're not as aggressive as they are when held by their human."

She put Taco on the stainless steel top of the exam table, and the dog scrambled furiously trying to dig his toenails into the table for traction. He slipped, fell hard, jumped to his feet, slipped again, regained his balance, and leaped at least two feet back into the safety of Mrs. Baldwin's arms. It happened so fast I never got close with the towel.

"OK," I said. "Let's try that again, and this time I'll have the towel spread out and ready. Try to hold onto him until I get him wrapped up."

I held the towel out lengthwise, by the opposing ends. Mrs. Baldwin placed Taco in the middle of the towel, and while she still held the animal, I covered him with the towel and managed to wrap it around him. She was still holding him on either side of his chest.

"OK, Mrs. Baldwin. You can let go. Then I'll have you hold him with the towel while I examine him."

She started to pull her hands away while I held the dog. She got her left hand out from under the towel. While extracting her right hand, she got too close, and he bit down on the base of her thumb.

"Yeeough!" she screamed. "He's biting me! Taco, STOP . . . NO!"

The dog's head was now out of the towel, and he still had her thumb trapped in four canines. I grabbed him over the muzzle with my left hand, holding the towel tight around him with my right. I pressed him down against the table while he squirmed and continued to gnaw on the thumb in his mouth.

Mrs. Baldwin was screaming and crying. Dick rushed into the room just as I managed to push the dog's upper lips over his teeth and force him to let go. I held onto his head forcing it down against the table with his body. He was trying to chew my fingers but his lips were between my fingers and his teeth, so the attempt was not nearly as forceful as he would have preferred.

Dick and I managed to wrap the towel completely around little Taco three times, leaving his head exposed but with enough towel around his neck that Dick could hold him. The thickness of the roll of towel around his neck prevented him from reaching Dick's hands.

"You got him?" I asked, releasing my grip.

"Uh, huh. Yeah, I'll hold the little SOB. Feisty, ain't he?"

I nodded my agreement and turned to attend to Mrs. Baldwin. She had slid to the floor and was holding her punctured thumb with her good hand and crying.

"It's too much," she sobbed. "We were only married for a year and a half when I lost our baby. Then Jimmy finds out he has to ship out. He gets me this little tiny puppy, and everything seemed better. Then because I can't find a decent job in San Diego, I can't manage the rent and living expenses, so we decide I should come back and live with my folks until Jimmy gets back. Moving was a disaster; the car broke down before Taco and I even got out of California. We finally get here and start to settle, and Taco starts losing his hair and trying to attack everyone who comes near me. He even snarled at my dad a couple of days ago. Dad said if the dog ever bit him, he'd wring his neck. He could and would. Now he bites me. It's just too much."

The tears were running down her cheeks, and I could see blood oozing from between the fingers of her left hand.

"Here, let me help you up and have a look at that bite. We need to wash it off and disinfect it. It's a good thing when puncture wounds bleed; that washes them out."

She looked down and saw her blood for the first time. "Shit, I can't believe he did that. Oh, now it's starting to really hurt."

I helped her to her feet by her elbows and then took her to the sink. She cried out when I milked blood from each of the puncture wounds.

"It's really important that we get blood to flow out of each of these," I explained. "There will be much less chance of infection."

I helped her soap and wash her hands and then rubbed some antibiotic ointment over the wounds and bandaged her thumb with some gauze.

"Have you had a tetanus shot recently?" I asked.

She stopped crying and was wiping at her face, her makeup coming off on the damp paper towel I had given her to dry her hands. "Not since I was a kid," she answered.

"Well, you need to see a doctor and get a tetanus shot. I suspect he'll want you to soak that hand in warm Epsom salts and water or something to draw out any possible infection. Taco's teeth are needle sharp, and puncture wounds can be dangerous. I don't think we'll have to quarantine him to observe for rabies. I'll call and see if it's OK for you to just keep him at home, but you'll have to keep him inside. Are you OK now?" I asked. "Why don't you go sit down in the waiting room? Dick can hold Taco for me. I need to do a skin scraping and examine it under the microscope. I think I know what the problem is, but I have to make certain."

I walked with her into the waiting room and made certain she was comfortable. When I went back into the examination room, I closed the door, making certain it was tight.

"OK, Dick, you still got a good hold on the little shit? Neither of us needs to get bitten."

"Yeah, I got him, Doc. Do what you need to."

"OK, but don't squeeze his scrawny neck too tight. These buggers can actually pop their eyes out over the lids. It's usually possible to replace them, but I don't want to have to explain how it happened."

Taco was no longer struggling. He appeared to be smart enough to realize he was no longer in charge of the situation.

I took a used scalpel blade and scraped some skin from the edge of the lesion around his left eye and a second scraping from the new lesion forming on top of his head. Then I spread the material from each scraping on separate microscope slides, added a drop of mineral oil, and covered each with a cover slip.

"Yep, there they are," I murmured. Moving about in both scrapings were the microscopic alligator-like mites I had expected to find.

Dick followed me into the room that functioned as our pharmacy, small animal treatment room, X-ray room, and clinical laboratory. He was holding Taco, still wrapped in the towel, in the crook of his left arm.

"It's demodectic mange, *Demodex canis*. Want to see them?"

He looked briefly into the microscope. "Is this the one called red mange?" Dick asked.

"Yep, it is. I'll go talk to Mrs. Baldwin."

I found her reading a magazine, still holding her thumb. She looked up when I came into the exam room.

"Well, Taco has a skin disease called demodectic mange, caused by a microscopic parasite that can be found on almost any dog if you look long enough and hard enough. We think some young dogs don't have a strong-enough immune system, and that kind of turns the parasite loose; they multiply like crazy and cause these skin lesions. Sometimes the dog can lose hair all over its body, develop secondary bacterial infections, and the disease can become a rather severe problem. However, I don't think that will happen with Taco. We should be able to treat him and get him better without too much problem."

"What about him being so nasty and biting? What can I do about that? My dad will probably want me to put him to sleep for biting me."

"That's a whole other issue," I explained. "Taco doesn't know he's a dog. He thinks he's the alpha male in a pack, and that behavior is reinforced whenever you pick him up, carry him around, and allow him to become aggressive whenever anybody comes close to you. He considers you his, and he's protecting what's his."

"How do I make him stop?" she asked.

"It's a matter of training," I said. "You've got to treat him like a dog. Make certain he understands that you are the alpha, not him."

I stood and reached over the counter taking one of Dick's message pads and a ballpoint pen from the reception desk. I wrote out "The Kohler Method of Dog Training by Kohler" on the top page, tore it off, and handed it to her.

"This is a very good book on how to train dogs. The author trained war dogs during World War II, and his methods work. I used them to train my own dog. I'm certain the bookstore can get it for you, and they might even have a copy in the library. If you can't find it any place, let me know, and I'll lend you my copy.

"The first thing you can start doing, even before using the book and training him properly, is to treat him like a dog, not a baby. Don't carry him around unless you have to. If he wants to jump into your lap to be petted fine, but make him get down when you are done. Make him walk whenever possible. You train him using a leash and a choke chain. He must learn to heal, sit, and stay on command. Most important, he has to learn to stop whatever he's doing when you tell him no. You tell him only once. If he continues, you grab him by the scruff of the neck, shake him, and say no again and then put him down on the floor."

"What if Taco bites me?" she asked.

"I don't think he will," I said. "I think this bite was an accident. He was in a very tense, strange situation. He was fearful and didn't know what was happening to him. Your thumb just happened to be in the wrong place at the wrong time. I don't really think he would bite you on purpose. Nevertheless, biting anyone is bad behavior. If he acts as if he's going to try to bite you or acts aggressive in any way towards you, be very firm with your command. If you have to, grab him and shake him hard. You must make him understand you are the boss. If you come on very strong, he will get the message and won't try it again. You must not allow him to challenge you. If you don't think you can do this, you might as well get rid of him. You don't want a dog you can't control."

She seemed to ponder these ideas and then nodded her head. "Yes, I see what you mean. Once, just after we got him, he snapped at Jimmy, but just that once. Jimmy grabbed him and shook him. From that time, he did what Jimmy wanted. If he was chewing on something he wasn't supposed to, all Jimmy had to do was frown at Taco, and he would stop and kind of crawl on his belly over to him."

"Exactly," I said. "You want Taco to be happy and playful, not cowed, so play with him, even rough house, but don't let him get away with challenging you. If you have to correct him about something, do it immediately and then get him to play. If he'll chase and retrieve a ball, that's great; maybe just play tug of war with one of his toys or an old sock, any kind of play that he seems to like. Always praise him when he does something good, comes when he's called, stops doing whatever it is when you say no. You can give him a treat to teach him tricks like shaking hands, rolling over, that sort of thing, but don't teach him obedience commands with a treat. He has to learn to do those things because you gave him a command. His reward for obeying is verbal praise, maybe a pat on the head. It's just as important to reinforce good behavior as to correct bad behavior.

"Now, do you want to look in the microscope and see what's causing his skin lesions?"

"Yes."

I showed her the mites.

"Those are really ugly," she said. "They look big and nasty in the microscope."

"Actually they are very small." I took a ten-centimeter ruler from a drawer below the microscope. "Each one of these larger divisions is one centimeter, about two and a half centimeters to an inch. On the ruler each centimeter is divided into ten millimeters. The mites are about one-fourth of a millimeter long.

"So," I continued, "here's what we're going to do." I reached up and took down a bottle containing a 1 percent solution of rotenone off a shelf. While Dick held Taco, still wrapped in the towel, I demonstrated how to apply the solution with a cotton ball, rubbing it into the lesions on his head and around his mouth. I showed her how to apply it around the eyes without getting any in the eyes. The dog seemed resigned, perhaps from the soothing sound of my voice telling him what a big brave fellow he was . . . but not likely.

Dick looked at me and shook his head, rolling his eyes.

Mrs. Baldwin smiled at our behavior and then asked, "Dick, do you have a leash and choke chain to fit Taco?"

"You bet," he responded. "Here, you hold him on the table, and I'll get them."

He returned quickly with a tiny choke chain and a very light leash. "These should do the trick." Dick made a loop with the chain and placed it over Taco's head, adjusted it on his neck and attached the leash.

"OK, tough guy," I said, "you're all set. Why don't you put him on the floor?" I instructed. "Let's see what he does."

Mrs. Baldwin removed the towel from around Taco, who licked her bandage, perhaps apologizing for his brutish behavior.

"You're sorry for what you did to me, Taco?" she asked. "You should be. I'm going to put you down now."

She placed the dog on the floor. He sat and looked up at her. He seemed confused about her not holding him. Then he scratched at the choke chain with his right hind paw, yelping when the paw caught in the chain. Mrs. Baldwin squatted to extricate him, and he immediately tried to climb into her arms.

"No, Taco," she said.

The dog, confused, sat down, cocking his head to look at her.

"That's very good," I said. "He knows what 'no' means. He's a smart dog. With a little work and consistency from you, he'll catch on fast."

"I'm also going to send these vitamins home with you. Give him one a day; just crumble it into his food. Dick also has some high-protein, canned dog food. You should feed him a couple of tablespoons, twice a day. I want to see him again next week to evaluate how he's progressing. Do you have any questions?"

"No, I don't think so, Doctor. Thanks. Come on, Taco," she said.

At first, the dog resisted, pulling back against the leash. The choke chain tightened around his neck as he resisted. Mrs. Baldwin looked at me.

"Just pull him along. He's on a slick floor. He'll get the idea."

After just a couple of steps, Taco gave up and trotted ahead of his mistress. She settled the bill with Dick, and she and Taco got into her old, two-door Chevy while I watched from the door. After pushing Taco off her lap, she raised her eyebrows and shrugged at me. I gave her the thumbs-up sign and retreated to the office.

The following week, Taco was significantly improved. Mrs. Baldwin brought him into the exam room on the leash. She bent over and lifted him to the table. I approached and offered him the back of my hand. He sniffed it and then wagged his tail. Now he was my buddy. I petted and praised him. He wasn't the least embarrassed about his unacceptable behavior during his previous visit.

"This is great progress, Mrs. Baldwin, and his mange is improving too. See here, under his eyes, the hair is starting to grow back. Let's keep up this treatment for two more weeks, and I'll check him again. If he improves at this same rate, he'll be back to normal by then."

"That dog training book is very good, Doctor. They had it at the library, and the bookstore has ordered me my own copy. Taco sits and heels on command pretty well, and he'll stay as long as I have a hold of the leash. He's been playing with my dad and hasn't been aggressive with anyone. I think he's going to turn out to be a good dog."

"How's your thumb?" I asked.

"Fine," she said and flexed it for me. "I went to the doctor, and he told me to soak it in Epsom salts and water as hot as I could stand twice a day for two days. He also gave me a tetanus booster shot. We're keeping Taco indoors, except when I take him for a walk on his leash to do his business."

"Great. It sounds as if everything is on track. Have you heard from your husband? Is he doing OK?"

"Yes. He can't tell me where he is, but I think someplace in Southeast Asia. He's fine. He says his squad is a good group who follow directions and do what they are told when they are told. I wrote him a long letter telling him everything that happened with Taco, but I don't think he's received it yet. He'll be happy that Taco is being trained. He's very big on proper training."

"Yeah, well, I wouldn't expect anything else from a marine sergeant," I said. "Keep up the treatment, and we'll see you both in a couple of weeks. Good boy, Taco." I lifted him off the table.

He pranced proudly out of the clinic.

PART IV:
SPRING 1961

CHAPTER 18:
TURLEY'S PIGS

EARLY MARCH BROUGHT LITTLE CHANGE in the weather. We continued to experience cold and occasional snow flurries. I was standing in the middle of a large pigpen looking down at two dead pigs, each weighing about a hundred pounds. That day, the sun was bright, the temperature in the mid-forties. Except for the dead pigs, it would have been a glorious day. There were at least forty other pigs in the pen, of various colors and breeding, but all about the same size.

I moved my feet. A mixture of mud and feces extended six inches over the top of my instep and sucked at my rubber boots. I was glad the rubber boots fit tight over my regular boots. It was a pain to get the rubber boots on and off, but that was better than ending up barefoot in the muck.

"These the only ones dead?" I asked John Turley.

Turley was a middle-aged bachelor who farmed a little over eighty acres of corn and alfalfa and worked as a minimum-wage gofer for Ike Williams and Jon Wilkins. He was honest, reliable, and able to complete simple tasks when they were explained to him in words he could understand.

"Uh, yeah, Young Doc, but I think some a th' others bein' sick though. They not be eatin' and just standin' round."

"How long do you think these two were ill?" I asked.

"Ill?"

"Sick, don't eat, just standing around."

"Oh, I dunno, maybe three, four days. I just put out the feed, and them that gets to the trough eats; don't pay much mind. But I think these uns was hangin' back, maybe a couple of other uns too."

I nudged one of the corpses with the toe of my rubber boot. "Well, Mr. Turley, we need to move these two out of the pen, someplace close to water and a hose. I'll do a necropsy on them and see if we can find out what happened."

"A what?"

"Necropsy. I need to cut them open, have a look at their innards, and see if I can figure out what killed them and if the rest are in any danger. We don't want to lose the whole herd."

I grabbed one of the dead pigs by a hind leg and started pulling it towards the gate. "You want to bring the other one along, Mr. Turley?"

"Uh, oh, yeah, Young Doc, I'll do that." He grabbed a hind leg of the other pig and followed.

"Is there a hose bib with a hose attached nearby?" I asked.

"Uh, yeah, straight ahead up by the barn." He pointed with his chin to a structure trying desperately to remain upright.

"OK, Mr. Turley, I'm going to get what I need from the truck. You can be a big help to me if you will put some feed in the troughs and move the ones that don't come up to feed to a separate pen. Do you think you can do that alone, or do I need to help?"

"Uh, no, Young Doc, I can do that. I'll get me a gate and can move them into that other pen alongside the one we were in. I can do that."

"That would be great," I said. "That will be a huge help. Meanwhile, I'll cut these two open and see what I can find."

I returned from the truck with my necropsy instruments, hooked up the hose lying on the ground next to the barn, and tried washing the muck off the two dead pigs. The hose leaked at the connection to the hose bib and small geysers erupted along its length. A weak stream of water made it out the end of the hose. I put my thumb over the end, attempting to direct a stream of water onto one of the dead pigs. The extra pressure increased the flow from the multiple lacerations along the length of the hose and stopped the flow from the end.

Using my long-handled boot brush and the dribbling hose, I managed to wash off one side of each corpse, turn them over, and wash off the other side. Next, I held each of the pigs on their backs to wash off the underside. They were stiff with *rigor mortis*, so I was able to clean most of the muck off them. A decent hose and a strong jet of water would have made it easier, but you work with what's available.

Once I got the pigs cleaned off, the diagnosis seemed apparent. There were raised, purplish lesions on the skin of the ears, snout, and abdomen of the first pig. The second animal had unmistakable diamond-shaped, raised, pink lesions on both sides and over the top of the rump.

When I opened up the first pig, I found enlarged lymph nodes, a swollen and congested spleen, and edema of the lungs. The second pig had fewer changes in the spleen, lymph nodes, and lungs, but I found granular growths on the mitral valve of the heart. I put samples of spleen, lymph nodes, heart valves, and lungs from both pigs into specimen jars half-filled with formaldehyde, marked the jars, and made certain their lids were tight. As I was cleaning the necropsy instruments, I heard a pathetic squealing from the pen where Turley was separating the sick pigs.

I walked over to the fence of the big pen and watched as Turley moved three pigs. He was herding them with a small wood gate towards an opening in the five-board fence and into an adjoining smaller pen. Four other pigs were already standing uncomfortably shifting their weight from foot to foot in the small pen. The three new arrivals were all reluctant to move. One of them squealed with pain every time Turley forced the three to move toward the opening. All three walked very stiff, up on their toes.

When the three pigs were finally in the pen, Turley shut them in by replacing the gate and turned to me. "That's all of 'em, Young Doc, I think. None of them others hung back from the trough. Hadn't seen these bein' so lame an' all."

"Well, Mr. Turley, I'm almost certain they've got a disease called erysipelas. I took some samples, and I'll check to see if I can find the organism after I get back to the hospital, but you need to keep a close watch on all the ones in the big pen. If any more of them stop eating or start to limp around, you need to move them into that pen with the other sick ones. This disease usually responds well to penicillin so I'll give the sick pigs a shot today and come back every other day to give them another shot. If you find more that act sick, call us, and I'll come treat those as soon as you find them. OK? They usually recover quickly after being treated, but we will need to give them at least four treatments to make certain the disease is under control. Do you understand what you need to do?"

"Uh, yeah, I watch 'em real close. If they don't eat or start limpin', I call you. Got it."

"Have you got any sows that are about ready to farrow?" I asked.

"Yup, got two o' 'em in the barn; should be any day now."

"Well, you need to keep a close watch on them too. If they stop eating, they could be coming down with this, and they could abort their piglets."

"Do what?" He asked.

"Abort them—the disease kills the piglets inside the mother, and then she gives birth to the dead babies before their time," I explained.

"Oh . . . OK, I'll watch 'em."

I went back to the truck and filled a syringe with long-acting penicillin. Turley helped me crowd each of the seven pigs against the fence, and I gave each a dose of the antibiotic.

"While you're here, Young Doc, think you can cut my boar? I've got me a new boar, and the old one's goin' for sausage after he heals from bein' cut and loses his boar stink."

"I've got some other calls to make but, let's have a look at him," I said. "Maybe there's enough time."

He led me around the barn to a pen where a huge Yorkshire boar calmly peered at me through the boards of a pen that barely contained him. When I came close to the pen to get a better look, the beast snorted, charged two steps, and banged his head into the

second board up. The whole pen reverberated. I was happy that the
pen was well made of rough-cut three-by-eight boards and six-by-six
posts sunk deep into the muck.

He must weigh close to a thousand pounds.

"Well, Mr. Turley, I think castrating this guy will take a little
more time than I have today. How would it be if we do this day after
tomorrow when I come back to treat the others? Maybe I can talk Dr.
Schultz into coming out to treat the sick ones and take care of the boar
for you. This guy looks to be a handful, and Dr. Schultz knows a lot
more about pigs than I do."

"Yeah, well, Old Doc knows his pigs aw right."

I didn't have a clue about how to go about castrating a boar that
size. Dr. Schultz was the pig expert, and I hoped he would be willing to
take care of this so I wouldn't have to. Under any circumstances, I was
not particularly fond of pig practice, too muddy, too dirty, and way
too smelly. Castrating this huge boar was not something I considered
a necessary challenge.

~

That evening, Rosalie and I celebrated a lonely Passover Seder.

"I invited the Rosensteins," she told me, "but they are going to a
Seder with some members of Beth Aaron who live in Glendive. Mrs.
R. said she was certain that the other two families would welcome us,
but with your schedule, I didn't know if you could get away."

"You're right. If we'd agreed to go, I would probably have had
several calls to go on and we wouldn't have made it. They would be
upset we didn't show, and we'd miss out completely. Where did you
get the Haggadahs and the matzos? The Haggadahs look familiar."

"They should. I called your mom and she sent a care package,
the Haggadahs and the matzo. She said she wanted the Haggadahs
back in case we can all be together again some year."

I led an abbreviated Seder service for the two of us but got all
the important stuff covered, especially the four different times to drink
wine. As the youngest at the table, Rosalie asked the four questions,
and it cost me five bucks to get the afikomen back so we could complete

the service. I couldn't remember ever getting more than a quarter for the afikomen from my dad.

~

I caught Dr. Schultz before he left the hospital the next morning and showed him a stained slide containing *Erysipelothrix rhusiopathiae* from one of the lymph nodes I had gathered the previous day.

"Good work," he said. "Turley's place has been endemic for erysipelas for as long as I can remember. I've told him about spotting the sick ones early and getting them treated, but he's like a duck—every day is an entirely new experience. Did he ask you to castrate his boar?"

"Yeah, that thing is huge. How the heck are you planning to restrain it?"

"I'm not," he responded. "You are. I've dealt with Turley enough for a lifetime. You need the experience."

"Well, I don't have a clue about how to restrain a boar that size. He'll kill both Turley and me."

"Naw, it's simple. You fill a sixty-milliliter syringe with pentobarbital. Get Turley to put a rope over the boar's snout and move him into the corner where the gate hinges. That gate opens into the pen, so you just open the gate and trap the pig in the corner. You can lash the gate to the fence to keep him pressed in. Then you inject the pentobarb into one of the testicles, refill the syringe, and inject the other testicle. By the time you get back from the truck with your instruments—and don't forget your emasculator; you'll need it for certain—he should be down. When you cut out the testicles, you'll remove any pentobarb that hasn't been absorbed, and he'll wake up on his own within a half-hour or so."

"You're kidding me?"

"Nope." He raised his right hand, palm facing me. "My hand to God, it'll work. I kid you not." He smiled, but I was skeptical. I didn't trust that particular smile.

The next day, there were two more sick pigs. I treated them and then it was time to tackle the monster boar. I followed Dr. Schultz's instructions verbatim, and it worked like a charm.

"That's the way Old Doc does it too," Turley observed. "Slick."

Chapter 19:
Calving Season

IT WAS A FEW MINUTES PAST EIGHT in the morning, mid-March, when I arrived at the hospital. The practice was still stuck in the winter lull. The previous week, I had treated a few cases of pneumonia, three colicky horses, and two horses and one dairy cow that injured themselves slipping on ice. There was also an outbreak of respiratory disease in both dogs and cats. The word was out that the new vet liked to work on small animals, so the practice was, in fact, busier than in previous years.

"You had best rest up as much as you can now," Don told me. "When calvin' season starts, there won't be time for sleep."

It started that very afternoon. By eight in the evening, I had treated four cattle dystocias, cows with calving problems. In all cases, the owner had tried to get the calf out, without success, so the cases required extra time, skill, and effort.

Don and Dr. Schultz were an experienced team. Schultz slept while Don drove. When they arrived at the farm or ranch, Schultz would tend to the dystocia while Don slept. Dick told me they could keep going for four or five days that way, if necessary. Their record, he said, was six days in a row.

For the next three days, I got less than four hours of sleep a night. If I got into trouble with a delivery, Dick linked the two-way radios so I could talk to Dr. Schultz or to Don and get some advice.

The fourth day, we handled twelve calls between us, but we each also had owners haul two cows into the clinic for caesarian sections. That night, I got home just after nine thirty and got a full five hours of sleep before the phone rang.

"This is how you want to live?" Rosalie complained. "This is nuts. You are going to fall asleep, drive off the road or worse—into someone and kill them and yourself."

That night, I took her along for company. I delivered a calf and dried him off. The animal got to his feet, ready for his first taste of milk with Rosalie watching.

Back in the truck I said, "That's what keeps me going, honey. Without my help, probably both the calf and the cow would have died, the calf for sure."

She smiled. "Yes, I understand. I love you even more, if that's possible, but you've got to figure out some way to get more rest. You can't keep up this pace."

"Yeah, I know. We just have to get through this calving season. If we keep the practice growing, I think Dr. Schultz will take me on as a partner, and we could hire another associate. He's been hinting at that."

The next day, Rosalie volunteered to take over the driving so I could sleep between calls. She napped while I was delivering the calves. We had been going for sixteen hours when we arrived at the Joneses' ranch at one in the morning. John and Skipper came out of the house to greet us.

"What's with Skipper?" I asked. "She's limping."

"The cold seems to be affecting her," John answered. "Ferdie convinced me to spoil her. We're letting her sleep in the mudroom."

We took off our boots and coats and entered the glowing kitchen. Kathy was waiting for us with hot coffee. There was also a huge pot of hot water on the stove.

"Jeez, Doc . . . Rosalie . . . you both look like shit warmed over," Kathy said. "I'm glad to see you Rosalie; didn't expect you to come along at this hour. This the only way you get to spend time together these days? Sit and have a cup-a. The heifer will wait another fifteen minutes."

"Hi, Kathy," answered Rosalie, hugging her. "I've been pressed into service driving the big galoot all over the country."

I collapsed onto one of the kitchen chairs. Kathy held out a mug of hot coffee. I took it from her and smiled. "Thanks. Got sugar?"

"I thought you took it straight." She pushed over a sugar bowl and a teaspoon and watched with concerned humor as I spooned in five teaspoons, stirring while dozing. "How long have you guys been going?" she asked.

"About ten years, I think," Rosalie said. "Actually just . . .," she consulted her watch, "sixteen hours."

Both John and Kathy shook their heads. "You two had better give it up before you fall over dead. Just forget the heifer and get some sleep," said Kathy.

John agreed. "You guys take our bed. Three or four hours of sound sleep, and you'll both be a lot better off. You're going to end up in a borrow-pit, upside down."

"Nope," I said. "Rosalie can get some sleep while I get this calf out." I stood up.

"Where is she? Inside the barn, I hope?"

"Hardly. She's out in a calving shed in the south forty, half a mile from here. You sit back down a minute, Doc. Tell me where your bucket is in the truck, and I'll fill it with hot water," John answered.

"Just inside the back door," I said, plopping down again.

John went out, not bothering to put on a coat, despite the wind and near zero temperature. I heard the truck door open and slam closed. John stomped back into the kitchen.

"Just a tad cool out there," he said. He filled the stainless steel bucket three-quarters full of steaming water and then looked at me.

I nodded and got to my feet, gulping down the remaining half-cup of dark syrup. "Let's do it," I said. "You drive."

I held the bucket between my feet, glad for the warmth when some of the hot water sloshed out over my rubber boots. Since most of the airflow from the heater was directed through the defrosters, there wasn't much heat near the floor. We lurched and bumped our way out to the three-sided calving shed.

At the open side of the shed, we stopped; the headlights provided the only light. I saw a Hereford-Angus-cross heifer down on her right side, her head tied to a post sunk deep in the center of the shed with one of John's throw ropes. The heifer was breathing hard and straining. One leg of the calf was sticking out.

The floor of the shed was a mixture of frozen mud and manure. The wind whistled through half-inch gaps between the boards on the north side. I looked up to see scuttling clouds and an occasional star where sections of the galvanized metal roof had blown away.

A sigh escaped. I went back to the truck, took out a syringe and needle, a bottle of procaine, Nolvasan disinfectant concentrate, surgical soap in a plastic squeeze bottle, and a set of OB chains. After dumping a shot of Nolvasan into the still-warm water, I threw the OB chains into the bucket. They clanked metal against metal.

"Well, John," I said, "do you think we can get her up? I need to give her an epidural, and it will be a lot easier if she's on her feet."

"We can try."

We rolled her onto her sternum tucking her legs under. With John on her head and me on her tail, we tried to lift. John slapped her head with one hand.

"Yeeough . . . up, up!" he shouted.

Nothing happened.

Next John took her left flank, and I her right. We lifted her hind end up into a praying position, most of her weight resting on her front knees. I held her up by the tail while John slapped her head and ears. She finally struggled to her feet and stood, trembling. Standing on her left side John reached across her back and grabbed her right flank, holding her up against his body.

"You had best get on with it, Doc. I don't know how long I can hold her like this."

I clipped the hair from her tail head with my bandage scissors, swabbed the exposed skin with alcohol, pulled procaine into the syringe, and pushed a twenty-gauge needle into the intervertebral space between the first and second lumbar vertebrae. I felt the needle pop through the ligamentum flavum and checked to make certain no spinal fluid came out of the needle hub. I injected the procaine and removed the needle. The heifer's tail went completely limp, and she started to sag.

John grunted, trying to hold her up.

"What's the matter, cowboy?" I asked. "Getting too old to hold up a little heifer?"

John let go, and she slumped back to the ground.

"Thanks, John. Jeez, now I'll have to lie on the ground to get that calf out," I teased.

John peered at my face. I cracked a smile to let him know I was joking.

John smiled in return. "Sorry, big guy. Guess I'm getting a little old."

I took off my coat, vest, and shirt and then rolled up the sleeves on my thermal undershirt. I put the vest, damp with blood and amniotic fluid back on.

"We need to roll her over onto her left side so I can work with my left arm," I said.

I splashed some of the now lukewarm water onto the heifer's perineum, washing off as much mud and feces as I could. A puddle of mud formed where I had to lie down. I lubricated my left hand and arm with a shot of surgical soap and reached into the heifer's warm vagina. The calf's head was twisted back to the right, and its right front leg was trapped. I carried two handfuls of the Nolvasan water and some soap into the vagina and lubricated the calf enough to push it back into the uterus. Only the foot of the left leg remained over the rim of the pelvis. I put one of the OB chains around the leg, just above the foot.

"You need to keep just enough tension on this chain to prevent it being pulled back. OK, John?"

I reached in again with my left hand putting my third finger in the left eye orbit and my thumb in the right. I squirmed in the puddle of mud until I got my right hand in and pushed back on the chest of the calf with my right hand while pulling its head into the pelvic canal. I got the neck almost straight, and the heifer strained, crushing my forearm against the side of her pelvic bone. When she finally relaxed, I managed to push with the right and pull with the left hand until the calf's nose came into position. I got another OB chain around the back of the calf's head and looped it through its mouth. I gave John the free end of that chain to hold the head in position. Finally, I slid my arm along the side of the calf and found the right front leg, still extended backward. I brought it into the proper position.

Both forelegs were now in the birth canal, and the calf's head was between them. I put the third OB chain on the other front leg and then went back to the truck for a jar of K-Y jelly and the calf puller. I scooped out a large handful of the K-Y and lubricated the head and shoulders of the huge calf. I placed the calf puller, a pole with a winch at one end and a curved metal "saddle" at the other, in position.

"I'm going to attach the OB chains to the winch as close to her as possible. When you crank, the winch will advance along the pole pulling on the calf while pushing on the heifer. I'll be guiding the calf, so I need you to crank, OK?"

"Sure."

I placed the saddle against the rear end of the heifer and attached the OB chains. On my command, John cranked two turns.

"Whoa," I said and adjusted the position of the calf's legs and head. "Go ahead a couple more." We repeated the process until the calf's shoulders stuck in the pelvic inlet. I removed the chain on the left leg from the winch, and John cranked out the right leg and head about an inch. I then released the right leg, reattached the left, and we pulled that side out a couple of inches, repeating the process until the shoulders cleared. The calf started to move his head as we pulled the chest and abdomen out, and then his hips hung up. I manipulated the puller from side to side, the heifer strained, and the calf came out in a rush of amniotic fluid tinged with blood.

John rubbed the bull calf with an almost-dry feed sack. I removed the OB chains and wiped the calf's nose and mouth with the clean towel I had stuffed into my back pocket on my last trip to the truck. The heifer stretched out on her side but lifted her head and turned to look at the bawling calf. She struggled to her sternum, voided a gallon of urine, and tried to reach around to her calf. John and I moved the calf where she could reach him.

My arms and hands were slimy. There was a thin film of ice on the water in the bucket. I took the bucket back to the truck, skimmed off the ice, and rinsed off and then took out two sulfa tablets. I deposited the sulfa tablets into the heifer's uterus and gave her an injection of Combiotic.

I soaped up and cleaned my hands and arms in the now filthy, cold water as best I could and then replaced my shirt and coat, shivering in the cold.

"Let's see if we can get her up before we leave," I told John, taking the cattle prod from the truck. "You tail her up; I'll give her a shot from the prod."

When tickled with the cattle prod, she bawled and struggled to her feet, then gathered strength, and started licking and nudging the calf. John lifted the calf to his feet, and he took a couple of shaky steps. The heifer nosed him to her flank. He nuzzled around and found a teat.

John helped me gather and stow all my stuff, and we headed back to the house.

Kathy was ready with two washbasins full of clean, hot water. I stripped to the waist again and cleaned up.

"Here, man," said John, "take this clean undershirt and shirt. You can't put that filthy stuff back on."

"How about another cup of coffee, something to eat?" asked Kathy. "Rosalie had some pie before she zonked."

"Nothing to eat, thanks, Kath, but I will have more coffee."

I finished the coffee; then we filled my thermos and woke Rosalie. I gave Kathy a hug and John a firm handshake. "You guys are the best, thanks!"

Rosalie and I were on our way home. I checked with Dick, but no new calls had come in. The night was dark, the stars, completely masked by high clouds. The headlights of the truck searched out the dirt road in front of us. Rosalie sat close, her head against my shoulder as I drove. No lights defined the horizon. We drove through the black void in the glow of the dashboard, isolated from the rest of the world.

CHAPTER 20:

DISTRACTED

THREE WEEK LATER, WE HAD BEEN ASLEEP for only half an hour when the phone rang.

"Harry Waltham has a horse that ran through a barbed wire fence." It was Dick Mathes.

I sighed and took down the directions.

"OK, Dick, thanks. Call him back, and tell him I've got the message and I'll get there as soon as I can. It should take me about twenty minutes."

"More like thirty if you leave right away," said Dick. "The road to their place is not in very good shape."

I hung up and looked over at Rosalie who was leaning on her elbow listening. "You want to come along?" I asked. "I could use some company."

"Sure," she said. "I don't want you falling asleep driving."

We got to the farm, drove around to the barn, and found Mr. Waltham holding a common-looking bay gelding by the halter rope. The horse's pectoral muscles were lacerated, three long gashes that extended across the entire front of his chest. There were also some lacerations high on both front legs, probably the result of the horse rearing back trying to extricate itself from the barbed wire.

I approached, and the horse shied away. Waltham jerked on the lead rope, making it worse.

I reached for the rope. "Here, Mr. Waltham, let me take that."

He seemed relieved to give it up.

I calmed the animal and examined the wounds.

"When did this happen?" I asked. "It's pretty much dried up, looks old."

"Dunno," Waltham answered. "I found him after dinner when I brought him up from the pasture. The wife and I argued some about calling. She didn't want to spend any money on him. She thinks I'm a fool to keep him around 'cause we don't ride or use him for anything. He was my son's afore he went and got his self killed in that truck accident."

"I'm sorry. I didn't know your son was killed," I said.

"Happened 'most two years ago, afore you got here."

"Sorry," I repeated. "Well, this looks a whole lot worse than it is. I have to clean him up and suture these wounds, but he hasn't cut anything vital. Wounds like this typically heal well. He'll have some scarring, but it shouldn't hamper his movement. He'll need some antibiotics and a tetanus shot, but he should do just fine. I'm going to give him some tranquilizer, and then I can work on him without anybody getting hurt."

There was a floodlight on over the door to the the barn, but it provided sparse light. The barn door was open. I saw a dirt floor and a lot of machinery.

"Looks as though there's no room in the barn to work on him inside, and I'll need more light than we have here. The floodlight is too high to be much help," I said. "Let's take him over in front of my truck. We'll use the headlights. I'll need you to hold the lead rope, to prevent him from moving around while I'm working on him. Just hold him loose, though; don't jerk on the rope, OK?"

I positioned the gelding about ten feet in front of the truck and went to the back of the truck for the Thorazine.

"Honey, will you turn on the headlights for me, please? I'm going to need them to see."

The headlights went on. Rosalie gasped when she saw the horse's wounds. "That's awful. Do you have to put him to sleep?"

"Nope, it looks a lot worse than it really is. I'm going to tranquilize him, clean everything up, and suture the wounds closed. He'll be fine."

"You're joking," she said.

I smiled. "Would I kid you?"

I went back to the horse, held off his jugular vein, slipped a needle into the vein, and administered the tranquilizer. Twenty seconds later, the horse was tranquil. I returned to the back of the truck for three bottles of local anesthetic, a sterile syringe, and a twenty-gauge needle. I grabbed a sterile minor surgical pack and opened it on the hood of the truck, along with a package of sterile four-by-four gauze sponges and a pair of sterile surgical gloves. The horse was standing with all four legs slightly spread out, its lower jaw only six inches from the ground.

"Mr. Waltham, you can help me a lot by holding his head up while I anesthetize the wounds and then clean them up."

I squatted like a baseball catcher, in front and slightly to the side of the horse, injecting Procaine into the tissues along the periphery of the wound. I shaved the hair away from all the wound edges and irrigated the wound with a mixture of saline and penicillin rubbing off dirt and debris with gauze sponges. After the wounds and wound edges were clean, I scrubbed my hands and arms and put on the surgical gloves. I took a thumb forceps and a Bard-Parker scalpel handle from the surgery pack and attached the sterile disposable blade to the handle. Cutting off dead tissue, I left bleeding but clean edges. Using a different pair of sterile forceps and a needle holder with a surgical needle threaded with braided nylon suture material, I started suturing.

After squatting for almost twenty minutes, my legs started aching. I pushed some small stones out of the way with my knees, found a comfortable kneeling position, and continued. From time to time, the horse roused from the tranquilizer and moved about. Each time that happened I stood and then repositioned on my knees.

I finally finished closing the pectoral muscles and the wounds on the left foreleg. I got up, stretched my back and legs, and moved around to the right side of the horse to finish suturing the right foreleg. The owner was now struggling to hold the gelding's head up.

"Just let his head go down," I told him. "I can work from the side."

I got down on my knees again and resumed suturing. A rock under my left knee elicited a stab of pain. I got up and then squatted to finish. The gelding suddenly roused himself, jerked his head up, and at the same moment, brought up his right hind leg and cow-kicked, catching me squarely in the middle of the chest.

Rosalie, dozing behind the steering wheel of the truck, heard the thump. Her eyes opened, and she watched me flying backward through the air. I landed on my rear end five feet from the horse. She was out of the truck and at my side before I caught my breath.

Trying desperately to inhale, I looked down and saw I was still holding the needle holder, and thumb forceps. I dropped them and rolled over to my hands and knees. I took a shallow breath and slowly exhaled.

Rosalie hovered over me, not knowing what to do.

I took three more short breaths, then rolled onto my side, knees up, and groaned.

"Dave," Rosalie said, "I'm calling for an ambulance. Can you breathe? Where does it hurt? I'll call Joe Lufkin. He'll be there when we get to the hospital."

I shook my head and waved one hand at her, trying to get enough air to talk.

"No, wait," I finally croaked. "I'll be OK; just had the wind knocked out." I sat up and stripped off the surgical gloves feeling around my sternum and ribs and then checked my pulse rate. "I'm going to be sore for a few days, but nothing's broken. My heart rate is still normal. I wasn't paying enough attention to him. I need to put some more local anesthetic in that wound. I must have hit a nerve end to make him react like that. Let me just sit here a minute or two, and then I'll finish up."

"You are not going to continue working on this animal," she said. "He could have killed you."

"Yeah, well, I am damned lucky I wasn't still kneeling when he let me have it. He would have crushed my sternum." I smiled at her and reached out a hand for her to help me up.

Waltham, mouth agape, was stunned to immobility. He finally let go of the lead rope and came over to us.

"Here, let me help, Doc. Jeez, I didn't know the worthless SOB could move that fast. Are you sure you're all right? Here let me help you up."

He grabbed me by the opposite elbow and helped Rosalie lift me to my feet.

I bent over at the waist and took some more deep breaths and then walked around the yard for a couple of minutes, hands on my hips. The gelding started to wander off, so I went over, took the lead rope, and led him back to the front of the truck.

"Here, take him again," I told Waltham. "He's still plenty tranquilized. I'm going to re-inject with local anesthetic and finish up."

Rosalie retrieved the dirty instruments from the ground and placed them on the hood of the truck, watching me carefully as I moved about. I scrubbed my hands and arms again, and put on another pair of sterile gloves. My surgical pack had another needle holder, but I had to wipe off the thumb forceps with sterile gauze.

"Honey, in the back of the truck in the case next to the wall on the left side, you'll find some bottles of alcohol. Would you get one, open it, and pour some on these thumb forceps? Thanks."

While she poured the alcohol, I looked her in the eye and smiled. "I'm all right, baby, really. I've been hurt worse. I'll be fine. I just want to finish up here and go home."

I re-anesthetized the wound edges and then finished suturing. After putting things away, I gave the gelding separate injections of penicillin and tetanus antitoxin.

"Just keep him up and keep the wound clean," I told Waltham. "After tomorrow, if it gets dirty, just wipe it off, gently with a clean, damp cloth. We want the scab to stay on. I'll be back in a couple of days to check on him."

It was approaching two in the morning when we got home. Rosalie insisted on examining my chest while I was in the shower. With her forefinger, she traced the perfect imprint of a horseshoe.

"We could save time if you got in here with me," I smiled.

She poked my sternum with the same forefinger, and I winced.

"Oh, I'm very impressed with how tough you are," she said, still serious and concerned.

I lifted her, fully clothed, over the edge of the tub and into the shower. She leaned her head, very gently, against my chest.

"I was so scared when that horse kicked you," she murmured.

I wrapped my arms around her. "I know. It was stupid. It never should have happened. I just got distracted. Tired, I guess. I promise to be more careful."

I started unbuttoning her wet blouse, fumbling.

"For an athlete, you certainly are a klutz," she giggled, helping me.

CHAPTER 21:
FRICK AND FRACK
AND WILMA THE CAT

IT WAS MID-MAY. I LEFT THE BASEMENT at six in the morning to get an early start on an assortment of routine calls. By ten, I finished the farm calls and was occupied with an ovariohistorectomy on a dog when a client brought in two bluetick hounds. Both the hounds' faces were unrecognizable, their muzzles full of porcupine quills.

Their owner was Tim Gervis, a gentleman in his mid-sixties, tall, loose limbed, lanky, with gnarled arthritic hands and graying hair. Later Dick explained to me that Gervis owned the ranch just north of Frank Tompkins's old place.

Frank Tompkins was a local legend. He was a famous rodeo cowboy in his early days, and he was a supporting character to Buffalo Bill in the later years of the Wild West Show. He was also a decorated pilot in World War I, an ace with ten verified kills. After the war, he returned to take over his family's ranch north and west of Sidney.

Gervis waited patiently, as did the two hounds, until I finished and came into the waiting room peeling off my surgical gown and cap. He got to his feet and extended his hand.

"Glad to meet you, Doc. Frick and Frack here never seem to learn about porcupines. Usually they only get one or two quills stuck, and I just pull them out with pliers, but this is a bit much."

"Frick and Frack, how did those names come about?"

"Hell, I don't know. They're brothers, about eight years old now. My youngest, Sadie, was ten when I brought 'em home. She named 'em. She turned eighteen a couple of months ago. I think she just liked the way the names sound together."

"Which one is Frick, and which one is Frack?" I asked.

"Hell, they're identical, even when their heads aren't all swelled up, and they're always together. I can't tell which is which. Sadie can. They're pretty much useless, just kinda hang around on the porch, except when they decide to hunt porcupines. If it were up to me, I'd just tell you to put 'em to sleep and be done with it, but Sadie would have a fit, and her mom would kick me out of the house."

How many poets have eulogized the relationships between people and their dogs? Why can't he just admit he's attached to them and that he wants me to relieve them of their pain and discomfort? He's just as attached to the two hounds as are his daughter and wife. What is it about our culture that does not permit him to admit it?

"No problem, Mr. Gervis. I'll anesthetize them, pull out the quills, treat them with some anti-inflammatory drugs and antibiotics, and they'll be ready to hunt porcupines again in no time. However, there's one hell of a lot of quills in each of them, and it's going to take some time to get 'em all out. I have to tell you I've never seen that many quills in an animal before."

"Is there any hope that these two have learned their lesson and will leave off these encounters?" Gervis asked.

"Sometimes they learn. This time, they obviously got close enough to both get smacked with the tail, or maybe there was more than one porcupine since they both seemed to have caught a full load. They're certainly old enough to learn that porcupines need to be left alone. We can hope for the best."

Gervis shook his head. "I don't know, Doc. I hope you're right and they learned their lesson this time."

After he left, I consulted with Dick. "Which one has the most quills?" I asked.

"You got to be kidding me. I've never seen so many quills in a dog before. Both of their heads are as swollen as basketballs. It's amazing they didn't get hit in the eyes and get blinded too."

"Well, they both have a few quills around the eyes. They must have squinted very tight just before being hit. This is liable to take a while. Let's start with Frick, or are you Frack?" I asked one of the dogs.

Both dogs cocked their heads listening, silently pleading for me to stop talking and get busy relieving them of their painful burden.

"OK, OK," I said, brandishing two syringes. "Here's some tranquilizer for each of you. That should take some of the hurt away until I get you anesthetized and get rid of the quills."

I spent the following three hours pulling quills, one by one, out of the hounds' faces. When I finished, each of the two dogs resembled bluetick hounds again but still with significantly swollen faces. I gave each an injection of prednisolone and antibiotics and then put them next to each other in separate large cages on the bottom of the three-cage tier. Since I had used a short-acting anesthetic for induction and the gas anesthesia machine, they were both up and about in short order, except they were howling. Imagine, if you can, the sound those two hounds made howling in unison, each inside a stainless steel cage in a closed room with a wall full of reverberating stainless steel cages! The howling caused all the other animals in the hospital—several dogs and cats with a variety of conditions and a bull in the barn that Dr. Schultz was treating for a ruptured penis—to add their voices to the pandemonium.

Dick covered his ears and gave me a look. "Do something, Doc, or I'll go shut those two up permanently."

It finally occurred to me that these dogs, like Skipper Jones, had never been inside a house or been locked in a cage. First, I made certain the barn door was closed and latched. Next, I took out Frick and Frack, one at a time, and put them in a stall together. A wave of silence engulfed the hospital. All was good with the world.

Dick handed me a couple of call slips.

"When I finish with these, I'm going home. Call me on the two-way if something else comes in before I get home."

Ike Williams and Jon Wilkins were partners, owners of Williams & Wilkins Blacksmiths and Mechanics. Theirs was a large, dirty shop occupying the property in front of the small, immaculate frame house they shared. The shop blocked the house from sight on the main road leading north and east from Sidney. Their considerable skills shielded them from the necessity of acknowledging who and what they were. What the community considered important was that they were able to repair, and if necessary fabricate, a part for any type of agricultural implement.

They had lived and worked together in Sidney for twenty-five years before my new bride and I arrived. Like an old married couple, Ike and Jon finished each other's thoughts, knew how to avoid conflict, and were comfortable in their own skin and with each other. They had made all the necessary accommodations years previously.

They both loved cats. I was never able to determine exactly, or even approximately, how many cats they cared for. There were shop cats, outside cats, and house cats, all seemingly equally loved.

They made certain their cats received all necessary vaccinations. From time to time, one or both would bring in a male for castration or a female for spaying. Those animals were destined for the house or shop. I guess they had a method for making that decision. The outside cats were apparently free to reproduce, but each new litter of kittens was brought in for vaccinations, and caring homes were found for them.

This day they were both in the waiting room when I returned from doing pregnancy exams on twenty-five head of half-wild range cattle. I rubbed my sore left arm as I greeted them.

"Mr. Williams, Mr. Wilkins, what have you got for us today?"

They stood up as if joined at the hip, Wilkins holding a huge tabby in his arms. The cat was meowing, whimpering actually, and obviously hurting.

"This is Wilma. She's a house cat. Dr. Schultz spayed her for us several years ago, and she's had all her shots every year. Today when we went to the house for lunch, we found her crying in pain. I think she's paralyzed."

Tears welled up in Wilkins's eyes.

Ike put his arm over his partner's shoulders. "It will be OK, Jon. Young Doc is good; everyone says so. He'll take care of Wilma for us, won't you, Doc?"

I held out my hands. "Here, let me take her. Let's go into the exam room and see what we can figure out."

Wilma was too soft, too fat, and too much in pain. Both hind limbs were flaccid. She was meowing louder now that Jon was no longer holding her. She was also hyperventilating. I examined her carefully, noting that the white nails on her hind paws were tinged blue and the paws were cold to the touch. I was unable to palpate a pulse in either femoral artery. I checked again and made certain there was no pulse.

I tapped on both patellar tendons with the handle of a bandage scissors. There was a delayed reflex response.

"This is not good," I told them. "I'm pretty certain she has what we call a saddle thrombus. It's a blood clot blocking the two main arteries to her legs. I've never seen a case before, but I remember the description from vet school. All the signs are there. She is partially paralyzed in the hind legs, in obvious pain, and there is little, if any, blood circulating to her hind legs."

"Is there something you can do to fix her?" asked Ike.

"Well, theoretically I could operate and remove the clot. However, I've never seen nor done anything even remotely like that before, never opened an artery on purpose and then tried to suture it closed afterwards. I don't think we even have any suture material small enough to do that kind of thing. We have no idea what causes this, and it could come right back. I'm sorry. I hate to say this. My job is to help animals, not kill them. In this case, I think the best thing I can do to help Wilma is to put her out of her misery."

They were devastated.

"Are you sure you don't want to even try?" pleaded Jon. "Cost is not a problem, you know. We'll pay whatever it costs." He looked to Ike for confirmation.

Ike nodded in agreement.

"OK, I'm willing to try anything, but I have to make certain you know this could be a disaster. I've only read about this kind of operation in a textbook. First let me look to see if we have any suture material small enough to suture an artery closed."

I was apprehensive as I searched through the cabinet of surgical supplies. I found one packet of 4-0 silk, with a needle attached. It looked to be several years old. I had no idea where it had come from or what Dr. Schultz had intended for it when he had bought it. I came back into the exam room and held up the packet.

"This might work; it might be fine enough, but it's old, and I'll need to sterilize it again. I have no idea how long it's been around. You are certain you want me to try? I'll have to dissect down to the end of the aorta, that's the main artery coming from the heart, where it branches to supply blood to both hind legs and the tail. Then I have to find the blockage, try to put a tourniquet around the artery above the obstruction, open the artery, remove the clot, and suture the artery back together. Chances are Wilma will bleed to death while I'm fumbling around."

"But she'll be anesthetized, right, Doc? She won't feel anything?" Ike asked.

"That's true. As soon as I anesthetize her, she'll feel no more pain until and unless we remove the clot and get everything repaired and let her wake up again. She could still be in a lot of pain after I'm done with the surgery. I don't know."

"But you can give her something for post-operative pain, right?" Jon pleaded.

"Sure, we can treat post-op pain, to some extent at least."

Ike spoke up. "OK, Doc. Go for it. Is it OK if we wait here? We already put a sign on the shop door saying we wouldn't be back until tomorrow."

"Sure, you're welcome to wait here. It will take me some time to put a surgical pack together to sterilize with the suture material. I have to think about what I might need by way of instruments. I know we don't have any specialized vascular surgical instruments, so I'll have to improvise. I'll let you know before I get started. Let me give her just a touch of tranquilizer to see if we can make her more comfortable. I'm afraid to give her anywhere near a full dose because her heart rate is so fast. The tranquilizer will slow her heart rate, and the high heart rate may be the only thing keeping her alive. There's too much I don't know about this."

It went about as I had anticipated. I got Wilma anesthetized, hooked up an intravenous drip, opened up her abdomen, packed off her abdominal organs, and gained access to the distal aorta. When I tried to dissect around the aorta, I managed to break off some small branches, and the abdomen quickly filled with arterial blood. The turkey baster I added to the pack was not an adequate suction device, and Wilma bled out in short order. The experience was the unmitigated disaster I had feared.

—◦—

Today we know that saddle thrombus is usually associated with a disease called dilated cardiomyopathy, a condition that probably has a genetic predisposition. Cats with cardiomyopathy have an enlarged and dilated heart that doesn't function properly.

Normally blood circulates continuously inside the heart, like swirling a drink in a glass. Even when the heart is in diastole, resting between beats, the blood is in constant motion, so clots do not form. With cardiomyopathy, the heart is unable to beat strong enough to maintain the constant motion of the blood, and areas of flow stasis develop within the heart chambers. Areas of flow stasis allow clots to develop.

These areas of flow stasis are like eddies in a creek. When a leaf falls into the water, it can get trapped in an eddy. If enough leaves collect in the eddy, they will bunch together and eventually wash downstream. When the clot grows enough, it eventually washes out of the heart. The clot then flows through one of the arteries until it lodges at a location too small for the size of the clot. In cats, the most common location for it to lodge is at the terminal trifurcation of the aorta. Today veterinary surgeons are prepared to do this surgery. If the diagnosis is made early enough and if the underlying heart disease is controlled, many of these animals can be saved and go on to live a reasonably normal life.

In 1961, saving Wilma would have been a miracle, especially in my hands. If I had a time machine and I could go back with the knowledge and skills I have now . . . wishful thinking.

⌒

Jon cradled Wilma in his arms, rocking her gently while Ike handed me a greasy ten and two crisp fives. He sniffed and then turned to Jon.

"You want me to carry her to the truck, or do you want to hold her?"

"I'll hold her; you drive."

Jon reached up with his right hand to remove his glasses. Wilma started to slip, and he squeezed her to his chest. He wiped his eyes with first his left and then his right upper arm.

"Do you want to bury her tonight?" asked Ike. "Or should we wait till morning?"

"I think tonight," Jon answered, replacing his glasses. "We can put her next to Tom and the others under the walnut tree."

"Yeah, we'll put up a marker for her, like we did for Tom," said Ike, holding the door to the waiting room open.

Their pickup roared to life, and the headlights came on. As the truck pulled onto the road, I waved at them through the window.

PART V:
SUMMER 1961

Chapter 22:

The Elkhorn Ranch

I WAS BACK IN THE BADLANDS, this time called to Bill Dow's ranch. I drove over the cattle guard and approached a group of scattered buildings about two hundred yards from the north bank of the Little Missouri River. The house was long, low, and narrow, built halfway up with hand-hewed logs and then finished with unpainted, rough-cut, horizontal planks. The roof was made of sapling poles covered with galvanized tin, covered with tarpaper, covered with sod. The front of the house and one side were festooned with elk, antelope, and deer racks. The barn and other buildings were sided with vertical, twelve-inch-wide, rough-cut planks, also unpainted.

Bill Dow fit John Jones's description, huge and hairy. His beard, midnight black, flecked with gray, covered his face, save his eyes and forehead. Long black hair, also flecked with gray, covered his ears. He extended a gnarled, callused, and weathered hand. His fingernails were broken fragments.

John Jones told me that Bill was the son of Wilmot Dow, who had died in the summer of 1891 when Bill was only five years old. When he was growing up, young Bill listened to the stories of his family's Badlands adventures as told by his great-uncle, Bill Seward. Seward and Wilmot Dow were partners with Theodore Roosevelt in the original Elkhorn Ranch.

After serving in World War I, Bill Dow decided to see the Badlands for himself. In 1921, only twenty-five years old, he put everything he had managed to save and borrow into an abandoned homestead and a few head of cattle. The place he purchased was not far from where his great-uncle and father had helped Roosevelt capture the notorious Redhead Finnegan gang.

Dow was sixty-five years old when I drove onto his place. The old bachelor followed his father and great-uncle's passion for hunting, fishing, and the outdoors. Ranching was the way he earned enough to feed his passion.

"Howdy, Doc. Glad you could come out. I usually manage to take care of m' own cattle, but I did the Coke bottle trick on these heifers, and they just popped out again."

On occasion, usually within a week after a range heifer has experienced difficulties calving, the uterus can evert, that is, prolapse by turning inside out. It is more unusual for this to happen in older cows. In beef cattle, usually just the vagina and cervix prolapse, but in dairy cattle, the entire uterus can turn inside out. Some ranchers addressed this problem by pushing the prolapse back into the animal, putting a soft-drink bottle in and sewing the vulva closed over the bottle, usually with bailing twine. The animals thus treated might continue to strain, perhaps because of the foreign object, bust through the sutures, and prolapse again.

"Pleased to meet you, Mr. Dow," I greeted him. "Let's have a look and see what you've got."

"Got 'em in th' corrals out back a th' barn. I put th' first un in the squeeze when I seen your dust on the road. Th' other un's in th' chute wait'n. You kin pull your truck round th' barn so's it's close."

"Great. You want to ride with me?"

"Naw, ma feet still work; I'll meet ya there."

I looked and saw the expected windmill half protruding above the roof of the barn, turning with hesitation in the slight breeze. "Is the water from the well good?" I asked.

"Yeah, clean water."

The two heifers were patiently waiting behind the barn. The one in the squeeze chute, her head held firm, had been prolapsed for at least a week, the extruded tissue swollen, scabbed, and oozing serum.

I filled my bucket from the intermittent stream emanating from the pipe empting into the water tank and added disinfectant. I fit a squeeze bottle of surgical soap, bandage scissors, and a sterile surgical pack containing scissors, tissue forceps, suture needles, and umbilical tape suture, along with some antibiotic boluses into the back pockets of my coveralls. I filled two syringes with Lidocaine, and those went into one top pocket, and an unopened package of sterile four-by-four gauze sponges in the other. I climbed over the rails of the chute and stood behind the heifer in the squeeze. The second heifer retreated, pushing against the pole Dow had placed behind her, giving me room to work on the one in the squeeze.

After giving the heifer an epidural, I used the bandage scissors to scrape scab, dirt, and foreign materials off the protruding tissue. I squeezed soap onto the prolapse and then opened the pack of gauze, soaked several sponges in the disinfectant water, and used them to clean the mass. Squeezing with both hands, I gradually worked the prolapsed tissue back into place and then deposited two antibiotic boluses into the vagina. I opened my surgical pack and used umbilical tape and a large suture needle to lace up and hold the inverted vulva in place with a shoelace suture. The epidural and the fact that she had been prolapsed for some time had a combined effect. The heifer didn't seem to have any feeling left in the region. She manifested no objection or embarrassment. I returned to the truck, filled a syringe with oxytocin and another with antibiotic, and administered them both to the first heifer. We released her and put the second heifer in the squeeze. While working on the second heifer, I started a conversation with the rancher.

"So, Mr. Dow, John Jones tells me your dad ranched near here as a partner with Theodore Roosevelt. How did that come about?"

Like many men who live a solitary life, he had a lot to say.

"Well," he responded, "while he wuz a student at Harvard, Mr. Roosevelt come t' Aroostook County in Northern Maine. He come t' hunt, an' 'is guide an' compadre wuz ma great-uncle William Sewall. I be named after 'im. Uncle Sewall's partner wuz also 'is nephew, Wilmot Dow, my pa. Pa wuz only twenty-three when he first met Mr. Roosevelt. Pa wuz just as big an' wild as Uncle Bill, but Uncle Bill al'ays said Pa's a better guide, better hunter, better fisherman, an' th' best shot in Aroostook County.

"Mr. Roosevelt come back fer a longer huntin' an' mountain climbin' trip with Uncle Bill an' Pa th' followin' year. They's mighty impressed with 'is stamina an' determination, even though he wuz kinda frail an' suffered from th' asthma.

"September 1883, Mr. Roosevelt first come out here on a buffaler hunt. He falled in love with th' country, an' by th' end a th' fifteen-day hunt, he ponied up fer th' Maltese Cross Ranch upstream o' here by Medora with Mr. Sylvane Ferris an' Mr. Bill Merrifield, 'is partners. 'Bout five months after that first visit, Mr. Roosevelt's wife an' mother both died on th' same day. He were purty distressed by that an' left New York t' devote 'is time t' th' cattle b'iness.

"March 1884, Mr. Roosevelt wrote Uncle Bill inviting him an' Pa t' help set up a second cattle ranch. He wuz t' put up all th' money, but they'd have shares in any profits. If they lost on th' deal, he said he'd swaller th' loss an' still pay 'em monthly wages. They both had mortgages on their properties in Maine. Mr. Roosevelt sweetened th' deal with three thousand dollars t' pay off them mortgages.

"The wives wuzn't happy t' be left home alone or t' be stuck out in th' Badlands out West, but Mr. Roosevelt promised t' pay fer their families t' join Uncle an' Pa if all went well that first year.

"Mr. Roosevelt went t' th' 1884 Republican convention that June, but th' candidate he backed got whupped. His cattle on th' Maltese Cross Ranch wintered good, so he got a thousand head more an' made ranchin' 'is primary b'iness. He come north a horseback from Medora, crossin' back 'n' forth th' Little Missouri searchin' fer a likely property. He 'ventually reached a stretch a bottomland on th' left bank that he liked well nuff. Grass spread out from th' river edge fer a hunderd yards, t' a cottonwood grove full a loud birds, Uncle Bill told it. Th' grove run west fer 'nother two hunderd yards.

"That wuz the site of th' 'riginal Elkhorn Ranch, 'bout thirty-five miles north a Medora an' th' Northern Pacific Railroad. He bought th' place fer four hunderd dollars. Him an' 'is four partners run three thousand head, or there'bouts, dependin' on how them owned with various partners wuz counted. In them days, this wuz all open range an' th' cattle wintered best they could on what grass an' what else they could find t' eat.

"That fall uv 1884, Uncle an' Pa got here an' started workin' on buildin' th' ranch house an' th' other buildin's. That winter they built th' main ranch house, thirty by sixty foot with seven-foot tall walls. It had eight rooms. A porch, big nuff fer a couple a rockin' chairs, by th' front door an' facin' east lookin' out crost th' river. Built a barn too that wuz two sixteen-by-twenty-foot stables an' a twelve-foot-wide breeze, roofed, 'tween th' two buildin's. They built 'em a cow shed, chicken house, an' blacksmith shop all tha' same winter."

"You're kidding me," I said. "They couldn't possibly build all of that in one winter and spring, just the two of them. Cut down the trees and built that many log structures, just the two of them?"

"Uncle never said they had any help. I'm purty certain it wuz just th' two uv 'em. In them days, a man worked hard and fast.

"At th' end a th' summer uv 1885, Pa went back home t' Maine an' brought back Ma an' Aunt Sewall an' ma cousin who wuz only a coupla year old."

"What was the story about the Redhead Finnegan gang?" I asked.

"Oh yeah. Heard 'bout that, uh? Well, most a th' year, th' Little Missouri be too shaller fer even a raft; you kin ride crost it horseback. In them days, th' river froze solid in winter, not so anymore. Early spring eighty-six, th' weather warmed, an' th' river wuz too high t' ford. Uncle an' Pa built 'em a sturdy boat t' crost over so's they could hunt an' check on th' livestock.

"That March, th' river edges wuz still choked wid ice, but a center stream a fast movin' water kept th' ice movin' in front a th' house. T' keep th' boat from bein' drug away if'n more ice melted,

Uncle had 'er tied t' a tree. Early mornin' a March 24, they come out an' seen th' rope cut an' th' boat be gone.

"Three outlaws had 'em a shack 'bout twenty miles upstream a th' Elkhorn, an' some a th' local cattlemen's association wuz threatenin' t' lynch 'em fer stealing livestock. Mr. Roosevelt, Uncle, an' Pa figured them three wuz sponsible fer stealin' their boat. Th' leader a th' gang wuz Redhead Finnegan, a vicious horse-thief an' gunman. Th' second wuz a half-breed name a Burnsted; th' third, a half-wit name a Pfaffenbach. Mr. Roosevelt wuz special pissed 'bout th' boat cuz he planned t' use 'er on a cougar hunt that day. Uncle an' Pa got busy right off an' built 'em a scow t' chase th' thieves, but a blizzard come, an' they wuzn't able t' strike out fer six days.

"Mr. Roosevelt wuz chairman a th' Stockmen's Association. Cuz a that, he wuz also a deputy sheriff a Billings County. Th' three a 'em took off ridin' th' fast current in th' scow. Uncle an' Pa did th' rowin' an' steerin'; Mr. Roosevelt huddled down in buffaler robes reading one o' th' two books he brought. Fer three days, they pushed on, fightin' th' cold, wind, an' rough water. It wuz a good thing Uncle an' Pa be expert at runnin' rivers, or it coulda bin a disaster. On th' fourth day, after shootin' a couple a deer an' eatin' a hearty breakfast, they gone on, not really expectin' t' catch th' three thieves cuz they had such a big lead. That afternoon, nearly a hundred miles north an' east a th' Elkhorn, they wuz a laughin' an' a talkin' as they rode th' river. They come round a bend an' most run int' a big ice jam an' see th' stole boat moored agins' th' riverbank.

"They quick looked 'bout an' spotted th' smoke from a campfire not fer off. They shed their overcoats an' snuck up t' surround the camp. The only one home wuz th' half-wit kraut; th' other two be out huntin'. They quick got th' drop on 'im an' took 'im prisoner. Uncle took charge o' th' kraut an' made certain he kept quiet. They hunkered down an' waited fer Finnegan and Burnsted t' return. The two uv 'em walked right int' camp talkin', unawares. The posse rose up an' shouted fer th' outlaws t' drop they's weapons an' reach fer th' sky. Burnsted give up right off, his knees ashakin'. Finnegan hesitated until Mr. Roosevelt walked t' within a few feet of 'im with 'is rifle aimed at th' center uv 'is chest. Mr. Roosevelt spoke to 'im real soft, Uncle said. Ordered him t' drop 'is weapons an' hold up 'is hands. Finnegan cussed a bunch but did as he wuz told.

"Uncle said th' three outlaws had a shit-pot full a rifles, revolvers, an' knives. They collected all th' hardware from 'em, but even after th' three wuz disarmed, they had 'em a problem. It wuz bitter cold. If'n they tied th' three tight nuff t' keep from gettin' away, they's hands an' feet wuz likely t' freeze. Mandan, th' first big town downriver, wuz still over a hunderd an' fifty miles. Th' river wuz chokin' up agin with ice floes as th' temperature dropped. They couldna go back upstream, an' they wuz runnin' outta grub.

"Fer th' next eight days, they had t' wait till most noon fer the ice jams t' start movin'. They worked their way downstream till th' water froze up agin towards nightfall. Redhead be th' most dangerous, so one a th' three always kept a sharp eye on 'im. April 7 they come up on a cow camp an' got more supplies. Mr. Roosevelt borrowed 'im a horse an' rode t' th' C-Diamond Ranch. He talked th' owner int' rentin' him th' use uv a covered wagon an' two horses. Then he promised th' rancher extra t' drive th' team. They headed fer the sheriff's office at Dickinson, forty-five miles south. Uncle an' Pa continued on t' Mandan with th' boat, an' after reachin' Mandan, they brought th' boat back t' Medora on th' railroad, then rode th' river back t' th' ranch.

"Mr. Roosevelt didn't trust th' rancher much, so he walked back o' th' wagon that wuz carrying his prisoners, with his rifle cocked an' ready. After sloggin' through th' mud all day, they put up that night at a homesteader's shack. Mr. Roosevelt stayed up, sittin' on the floor of th' shack, his back agin th' door, keepin' watch. Th' followin' day, they made it t' Dickinson, an' Mr. Roosevelt turned them three over t' th' sheriff. Mr. Roosevelt got him a fee as a deputy sheriff fer making th' arrests plus mileage fer th' three hunderd miles he traveled. Uncle said the total wuz fifty dollars an' 'im an' Pa got shares.

"Mr. Roosevelt come back to Mandan fer th' trial a them outlaws. He done a lot a talkin' t' th' newspaper fellas. Th' stories they wrote did a lot fer 'is prestige an' reputation.

"Redhead Finnegan an' Burnsted both got three years in prison, but Mr. Roosevelt withdrew 'is charge agin Pfaffenbach. He said th' kraut didn't have nuff sense t' do anythin', good or bad. Th' half-wit thanked 'im, an' Mr. Roosevelt told the reporters it wuz th' first time he wuz thanked fer callin' a man a fool.

"That same August at th' Elkhorn, Aunt Sewall an' my ma give birth to sons, me an' my cousin Wil, but bad times were a-comin'. Th' buffaler herds wuz killed off by hunters comin' in on th' railroad an' by th' Texas cattle fever. Too many cattle wuz brought in, an' th' range got over-grazed. A drought come an' made everythin' worst. Th' price a cattle fer slaughter in Chicago fell cuz a th' oversupply, an' th' Elkhorn wuz bleedin' money. When Mr. Roosevelt come back from doin' some family b'iness in New York, him, Uncle, an' Pa talked over th' situation. Uncle an' Pa wuz fer quittin' an' goin' back t' Maine. Th' three uv 'em squared accounts, an' we come back t' Maine where I grew up. That wuz th' fall uv eighty-six.

"The next winter wuz real bad, an' Mr. Roosevelt lost 'bout 60 percent uv 'is cattle. By then he wuz livin' full time in New York, back t' writin' 'is books an' politickin'. He turned over th' cattle b'iness, including th' Elkhorn, t' 'is partners in th' Maltese Cross, Mr. Ferris an' Mr. Merrifield. He come back t' help with roundups an' t' do some huntin' but left all th' runnin' a th' ranch t' 'is partners. After a late summer visit in 1890, he left th' Elkhorn fer good an' ended 'is partnership with Merrifield, leavin' Ferris t' run th' remainin' cattle."

"Well, that's some story. So how did you end up with this place?" I asked.

"Ah wuz out huntin' an' lookin' fer th' spot where they captured Redhead an' 'is gang. Think ah found th' place downstream from here. This place wuz fer sale, an' ah saved most a ma pay from soldierin'. Th' bank had some money, so me an' th' bank bought 'er. She's free an' clear now an' suits me; don't need much."

"Have you found where the original Elkhorn was?"

"Yeah, but nothin' there; th' buildin's be ruins. Ah stood where th' house wuz an' could see th' view that Pa an' Uncle had crost th' river."

I had finished with the second heifer, put everything back in the truck, picked up my receipt book, and leaned over to check the mileage.

"What do ah owe you, Doc?"

"Just a minute, and I'll total it up. Looks like just over thirty miles from the hospital to here. That sound right?"

"Yeah, that's 'bout right."

"OK, I'm going to leave you this bottle of Combiotic. You need to keep those two in for the next couple of weeks and give them each ten cc of the Combiotic a day. Have you got syringes and needles?"

"Yeah, sure, might be stuck from th' last time I used 'em."

"Well, you need to wash them up good with soap and water, get them unstuck, and then boil them for at least ten minutes before you use them. You should cut out the sutures I put in ten days from now and then keep the heifers up for a couple of days to make certain they don't prolapse again."

I finished adding up the bill. "We've got twelve dollars mileage and fifteen each for the prolapse repair. That's forty-two dollars."

Dow counted out crumpled bills into my hand, smoothing each of them as he did so.

"OK, Mr. Dow. Call if you have any more problems. That's a great President Roosevelt story."

CHAPTER 23:
LEG PROBLEMS

I T WAS HOT. THE WET SPRING had turned all plant life a luxuriant green, but after six weeks, the sky was cloudless, and the wind shifted, blowing in from the southwest. The sun burned the green to brittle brown.

Jim Shapley owned the pharmacy three blocks from the animal hospital. He was distraught. A car had hit his blond cocker spaniel, Scamp, when the dog was returning from the field across the road from his house.

"I let him out at seven this morning as usual. He's always been very careful getting across the road to the field. He goes over every morning and follows rabbits, but he's yet to catch one. I didn't see who hit him, just heard a thump and him howling. The bastard just kept on going. I never even saw what kind of car it was."

Scamp was a crybaby. He started whining as soon as I approached him. I didn't have to palpate his left hind leg to diagnose the obvious femoral fracture.

"It'll be OK, Scamp," I said. "We'll give you some short-acting anesthetic, intubate your trachea, and anesthetize you, and when you wake up, everything will be fixed up." I reached out to pet the dog on his head, but with no warning, he snapped at my fingers. I pulled back just in time. "OK, we'll muzzle you before I do anything."

"He must be hurting bad," the pharmacist said. "We've had him since he was a pup, and that's the first time he ever snapped at anyone."

"Not a problem," I said. "He's no doubt in considerable pain, and he doesn't know me. It's not an unusual reaction. I'll just tie this loop of gauze around his muzzle and then tie it in back of his head, like this. He'll be fine."

I examined the dog and determined he was only in mild shock with a normal heart rate and pulse and normal breathing. I hooked up an IV saline drip, anesthetized him, put an endotracheal tube into his trachea, and then hooked him up to the gas anesthetic machine.

"OK, Mr. Shapely, I'm going to take some radiographs, and then we'll be able to decide how best to handle this."

The radiographs showed a spiral mid-shaft fracture of the left femur.

"With this kind of fracture," I explained, "it's difficult to keep the bone ends aligned with a splint of any kind. The best way to handle this is to do an open reduction and put a stainless steel pin in the bone. After it heals, I'll remove the pin. We'll also put a Thomas splint on him for added protection and stability. He should do just fine."

"Whatever it takes, Doc. He's a good dog, and my wife loves him. She was so upset she wouldn't even come along, afraid you were going to put him to sleep. Go ahead and fix him up."

He cares for the dog at least as much as his wife does, maybe more.

"Will do, Mr. Shapely, I'll start working on him right away. I expect you need to go and open your store, so I'll call you as soon as I'm finished and let you know how things went."

"Thanks, Doc. I appreciate that."

The open reduction was straightforward. I hadn't done one on my own but had assisted Dr. Smith in vet school twice. It involved dissecting down over the fracture site, removing the inevitable blood clot, pushing the pin down through the upper portion of the bone, aligning the fracture, and pushing the pin down into the lower portion until it was firmly in place. After cutting the remainder of the pin off just below the skin, I sutured the tissues over the fracture site and closed the skin. I fitted a Thomas splint, put Scamp into a cage, and called the pharmacist.

"Scamp's out of surgery and doing well. He is awake, his color is good, his heart rate and pulse are normal, and his breathing is regular. He should be ready to go home in a couple of days."

I saw Scamp every two weeks after he went home to repair the tape on the Thomas splint and to make certain he was doing well. After five weeks, I removed the Steinman pin and the Thomas splint, and Scamp walked out of the clinic with only the hint of a limp.

∾

"Old man Jackson told me they would be in town today," Dick told me. "He said the bull is easy to handle. He left him in the corral back of the barn, tied up. Said the bull's been limping around for several days."

I found the lame Hereford bull snubbed to the railing of a corral behind the barn. He was standing with just the tip of the toes of his left forefoot touching the ground. The wind kicked up swirling dried dirt and pulverized manure through the corral, and I spit some black stuff out of my mouth.

Lifting the bull's left forefoot, I pushed on the swollen area between the toes. Pus came out. The bull flinched and jerked his foot away.

Having anticipated that foot rot was the problem, I had brought a soft cotton rope with me from the truck. I looped it over the leg, just above the sore foot, placed the rope over the bull's back and around and under his chest. I pulled on the rope, bringing the foot up, and then tied the rope in place. I cleaned away dead tissue with a hoof knife and then poured 7 percent tincture of iodine into the wound. The bull bellowed and pulled away, fell to his knees, and scrambled up on three legs again, snorting. He looked at me with anger in his eyes.

"Sorry, old boy. It hurts like hell, I know, but it will be much better soon."

I stuffed gauze soaked in iodine into the now open abscess and then bandaged the foot using the gauze and tape I had stuffed into the pockets of my coveralls. After the bandage was in place, I went back to the truck for some antibiotics. I slapped a sixteen-gauge, two-inch-long needle into the bull's left rump, attached the steel and glass syringe to the hub of the needle, and injected the long-acting penicillin.

—

The day proved to be busy, and the weather got nastier, as the radio announcer had predicted. After a late lunch, I treated four mastitis cases and a retained placenta, each on a different farm. In the early evening, clouds built to the west, the wind shifted to the northwest, and for fifteen minutes, it rained mud as I drove. The last call of the day was a lame saddle horse.

I carefully observed the mare as the owner, at my direction, led her at a walk and then a trot, going away and then coming towards me. Finally, I observed from the side as the owner walked and trotted her for me to diagnose the lameness.

"Jeez, Doc," wheezed Frank Tompkins, "I hope you've seen enough. I kept this mare so I wouldn't have to use my own feet to get around."

Tompkins, the famous rodeo and Wild West show cowboy, had raised wheat and cattle on the high plains twenty-five miles north and west of town. He was now eighty-two, he told me, a widower for five years. His son had graduated from the University of Montana and come back to help his dad operate the ranch. After turning sixty-six, Tompkins had turned the ranching operation over to his son, leasing him the land and selling him the cattle herd. Frank and his wife had spent winters in Arizona and the rest of the year on the ranch; their house was just a hundred yards away from the home his son had built for his own family.

The son died after a six-month fight against pancreatic cancer. Tompkins's wife lived only one year after their son died. Their daughter, who had also finished college, was married, had her own family, and lived in Denver. After his son died, Frank resumed the ranch operations, taking care of his son's young family as best he could, but it got to be too much for him. His daughter-in-law and grandchildren moved back to be with her family in Billings where she started a new life.

Frank sold the ranch and moved to the house he had purchased when his children were going to high school. While they had been in school, his wife had stayed with the two children in town during the school week, so they would not have to drive in every day from the ranch. After his daughter had finished high school, they had kept the town place as a rental. Renters hadn't taken care of the house or the barn, and the five-acre place had been in sad shape when he had moved in, but he was gradually restoring it.

We moved into the barn to get out of the wind and blowing dust. Frank had started his renovation projects with the barn to make things comfortable for his animals before taking care of the house and his own needs. There were three renovated stalls. He had converted the fourth stall into a well-organized workshop. There were a lot of antique but well-cared-for carpentry tools, organized according to purpose. I noticed new paint and a new roof on the barn as I walked over and took a ripsaw off its peg on the wall. It was sharp, covered with a protective seal of beeswax. A wood-handled chisel was as sharp as a razor.

"I see you take very good care of your tools, Mr. Tompkins. My granddad was a carpenter, and he always talked about how important that was."

"Well, a man can't do good work without good tools, and this mare was one of the tools of my trade. Some jobs just need doing on horseback. This mare is one of the best cow horses I had over the years. It's a little hard for me to get around these days, but when I get up on her, I feel like I'm doing something worthwhile again."

"You miss the ranch then?"

"Oh yeah, but it was too much for me, too many things to be done. When my boy died and I had to take over again, I realized that and my heart wasn't in it. Nobody to leave it to."

We were standing in the wide alley of the barn. I continued my evaluation of the mare. "Right foreleg, it seems," I murmured. I used a hoof tester to rule out soreness in the hoof. When I palpated up the leg, I thought I felt some heat in the region of the sesamoid bones.

"I'll need some radiographs before I can make a diagnosis or give a prognosis. If you'll call the hospital, you can make arrangements with Dick Mathes for a time to bring her in for the X-rays. Do you have a trailer to bring her in?"

"Yeah, I've still got one out at the ranch. Haven't bothered to bring it in, didn't think I would need to haul her anyplace. I can go get it."

"Does she load easy?"

"Oh yeah, she'll load right up, no problem."

"Well, I don't think it's anything too serious, but we have to rule out a fractured sesamoid bone. If it's just the bad strain I think it is, three or four weeks of stall rest and some liniment rubbed on each day should take care of it."

"Sounds good to me," Tompkins said. "Taking care of her is more important to me than riding her these days."

CHAPTER 24:

MY SON, THE DOCTOR

HANK RANDALL RETIRED AS THE EDITOR of in-house publications at the Allis Chalmers Company. During his career at Allis Chalmers, he was also a free-lance cartoonist, selling cartoons to trade magazines. After retirement, he continued free-lance cartooning but spent most of his time doing serious paintings, acrylics on mason board. Most of his paintings were colorful western themes featuring stylized caricatures of people, buildings, and animals.

He was a quiet, regular man. During the week, he worked from eight in the morning until noon. When he broke for lunch, Emily, his wife of forty-some years, would have a tuna and mayonnaise sandwich and one sweet pickle ready and waiting for him. At twelve-thirty, he was back in his converted garage studio, hard at work. At five in the evening, he stopped what he was working on, cleaned his brushes and other paraphernalia, returned to the house, showered, and helped Emily prepare dinner.

Except on Fridays. On those days, he stopped working at four o'clock. At five, Alex Washburn, the owner of Freddy's would take out three bottles of Blatz beer and line them up on the end of the bar closest to the wall. On the wall was a hand-lettered sign saying "Hank's stool, Friday evenings." If anyone were occupying the stool on Friday at five fifteen, Alex would shoo him or her off.

At five thirty, Emily would drive up, and Hank would get out of the car and walk through the bar's door. Alex would pop the top on the beer bottle closest to the wall. Hank would assume his position on the stool and take a long drink from the opened bottle.

During the evening, a succession of regulars would join Hank on the stool to his left engaging in spirited, thirsty conversation. When he finished a bottle, Hank would stand on the runners of his stool and put the bottle in the open cardboard case Alex had placed within reach behind the bar for that purpose. That was the signal for Alex to place a fresh bottle in line, next to the remaining two and open the one closest to the wall. When Hank had enough, he would leave the empty on the bar. At midnight, Emily would arrive, honk the car horn once, and Hank would be gone for another week.

Years before our arrival, Hank had earned this special attention and the six to eight beers he drank each Friday evening by decorating the walls of Freddy's with life-sized caricatures of the regulars engaged in either their favorite pastimes or occupations. Alex had told me about the sign, the stool, and Hank's routine when I had stopped for a cold beer on a particularly hot afternoon.

Hank and Emily owned a wirehaired-terrier mix, Sparky. I met Sparky and Hank when his master brought the dog in for his annual rabies shot. I met Emily when I went to their place to give her pinto mare, Patches, encephalitis and tetanus vaccinations late that spring.

Emily's face was etched with permanent smile wrinkles. She bubbled, especially so when riding or taking care of her mare. Patches's personality matched Hank's, calm, steady, taciturn. Sparky was more like Emily.

～

Rosalie and I were just starting to get ready for bed a little after eleven in the evening when the phone rang.

"Doc," Dick said, "Hank Randall just called. His wife's mare is colicky."

"OK, call and tell them I'm on my way. Did you tell them to keep her up and walking?"

"Of course." He sounded a little irritated that I had asked.

Colic is another name for a bellyache. It can have many causes and is a serious emergency in horses because horses manifest abdominal pain by rolling. They get to the ground, sometimes falling heavily, and roll to their back and side-to-side. Because of the manner in which the bowel is suspended in the abdomen of horses, when the animal rolls with abdominal pain, the intestinal tract can twist on itself, roll on itself, or sometimes telescope into itself. When any of these happen, the blood supply to the affected portion of the bowel is interrupted, and that portion of the bowel dies. Once this happens, if not surgically corrected, the lesion is fatal.

In the early 1960s, there were very few veterinary hospitals prepared and experienced in doing abdominal surgery in horses. The Sidney Animal Hospital was not one of them.

The emergency treatment for colic is to keep the horse on its feet by forcing it to walk until the veterinarian arrives. Once the veterinarian is on site, it is necessary to make a diagnosis of the cause and treat accordingly. In many, if not the majority, of cases, the exact cause is not readily apparent, and the standard treatment in the early 1960s was to dose the animal via stomach tube with mineral oil, adding a degassing or surface-tension-reducing agent, and to administer an analgesic agent. Today we have available many more choices of antispasmodic and analgesic drugs for this still serious emergency.

A more societal aspect of colic in horses, depending upon the neighborhood and time of year, is the colic block party. Hank and Emily lived in an eclectic area just outside of town, characterized by five- and ten-acre plots of land and a wide variety of housing. There were mobile homes still on wheels, manufactured homes on solid foundations, modest frame houses, and some expensive custom homes. A similar mix of barns and corrals accompanied the houses and reflected the financial resources of the owners. It was summer, hot, dry, shirtsleeve weather, perfect conditions for a colic block party.

I arrived just after eleven thirty. There was a lit Coleman lantern standing on an inverted fifty-five-gallon drum in the middle of the Randall's half-acre corral. I noticed at least half a dozen neighbors sitting on cheap aluminum lawn chairs, most with a can in their hand.

There was a cooler filled with cans of beer and soft drinks floating in ice water. Frank Tompkins, whose place was just down the road from the Randalls', was leading Patches around the periphery inside the corral. Hank followed, a length of rope in his hand, occasionally flicking the mare's rump to keep her moving.

I performed a quick physical exam on the mare. Her mucous membranes showed no sign of toxicity. Her heart rate was elevated, but her lung and heart sounds were normal. I listened over her abdomen for several minutes but heard no signs of borborygmus, the normal rumbling noises caused by the propulsion of gas and ingesta through the intestines.

Patches kept looking around at her belly. As I put my stethoscope back around my neck, she started to collapse.

"No, . . . up girl," Frank shouted, pulling on her halter rope.

I slapped her hard on the rump. "I still have to do a rectal exam. Keep her up and moving, Mr. Tompkins. I'll get what I need from the truck."

I pulled the plastic rectal sleeve over my left hand and arm while following the two men and the mare around the corral. Still walking, I removed the plastic squeeze bottle with mineral oil out of the back pocket of my Wranglers and oiled up the sleeve.

"OK, stop and hold her, and I'll do this," I said. I stood on the right side of the mare and grabbed the base of her tail with my right hand pushing my left hand into her rectum. Without instruction, Frank Tompkins moved to the right side of Patches's head. He held her with one of his hands on either side of her halter. The old cowboy knew that if the mare decided to spook she would move away from both of us. If we were not standing on the same side, someone was likely to get hurt.

I gradually worked my arm in further until I touched the transverse colon. I could feel a large fecal obstruction with a lot of gas upstream. Patches was impacted. I pulled out my arm turning the sleeve inside out.

"Well, she's got an impaction," I explained. "I'm going to give her some mineral oil. She's got a lot of gas accumulating ahead of the blockage, and that's what's causing the pain. I'll give her something to try to reduce the gas formation and a touch of tranquilizer to take the edge off the pain. Keep her moving while I get everything ready. We don't want her to go down and twist a gut."

Both men nodded and started walking the mare while I went back to the truck. I poured a gallon jug of mineral oil into a stainless steel bucket and added a dash of the new surface-tension-reducing agent that one of the drug company detail men had recently touted. I had used it on two previous cases, and it had seemed to be effective. I put my stainless steel pump into the bucket, put a Tygon stomach tube around my neck, and pulled a dose of Acepromazine into a syringe.

I waited inside the gate until the two men brought Patches around again. I gave her the tranquilizer in the jugular vein and then carefully started the stomach tube through her left nostril while blowing gently into the other end of the tube as I advanced it. She started swallowing, a good sign that I was in the esophagus, not the trachea. I watched carefully and saw the end of the tube moving down her neck, another sign I was in the esophagus. When I felt the tube was in her stomach, I took my end of it out of my mouth and listened while watching her chest. I didn't want to hear air moving in and out of the tube with her respirations.

Pumping mineral oil, or anything else, into the trachea or lungs, could—probably would—result in inhalation pneumonia and death. For a veterinarian to do that is negligent at best, malpractice at worst.

"OK, just hold her steady while I pump this in; won't take but a minute." After emptying the bucket, I kinked the tube, removed it from the pump, unkinked it, then blew into it to empty it, kinked it again, and withdrew it from the mare's stomach and out through her nose. She snorted some mucous but no blood. This meant I hadn't ruptured any blood vessels in the turbinate bones of her nose while getting the tube in or taking it out, a reassuring sign of moderate competence.

"OK, let's keep her walking while I clean and put everything away. It's going to take some time for the oil to work its way through. Until then, all we can do is prevent her from going down and rolling."

"You want me to lead her for a while, Frank?" Hank asked. "Emily can follow and help keep her up." He looked over to his wife who was standing just inside the gate."

"Certainly," Emily said. "Please take my chair for a while, Frank. You've been walking her for an hour already. Hank and I will keep her up."

"You sure?" Frank asked. "My knee is getting a little sore."

"Of course. Please, go sit down."

"Keep her head up, Hank. She'll try to lower it before going down," Frank instructed.

For the next two hours, various neighbors took turns leading Patches and following with the rope. Twice she managed to go down, but when she did, several people, including myself, rushed in to keep her from rolling, and we got her back on her feet.

At about three in the morning, I walked through the gate pulling on yet another rectal sleeve. I waited until they brought Patches around to me. Hank was on her head again.

"Hold on to her head and stand on the same side of her as I'm on, Hank. I'm going to do another rectal and see if anything is happening." As I put my hand in her rectum I noticed a tiny bit of oil.

"This is good, there's a little oil in her rectum. It's getting around the impaction. That's a good sign." However, the impaction seemed to be in the same place and was just as firm as when I had first palpated it. I withdrew my arm. "Well, the impaction hasn't broken down or moved. Since the oil is moving around it some, I'm going to try something else, a soapy water enema, and see if we can move it that way."

I prepared a gallon of warm soapy water, placed an old stomach tube through her anus and into the rectum, and pumped in the enema. She evacuated everything in the first five steps as they took her for another circuit of the corral. I did another rectal when they brought her back around.

"No change," I announced. "Let's try it again. This time I'm going to try to hold it in with my arm and work it forward." I filled the bucket again, and this time took the tube in with my arm as far as I could reach.

Without saying anything, Frank Tomkins took charge of the bucket and pump. I nodded at him, and he pumped the contents of the bucket into the mare.

"OK," I said. "I'm going to pull out the tube but keep my arm in and see if I can break up the impaction."

Some soapy water leaked out of her anus and onto my shirt, but most stayed in. She suddenly started to sink down, hind legs first.

"NO, no, . . . get her moving," I shouted. Frank slapped her on the rump repeatedly while Hank pulled on her halter rope. She sighed and started walking with me holding the base of her tail and maneuvering my left arm and hand inside her, massaging the impaction. After two laps around the corral, I started laughing.

"What the hell are you laughing at, Doc?" Frank asked.

"I just had this mental picture of my mom in a rocking chair, smiling and proudly thinking, 'My son, the doctor.' I don't think what I'm doing at this moment fits her image of me."

I felt the impaction starting to break up under the prodding of my fingers. "Ah, I think we've got it," I said. "It should move through now."

I removed my arm, inverting the sleeve. "Keep her up, and we'll see if she passes anything."

Three laps later, Patches defecated soapy water and feces. A cheer went up from the assembled.

"Let her go, and let's see what she does," I said.

As soon as Hank unclipped the halter rope, Patches went to her hay trough and started munching.

"Great," I said. "I haven't yet had a horse die while eating. I think she's going to be fine."

❧

Two days later, I was in the office reading a journal article about aortic valve stenosis in German shepherd dogs. The author said it was possible to diagnose the condition by hearing a systolic murmur on top of the dog's head. Dick poked his head through the door.

"Hank Randall is here. He paid his bill and has something for you."

"OK," I said getting up and walking into the reception area. "Hi, Hank. How's Patches doing?"

"Great, Doc. She hasn't missed a meal. Emily is very happy and relieved. She's very attached to that mare." He reached into the briefcase on the counter. "Got this for you," he said, handing me a ten-by-fourteen-inch poster board.

It was a cartoon. In the right foreground, a woman with gray, curly hair and glasses was sitting in a rocking chair, smiling contentedly. To the left, filling most of the scene was a cloud containing a caricature of me, long sideburns, Resistol hat, cowboy boots, with my arm inside a caricature of Patches. The mare has her head turned, looking at me with an evil grin on her face. At my feet was a medical bag with a syringe and stethoscope hanging out, "D. R. Gross DVM" printed on the side. Over my mom's head was the caption, "My Son, the Doctor!"

Hank had never met or seen a photograph of my mom, but his caricature of her was right on, the hair, the glasses, even the expression.

As I write this, I'm looking up at that framed cartoon hanging on the wall of my office. The bottom left-hand corner is signed, "Hank R." The colors have faded, as have we all.

CHAPTER 25:
CASTRATING

"Dave, I don't know what I have to do to make her happy."

Dr. Schultz had recently started addressing me as Dave. I couldn't bring myself to address him as Marcus; he would always be Dr. Schultz. We were in the office organizing our day's work for maximal efficiency and minimal mileage. This organizing activity was a daily but futile exercise since the schedule inevitably altered to accommodate emergencies.

"Uh, I'm sorry, Dr. Schultz. My mind was elsewhere. What did you say?"

"It's Cheryl. She's not speaking to me again. She's giving me the dreaded silent treatment. I have no idea what pissed her off this time."

Uh-oh, how do I stay out of this?

"Well, did you miss a birthday or anniversary or something?

He thought for three or four minutes while drumming his fingers on the top of his desk. Three or four minutes of finger drumming is a long time. I said nothing.

"No, her birthday, all the kids' birthdays, our anniversary, no I haven't forgotten. I can't think of anything."

Dick saved me.

"Doc Gross, I just got a call from Fred Homer. You were supposed to be at his place at eight this morning, and it's almost eighty-thirty. He wants to know if we need to reschedule."

"No, Dick," I said. "I'm on my way."

~

Castrating calves is not a complicated procedure. Sometimes instead of incising the scrotum, the bottom portion is just cut off. Usually the spermatic cord is clamped with a hemostat or in larger animals with an emasculator. Then the cord is cut or scraped with a knife until it breaks, or the testicle is just pulled until the cord breaks. Lambs are castrated using the same techniques, although I have witnessed sheepherders grabbing the testicles in their teeth and chewing the spermatic cord or just pulling back until the cord breaks. The key is speed; get it done fast.

There is also the rubber-band technique, one I have never approved of. This method uses an applicator to apply a tight rubber band around the scrotum on top of the testicles. The blood supply to the testicles is interrupted, all the tissues distal to the band die, and eventually, everything sloughs off.

All these techniques sound brutal, and they are, but when done by experienced people, they take only moments, except for the rubber band method, and the animals rarely, if ever, have any discernable lasting adverse effects, psychological or otherwise.

During the forty-fifth reunion of my veterinary class, one of my colleagues, a veteran large-animal practitioner, told me the story of a new client who had purchased a few acres outside of town and was determined to be part of the back-to-earth movement. He insisted that a recently purchased bull calf, a 4-H project for his daughter, be castrated using general anesthesia. In fact, both father and daughter insisted. My classmate, who also happens to be a past-president of the AVMA and highly respected in the profession, explained he would have to charge the same as he would to perform surgery under general anesthesia for any animal. The client acknowledged the rationale and agreed. My colleague anesthetized the calf, completed the procedure, and monitored the calf until it recovered, all without incident.

The bill was over four hundred dollars, and the client paid it, his conscience clear.

When I joined the practice, Dr. Schultz charged a dollar a head to castrate calves. Most clients thought that charge was rather excessive and did the job themselves.

～

I was back on Fred Homer's place. Being a beet farmer, only recently into the dairy business, he was not familiar with all the husbandry skills necessary for running a dairy farm.

"I know most folks castrate calves themselves, but I've never done it," he told me. "Thought I best have you do it this time so's I could learn."

"No problem, Mr. Homer. It's not very complicated. How many calves do you have for us to work on?"

"Got fifteen of 'em saved up," he responded. "Come on. I'll show you where they are."

I had everything I would need in two stainless buckets, so I followed him to a steel-pipe corral behind the implement barn.

"Here we are," he said, opening the corner gate for us to enter. The corral was about forty feet square but with no chute or other mechanism for catching and holding the fifteen Holstein calves. A shed roof covered the corner of the corral opposite the gate. Most of the calves were small, between 120 and 170 pounds. One big guy was closer to four hundred.

"Nice corral," I said. "Have you given any thought to how the two of us are going to catch, hold, and castrate these critters?"

"Uh, no, I kinda thought you'd have a way to do that," he responded.

"OK," I said. "Do you have any extra gates we can use to crowd them together?"

"Nope."

I shook my head. This fifteen-dollar call, plus mileage, was likely to take most of the day, and a four-hundred-pound bull calf could hurt somebody, probably me.

"Well, how about some extra steel poles, left over from building this corral?" I asked.

"Yeah, I think there are three or four of them left. They'll be in the barn. Want to have a look?"

"Yes, please. How long are they?"

"Twelve foot, as I recall," he said.

I paced off the distance between the two posts holding up the high part of the shed roof over the corner. It was a little over ten feet.

"That might work," I said. "If the posts are actually twelve feet long, we can lash them inside these posts and make a small triangular catch pen to hold the calves. Chasing them around the whole corral will not be very productive. Have you got something to tie the poles to the posts with?"

"Baling wire?"

"Yeah, that should work. Let's get the pipes."

There were four twelve-foot-lengths of pipe. We carried them to the corral. I herded the calves into the corner we were going to close off and held them in there while Mr. Homer wired three of the pipes in place to form a triangular holding pen. It was close, but there was just enough room with the calves crowded into the corner to grab one at a time, move him to a clear area, throw him down, and hog-tie and castrate him. I went back to my truck for a braided pigging string and a throw rope.

"OK, Mr. Homer. Have you ever thrown a calf and hog-tied it?"

"No, sir."

"OK then, let me do the first couple; then you can try it. Is that all right with you?"

"Yes, sir."

I put the pigging string, coiled, in my mouth and grabbed the closest calf. Reaching across his neck with my left hand I grabbed his right ear and then reached my right hand over his back grabbing the loose skin at his flank. I pulled him against me, then lifted and pushed with my right knee, and slammed him on the ground away from the milling herd of calves. I slipped the loop of the pigging string over one front leg just above the hoof, then using my right leg brought both of his hind legs up, wrapped them tightly three times, and threw a half hitch around the front leg. The calf was restrained.

"Very impressive, Doc," smiled Mr. Homer. "You do some rodeoing, do you?"

"Nope," I responded, "just observation and a little practice."

I retrieved my instruments and made quick work of turning the bull calf into a steer calf. Then I used a marking crayon to put a yellow stripe on his back. "That'll identify the ones we finish with," I said.

After throwing, tying, and castrating the second calf, I let Mr. Homer throw and tie the next one. He fumbled a bit but seemed to get it done. The calf kicked loose just as I made the first incision, and I had to retie his legs. After that, Mr. Homer got the hang of it pretty well, and none of the others he tied got loose.

I castrated the eleventh calf and then suggested he do the rest.

"We'll save the big fella for last."

Homer was hesitant making the first cut through the scrotum, nibbling at it.

"Make it bold," I said. "You're going to take out that testicle anyhow; don't be afraid to cut into it. The trick is to get through the skin of the scrotum fast, in one cut, but hold the testicle in your left hand and slice away from your hand. Good."

He managed to get the first testicle out and applied the emasculator.

"Up higher," I instructed.

"There?"

"Yeah, now close it hard and hold it for a couple of seconds. Good! Now take the second one."

He was more certain of himself the second time and reasonably expert by the time he did the remaining small calves.

Only the four-hundred-pound calf remained. I put my throw rope around his neck and tied him to one of the posts of the shed roof.

"He's way too big to try to throw down. I've got another way to handle him."

"OK. I wondered how you were going to throw him down. I certainly wasn't gonna try it," said Mr. Homer.

"Let's turn the rest of these loose and give them some feed," I suggested. "I have to get another rope from the truck."

I helped Mr. Homer remove the pipes we used to make the catch pen, and he went to fetch a bale of hay. I retrieved an inch-thick cotton rope from the truck and tied a bowline loop around the big calf's neck while Mr. Homer spread a bale of hay out for the other calves. Most of them commenced nibbling without an apparent care in their world.

"Well, Doc, I'm going to be real interested in how you handle this one."

"Watch and learn, Mr. Homer. The trick is to be just enough smarter than the animal."

I used the free end of the rope to tie a half hitch around the calf's chest, just behind his front legs and a second half hitch around his abdomen just in front of his hind legs. Then I took a couple of steps until I was directly behind him and leaned back into the rope. The calf sank gently to the ground.

"Here, keep some tension on this, Mr. Homer, while I turn him on his side and tie up his legs."

"Doc, you are something. Just full of tricks, aren't you? That's just real impressive, not as much as the cow with the milk fever, but pretty impressive."

I reached over, grabbed his flank, rolled the bull onto his side, and hog-tied him. As I made the first incision into the scrotum over the down side testicle, the calf bawled and struggled loosening the pigging string and kicking wildly. I jumped back and, in the process, somehow managed to slice through the skin directly over the last joint of the third finger on my left hand, cutting through the extensor tendons. Angry with myself, I retied the calf, cinching the pigging string down very tight and throwing three half hitches to hold him. When I stood up, there was blood all over the calf's legs, my shirt, and flowing freely from my finger onto the ground.

"That doesn't look so good, Doc. Seems you cut yourself pretty bad."

I inspected the damage. "Looks like I did. Be back in a minute after I put a bandage on it."

I went to the truck, cleaned the wound, put a sterile gauze pad over my self-induced laceration, and wrapped it tightly with adhesive tape. Needing waterproof protection for it, I tried to fit a surgical glove over the hand but couldn't get the glove over the heavily bandaged finger. I squeezed the finger keeping pressure on it until I figured the bleeding stopped, then removed the bandage, and inspected the dry wound. I applied some antibiotic mastitis ointment to the wound and bandaged it with a significantly smaller bandage. This time I was able to get the surgical glove over the finger. I returned to the fray, irritated with my clumsiness.

"You OK, Doc? Looks like you got the bleeding stopped."

"Yeah, it'll be fine," I said. "Let's get done with this."

I completed the castration and turned the calf loose. He joined his brethren eating what was left of the bale of hay.

I had to re-bandage the finger several times during the day. Seems I washed my hands or got them wet more often than I realized, and once the bandage got wet, it was useless.

That evening Rosalie remonstrated, "Dave, you need to have Joe Lufkin look at that and suture it up properly. The end of your finger is pointing down; that's not right. Let's go to the emergency room and have it taken care of."

"Naw, it'll be fine," I insisted. I'm going to bandage it with a tongue depressor to straighten out the finger; it'll heal just fine, no problem."

～

I'm looking at the permanently hooked last joint on the third finger of my left hand. Of course, the cut tendons didn't miraculously realign, and the end of my finger never did straighten out, although the incision healed quite nicely. I can press down and straighten the finger, and the hook has full strength when I pull back on it. Over the years, I found it quite handy when pulling calves and foals. I can hook that crooked finger into one eye socket and my thumb into the other and have plenty of strength to straighten and pull the animal's head forward into the proper position in the birth canal.

CHAPTER 26:
A FUTURE VET

As I drove into the hospital garage, I saw Sammy Grant in the parking lot struggling to unload a huge wood box from the bed of his father's pickup. Sammy was a tall, skinny sixteen-year-old with the straggly beginnings of a dark mustache and beard that shared his face with acne sores. I knew him from a variety of calls I had made to his family's marginal farm. His father worked as a mechanic at the local John Deere dealership in town, and Sammy was responsible for the care of all the livestock on the farm. He was usually the one who called when they had a problem. Whenever I arrived at their place, he attached himself to me. What and why questions came fast and furious.

"Here, let me help you with that, Sammy," I offered. "What's in it?"

"Rabbits," he grunted. "Easier if you could just do 'em here without me having to get them inside, but Dick said I have to bring 'em in."

"He's probably right. There's a good chance they could escape out here," I said. "What seems to be the problem with them?"

"Nothin'. I just bought 'em off a guy, and he didn't know which were males and which were females. Got to get that sorted out before I can start raising them. I looked but couldn't really tell for sure. They're all young."

"So," I asked, "this your new FFA project?"

"Yeah, thought I'd try it. They're Flemish giants. The kits are supposed to bring a good price, and I got 'em cheap 'cause the guy needed cash. If I can get some ribbons on them at the county fair this fall, the kits should sell well."

I had never seen a Flemish giant rabbit.

"You grab one end of the box; I'll take the other," I instructed. "We can bring them in through the garage. We'll take them into the treatment room, and I'll show you what to look for."

We balanced the box on the treatment table, overlapping on all four sides. I lifted the lid a couple of inches and peeked inside. There were seven huge rabbits crowded into one corner.

"My word, Sammy, they are gigantic! Those are the biggest rabbits I've ever seen. Tell me about them; educate me."

He smiled, obviously proud and happy to be, for a change, the dispenser of knowledge. "Some think they were first bred in Eastern Europe in the 1890s. Others think they were derived from leporine rabbits and imported into England in the mid-1800s. Either way, they arrived in the States from both Belgium and England around the beginning of the twentieth century. The bucks are supposed to have bigger heads than the does, but these all look about the same to me."

He reached into the box and took out a steel-gray rabbit. He held it with his right arm cradling the animal against his chest. His right hand supported the rabbit's thorax with his second finger between the front legs, the first and third finger outside the legs holding them tight. The rabbit was at least twenty, maybe twenty-four inches long.

"These are all supposed to be less than six months old," Sammy said. "They call these juniors. I'll show them this fall as seniors, over nine months old. The book I got from the library says I need to breed the does before they are a year old. They're supposed to come into heat for the first time at about nine months. The pelvis of the does is supposed to fuse at about a year, so it's best to breed them during their first heat. The book says if they're bred early it prevents the pelvis from fusing and they will have fewer problems giving birth from then on.

"Look at this fur, Doc." He stroked the animal with his free hand, pushing the fur up from the rump to the head. The glossy, dense fur rolled back to its original position. I copied the motion and found the fur was indeed luxurious, soft and silky.

"The adults get even bigger than this," Sammy continued. "An adult buck has to weigh at least thirteen pounds to be shown, and an adult doe fourteen. Some of them can get up to thirty pounds."

"Unbelievable," I murmured. "I guess that's why they're called giants. Well, here, sit on this chair, and turn that beast over on his or her back. That's supposed to kind of mesmerize regular rabbits; we'll see if it will work on these guys."

He rolled the rabbit over onto its back, hind legs facing me. The rabbit was quiet and appeared comfortable.

"That's good," I said. "Now just hold the head, and we should be OK."

I used both hands to part the fur and apply gentle pressure on either side of the vent.

"OK," I said, "you see this opening just below the tail?"

Sammy leaned over and nodded.

"That's the anus. Here, below, that is another opening."

"Yeah, I see it," he said.

"That's the vent. If it's a male when I press, very gently on both sides of the vent, here, we should see the penis exposed. It's a tube with a small round opening. In the females, some tissue may also protrude, but it will be more oval and have a slit rather than a round opening. What do you see?"

"Looks like a tube with a round opening, a penis."

"That's what I think too."

"OK, Doc. Yeah, I can do this."

"Good, of course you can," I said. "Let's put him in one of the dog cages in the ward, and we'll do the rest of them, seven did you say?"

"Yeah, seven."

"You can do them sitting down. Once you get them settled on their back, you should be able to hold their head with one hand and use the other to find and examine the vent. You tell me what you think, and I'll verify. By the time we finish with these seven you'll be an expert."

Sammy put the buck into one of the dog cages and then removed a dark-black rabbit from the box. He took his seat on the chair and after a little fumbling was able to hold the head with his left hand and expose the vent with his right.

"This one's a doe, I think," he said.

"I concur."

He ended up with five females, two blacks, a fawn, a white, and the fifth a sandy tan color. The last rabbit we examined was another male, white in color. After Sammy returned all his rabbits to the box, I helped him carry it back to his dad's pickup.

"You all set on how to take care of them and what to feed them?" I asked.

"Yep, the book I got from the library has all that. Feed 'em grass hay, rabbit pellets, and fresh green vegetables when we have 'em. I can also feed 'em carrots and some fruits, but supposed to stay away from cabbage and cauliflower and such; gives 'em gas. I've got to make sure they have plenty of fresh, clean water and room enough to exercise. My plan is to build 'em a little yard they can run around in and a house for 'em to get into. I'll also make some whelping boxes for 'em. I'm gonna turn this box into a breeding cage; should work."

"Sounds as if you have everything under control, Sammy. When you make the pen for them, make certain you bury enough of the fencing all around to keep out the coyotes and other critters. It will have to have a top, too, to keep the hawks out. Chicken wire should do for the top. The main thing is to make sure you keep everything clean. You should disinfect anything you have them in at least every week or two but clean everything real good first with soap and water."

"What should I use to disinfect with?" he asked.

"A couple of tablespoons of Clorox in a gallon of water should do it."

～

Two Friday evenings after helping Sammy with his rabbits, I got a call to the Grant farm concerning one of their three milk cows.

I drove into the yard between the house and barn. The house was badly in need of scraping and a new paint job. The barn was in similar condition.

I got out of the truck, and Sammy came out of the barn at the same time his father walked down the stairs from the back, screened-in porch. The bang of the screen door slamming shut echoed in the small area between the barn and the house.

Mr. Grant showed me his hands, covered in black grease from his regular job. "I haven't had a chance to clean up from work yet, Doc. Don't think you want to get all dirty shaking hands before you see Bessie. Sammy milked her this morning before going to school and said he saw a couple of clots of blood in the pail. After he went to milk her this evening he called me at work to tell me her bag was hot to the touch and she was hurtin' bad when he milked her. I told him to call you. I just now got home, haven't seen her yet."

"Did she eat anything when you brought her in, Sammy?" I asked.

"Nope, she's acting really mopey too, Doc. Her udder is hot to the touch. What I milked out of her came out looking more like cottage cheese than milk. There were some blood clots, and it hurt her. She kicked at me, and Bessie never kicks. It's acute mastitis, right, Doc?"

"Well, before I give a diagnosis, let's go have a look at her. Sounds like acute mastitis, though."

Bessie's head was locked in a stanchion in the barn. The feed trough in front of her nose held a full scoop of a nice-looking mixture of corn and oats. She ignored it. Her rectal temperature was elevated two degrees. Her inguinal lymph nodes were normal. All four quarters of her udder were firm and hot to the touch. I milked each teat a little, and what came out did resemble blood-tinged cottage cheese.

"How long has she been fresh?" I asked.

"She calved almost three months ago," Sammy answered.

"Well, it's unusual for acute mastitis to develop so long after calving, but it happens. I think you got the diagnosis correct, Sammy. How did you come up with it?"

"I looked it up in that old *Merck Manual* you gave me," he answered. "That's really an interesting book, Doc. It's got about every disease a farm animal can get, doesn't it?"

"Well, it has most of them," I answered, "but if you keep your grades up through high school and pre-vet in college and get into vet school, you'll learn a lot that isn't in the *Merck Manual*. Remember, your high school activities and all that stuff are important, but the main determinant for getting accepted into vet school is excellent grades."

"I hear it's harder to get into vet school than into medical school. Is that right, Doc?" Mr. Grant asked.

"Well, I don't know about that, but there are a lot fewer vet schools than medical schools. I think between the States and Canada there are only about eighteen or twenty. There aren't any vet schools in Montana, North Dakota, South Dakota, Utah, Wyoming, or Idaho. The closest are Colorado State and Washington State. Iowa State has one, also the University of California at Davis, Michigan State, and Wisconsin. On the other hand, almost every state has at least one medical school, and many of them have more than one. Of course a lot more people apply for medical school than for veterinary school, so I don't know if the competition is really tougher or not. I can tell you that Sammy will need at least a B-plus average in college. In most colleges, they score four points for an A, one point for a D. The average for my class was about a 3.4 or 3.5. Having experience with animals helps, but the main thing is grades.

"Anyhow, Sammy, I'm going to show you how to put mastitis ointment inside each teat after you milk out as much as you can. I'm also going to give Bessie a shot of antibiotic. I'll leave a partial bottle of the antibiotic for you to give her an intramuscular injection twice a day until it's gone, and I'll leave plenty of mastitis ointment. The mastitis ointment comes pre-packaged in these syringes."

I removed the protector over the blunt injector probe at the end of the plastic dispenser of antibiotic ointment. "See, this cap comes off. You stick the tip of the probe up into the teat canal and inject the ointment; then massage the quarter like this.

"You go ahead and milk out all four quarters while I go to the truck for the antibiotic and more tubes of mastitis ointment."

I returned and filled a glass barrel syringe with Combiotic and removed the eighteen-gauge needle from the syringe.

"OK, Sammy, remember how we do this? Hold the needle between your thumb and finger like this. Hit her on the rump, here, twice with the heel of your hand, and then on the third strike, pop in the needle." I removed the needle from Bessie and handed it by the hub to Sammy.

"You do it, but then leave it in."

He did exactly as I had demonstrated.

"Good, now attach the syringe to the needle hub." I handed him the syringe full of antibiotic. "Now first withdraw on the syringe to make sure you're not in a vein. No blood? Good. Now inject the antibiotic into the muscle and remove the whole thing. That's good."

Next, I watched him finish milking her out and then treat each quarter of her udder with the mastitis ointment.

"OK, perfect. You'll need to milk her out and treat her at least three times a day, but don't use the milk for anything."

"Can I feed the milk to the pigs?" asked my protégé.

"Not a good idea," I said. "Any bacteria in the milk will build up resistance to the antibiotics, and the pigs could develop some new resistant strains that could cause problems in the future. It would be the same as feeding the pigs pus. Just throw it on the manure pile.

"You should milk her out and treat each quarter before school in the morning, as soon as you get home, and before you go to bed. Give her two shots of the antibiotic each day, morning and evening. You'll have to take apart the syringe and clean it each time after you use it, then boil it in water for at least ten minutes before you put it back together. I'll leave you a couple of extra needles in case you drop one or it gets a hook. You can take a hook off using a sharpening stone. Think you can do all of that?"

"Yeah, Doc, sure and thanks for showing me how to do all this stuff."

"No problem. I'm certain you can handle it. How are your rabbits doing?

"Oh, they're doing great. Want to see the pen I built for 'em?

"Yes, I would."

Sammy took me around to the back of the barn, his father trailing us. Mr. Grant was wearing a proud grin on his face. The rabbit enclosure was on ground covered in prairie grass. It was large, probably ten to twelve feet wide and thirty or more feet long. He had built a nice-looking hutch at one end, roofed with new-looking asphalt shingles.

"This is a fine-looking setup, Sammy," I said. "These rabbits are going to do very well under your care.

Mr. Grant's grin expanded. "Did it all himself," said the proud dad.

❧

When the county fair opened, Rosalie and I visited the rabbit barn where we found blue and red ribbons on most of Sammy's cages. The cages' inhabitants seemed unaware, even disinterested.

PART VI:
FALL 1961

CHAPTER 27:

A HUNTING ACCIDENT?

"THIS MIGHT BE MESSY," Dick said, handing me a call slip. It was 7:00 a.m. I had just walked in, and my coat was still buttoned. I read the slip. "Sam Samuelson, Box 24, Old Cottonwood Road, Shetland pony, gunshot wound."

"Didn't antelope season start yesterday?" I asked Dick. "How can someone mistake a Shetland pony for an antelope?" I shook my head. "Is it shot in the belly or something? Why messy?"

"Sam's a lawyer, a shark actually, super aggressive. He'll have the sheriff's office out collecting evidence. More than likely, he already has an idea who shot his daughter's pony and is building a case for the state attorney. If I were you, I'd be careful about anything you say to him. You'll find yourself in a courtroom testifying, wasting a day."

"OK, I'm forewarned; I'll be careful. This is out in that same neighborhood where Hank Randall and Frank Tompkins live, isn't it?"

"Yeah, Sam's place is about a half-mile north of the Randalls', up on the edge of the bluff overlooking all those little five- and ten-acre plots. Actually, I think Sam's the one that subdivided that property. He still owns a hundred acres or so up on the bluff. Just buffalo grass, and he doesn't do anything with it. I guess he's waiting for property values to increase. Then he'll subdivide more of those little mini-ranches."

I found an overlarge mailbox with "Box 24 Green Acres Ranch" painted in large green letters. A long gravel driveway snaked to the top of the bluff. When I reached the top, the driveway forked. The left fork ended in a circle in front of a large, brick, single-story house. I took the right fork and drove to the back of the house, parking next to a board-fence corral with a low three-sided shed in the far corner. Every piece of wood that I could see on the place, including the exterior woodwork on the house, was painted bright green.

A large man, his stomach protruding over his jeans, stood holding a black, brown, and white Shetland pony. A plump little girl, maybe four or five years old, with reddish-brown, curly hair stood next to him petting the pony's nose. Dried blood made a trail from the left shoulder down the outside of the pony's leg. The little mare was holding the leg with just the tip of the hoof resting on the ground, not bearing any weight on it.

I got out of the truck and walked over. "Mr. Samuelson, I'm Dr. Gross."

He extended a meaty right hand with short thick fingers. I took the proffered hand. His palm was soft, but his hand was too big for my long fingers to encircle. His handshake was perfunctory.

"Glad to meet you, Dr. Gross. What do you think of this mess?" He didn't wait for an answer. "Came out with Missy to feed the mare this morning and found the pony like this. Can you believe it? The wife and I woke up early to some guns firing. Some of the idiot hunters around here will shoot at anything moving. They were too close to the house. I've got the sheriff and the game warden out looking for whoever did this. They could have shot my little girl." He put his hand on his daughter's head, protectively. "I just don't understand these people. Why do they need to hunt in the first place, especially this close to town? No self-respecting wild animal is going to be this close to civilization. I guess they think they are macho men."

"Well," I said, "hunting is a long-standing tradition, especially, as you know in this part of the world. The Native Americans and mountain men all hunted to live. Almost all the Europeans who settled the West embraced it as a necessity."

He squinted at me, pulled his chin in, and furrowed his brow. I guessed my response was not what he expected or wanted.

"But I agree with you," I tried to recover. "There is no reason why anybody needs to be firing a rifle this close to people's homes. I guess I can understand intellectually why people want to hunt, but it's not for me. I have trouble putting an animal down with a lethal injection when there is no other humane alternative."

"Well, I don't understand it at all," he said. "I suppose if your family had no other source of meat, I might understand it, but the hunters around here aren't starving."

"Of course, there's also the issue of population control," I said. We've wiped out almost all the natural predators, so if hunters didn't thin the herds, it wouldn't take long for populations to increase to the point where the habitat wouldn't support them."

Mr. Samuelson peered at me and then smiled. "You have a law degree too?"

"No, sorry, I agree that there is no excuse for anyone to shoot an animal like this, unless this was an accident."

"You think it was an accident?" he asked.

"No, stupidity," I responded.

I moved to the pony and gently palpated the area around the wound. She flinched and half-reared moving away.

"OK, girl, sorry." I held her head and lifted her lips, looking at her incisors. "She's young," I said, "between three and four years looks like."

"That's what we were told," Samuelson said. "We've only had her for about nine months; got her for Missy's fifth birthday, didn't we, baby?"

"She's not going to die, is she?" asked the little girl.

"No, Missy," I said. "We can fix her up as good as new. I'm going to give her some medicine so she won't hurt so much. Then I'm going to take out the bullet, and she should be just fine in a couple of weeks. Can you wait that long before you ride her again?"

"Yes, I won't ride her if she's hurt."

"Good girl. Here, you pet her here on the neck so she'll know she's OK while I get the medicine."

I turned to the lawyer. "Is there water close by so I can scrub? I'll also need an electrical outlet for my clippers. I need to shave the hair away from the surgical site."

"The closest outlet is up at the house. We can take her up there on the lawn by the kitchen door. Will that do?"

"Absolutely, that'll be great."

We led the little mare to within six feet of the back door. Mr. Samuelson took the plug end of my clipper cord into the kitchen and plugged it in.

"You're all set, Doc."

I loaded a syringe with the appropriate dose of tranquilizer and injected it into the mare's jugular vein. After the tranquilizer took full effect, I used a number-forty blade to shave a ten-inch area around the bullet wound. Then I washed and prepared the skin with water-soluble iodine. Finally, I infiltrated all around the wound with lidocaine. I felt the tip of the inch-and-a-half-long needle I was using to infuse the local anesthetic scrape across something metallic. I removed the needle and palpated the area where I thought I had hit the bullet. Just below the spine of the scapula, I felt a hard object that moved against the bone.

"OK, I'm pretty certain I can feel the bullet there. She must have been shot from a long way away because the bullet didn't penetrate the bone of her shoulder. It should be easy to remove. I'm going to get my instruments from the truck. Do you have a card table or something I can set them on while I work? Alternatively I can pull the truck up close and work off the hood."

"We've got a little utility cart in the kitchen. I'll get it for you," Mr. Samuelson answered.

"Great."

After opening the surgical pack and setting out some suture material, a new scalpel blade, and a pair of sterile gloves, I prepped the surgical site again.

"You can use the kitchen sink to scrub," Samuelson suggested.

"That would be great," I said.

I put a surgical scrub brush and some surgical soap in a squeeze bottle into a back pocket of my coveralls. Before entering the kitchen, I scraped my feet carefully on an iron mud bar that was cemented into the stoop next to the kitchen door. Then I carefully wiped my feet on the mat in front of the door. Inside a smiling, plump young woman with the same reddish-brown, curly hair as Missy greeted me.

"Hello, Mrs. Samuelson. We'll have your daughter's pony fixed up straight away."

"Hello, Dr. Gross." Her smile was genuinely welcoming. "I've cleared everything away for you."

I glanced around the immaculate kitchen and saw a dish drain filled with pots on the kitchen table. The counter on both sides of the sink was clear. I looked down to make certain I wasn't tracking any mud or manure onto her clean floor.

"Don't worry about tracking anything in, Doctor. I can clean it up with no trouble."

I scrubbed up, and Mrs. Samuelson held the door open for me. I put on the surgical gloves, attached the blade to the scalpel, picked up a thumb forceps, and made an incision in the skin over the place where I had palpated the bullet. It only took a moment to bluntly dissect through the muscle with a forceps, locate the bullet, and remove it. I sutured the incision closed and then infiltrated all around the surgical site and the bullet hole with antibiotic. Finally I gave the mare an injection of antibiotic and a tetanus shot.

"That should do it," I said. "If you see any kind of discharge coming out of the bullet hole or the incision, give me a call; otherwise, I'll be back in ten days to remove the sutures."

Sounds good," he said. "That was a very impressive demonstration. Please leave me the bullet. If the sheriff finds a suspect, maybe we can match that bullet to his rifle. Have you got time for a cup of coffee?"

"Yeah, I think so. Let me check with the office."

I called in on the two-way.

"All I've got you down for this morning is to visit Turley's. He's got another batch of hogs ready for cholera vaccinations."

"OK, Dick, you can call Turley and tell him I'll be there in a half-hour or so."

"No need, he'll wait for you."

"Right, OK, I'll check in again when I'm done at his place."

Again, I took special care to make certain my boots were clean before entering the Samuelson kitchen. Mr. Samuelson held the door open for me.

The dish drain was back on the counter. The table was set with four place mats, cups and saucers at three places, and a glass of milk at the fourth. There was also a plate with a large piece of pastry at each place.

"Sit down; please sit down, Doc. Listen, no need for formalities. I'm Sam, this is Ida, and you've met Missy."

I smiled. "Thanks, I'm Dave. That pastry looks wonderful. What is it, Mrs. Samuelson, sorry, Ida?"

The three Samuelsons laughed.

"It's called pecan cookie crunch, my take-off on a pecan pie but with a cookie base. How do you take your coffee, Dave?" Ida asked.

"Black, please," I answered.

She poured coffee for the three adults. Sam spooned in three teaspoons of sugar and a generous dollop of cream. Ida did the same.

I took a bite of the pecan cookie crunch. "This is wonderful," I exclaimed, and it was. It was a thick cookie covered with a gooey caramel filling of brown sugar, molasses, and lots of sweet pecans.

"Can I get the recipe for this? My wife is learning to bake, and I'm sure she would love this. Is it difficult to make?"

"Of course, I'll be happy to give her the recipe," Ida answered. She stood up. "I'll write it down for her. It's a little time-consuming but not very difficult."

"It's obviously very low calorie," I said.

They both laughed. Missy looked at both parents and then belatedly joined in.

"Oh yeah, everything Ida cooks is low calorie," said Sam. "I'm an obvious testimony to that."

We spent a very pleasant twenty minutes chatting. It wasn't until I got in the truck and was halfway to Turley's that I realized Sam had extracted most of my life history, as well as Rosalie's, and I had found out practically nothing about the Samuelsons. I did know that if I needed a lawyer for anything, he was going to be the one I called.

CHAPTER 28:

FRICK AND FRACK ARE BACK

"Hi, Doc," said Tim Gervis. "This is getting to be more than a little weird. I run almost five hundred head of mother cows on my place, and the only times I've seen you is for these stupid hounds."

"Hello, Mr. Gervis. I thought I saw your ranch on the schedule for pregnancy exams next week."

"Yeah, we'll start next Tuesday, so maybe we'll get some real work out of you. Meantime these guys have been shaking their heads, digging at their ears, and chewing on their feet for over a week now. It's driving the family crazy."

～

The more innovative and successful ranchers in our area had enthusiastically accepted a relatively new service that Dr. Schultz had introduced four years before my arrival. For a dollar a head, we did rectal examinations on cows starting in late summer and early fall.

Dr. Schultz could identify a fetus in the uterus when it was only six weeks old. I wasn't as skilled but didn't miss many that were eight weeks or more. At the end of the breeding season, we would palpate herds of cows and separate out the ones that were pregnant. We checked the others again a month later to identify any that were not far enough along or that we had missed the first time. The rancher was thus able to identify those cows that were pregnant and going to produce a calf the next year. This meant they could sell the non-productive cows, thus avoiding the expense of feeding them over the winter. This was especially helpful for ranchers who had to purchase feed to get their cattle through the winter.

The process was simple but involved a long, hard day's work. The rancher and his hired hands brought the cattle to corrals with chutes leading off them, a setup essential for any working ranch. These chutes led to a ramp where the animals could be loaded into a truck or, alternatively, through a chute leading to a squeeze chute. The upright posts for the chutes were usually only about six feet apart, and the rails were close enough together to prevent an animal from sticking its head out. The posts were far enough apart to insert a pole between animals. The cows were herded into the chute and then blocked off with poles between the posts, so each cow was separated from the one in front of her.

We climbed over the chute, got in behind a cow and did the rectal exam. Pregnant cows were marked with a colored dye and separated from the non-pregnant or questionable cows. It was dirty work. Getting stepped on was part of the deal, being kicked was not uncommon, getting an arm twisted or jammed into a rail was routine, and being covered from head to foot in loose, grass-green feces was a given.

If the people working the cows were experienced and efficient, each of us could diagnose twelve to fifteen cows in an hour. The Gervis ranch was set up very well, and Tim had experienced men working for him. He had a double-chute setup, and the chute leading to the loading ramp had an escape gate, so we could divert the cows from that ramp into pregnant or non-pregnant corrals. The chute leading to the squeeze had a similar arrangement. The two of us would be able to work in separate chutes and get through his herd in two long days.

Today, technology has advanced, and pregnancy exams using an ultrasound machine with a rectal probe are common. The results are more certain, less dependent upon the skill of the veterinarian, a permanent record is possible, and pregnancy is diagnosed earlier, all huge advantages in breeding management, but the cost is more than a dollar a head.

~

"So, do we know Frick from Frack yet?" I inquired.

"Oh yeah," Gervis answered. "They have name plates on their collars now. My daughter bought them at the feed store."

He pulled one of the hounds close, sliding him along the floor. He grabbed the dog by the scruff of the neck and showed me a brass plate riveted to the inch-wide leather collar with the name "Frick" engraved on the plate.

"Very nice," I said. "I've seen name plates like this on horse halters but never before on a dog collar. I might have to get one of these for my dog. So, both Frick and Frack are scratching at their ears?"

"Yeah and biting at their feet."

"OK," I said. "Let's have a look."

I lifted Frick, my arms cradling both his front and rear legs, and put him on the exam table. The table jiggled and rocked with his shaking. I petted him and got him to lie down on the table. The shaking stopped. I lifted up his left ear and smelled the foul odor I expected. I took a step back.

"Whoa, that's not good. He's got an ear infection." I lifted his right ear, and that was just as bad. "We'll have to flush these ears out before we can determine the cause."

I separated the hound's toes on his left forepaw and found an infected tract between his third and fourth toes. The other three paws seemed to be normal.

"I think the same thing might be causing the ear and paw problems. If you'll put Frick back on the floor, I'll have a look at Frack."

The second hound gave my face a slurpy lick as I gathered him in my arms and lifted him to the table. Both of Frack's ear canals were also full of foul-smelling exudate.

"I'm going to try to clean this up without anesthetizing them," I said, "but ear infections can be painful. If it bothers them too much, I might have to anesthetize them to get this done."

I took a small stainless steel bowl, half-filled it with warm water, and added a cap full of dishwashing detergent. Next, I took a twenty cc syringe, filled it with the soapy water, and flushed it into Frack's left ear while massaging the ear canal from the outside. The dog tried to shake his head, but I managed to hold onto his head and prevented him from flapping his ears. I wiped out the now filthy excess fluid, repeating the process several times for both ears. Next, I added a few drops of warm mineral oil to each ear and massaged the ear canal again. Frack yelped once as I massaged the oil into his left ear and tried to scratch at the ear with his left hind paw. Gervis grabbed Frack's leg and held it down.

"Thanks," I said. "I think there are foreign objects in their ears causing the infection and making them so sore. Let's have a look."

I held onto the dog's ear at the base and manipulated my otoscope down and then at a right angle. Pushing against his eardrum were at least three objects.

"OK, it's as I expected. It looks like foxtail seeds. I'm going to remove them with these." I picked up an alligator forceps to show the rancher. "We'll be right at his ear drum, and I don't want to puncture it. Do you think you can hold him really still?"

The rancher tied Frick to the base of the table, then reached over Frack's neck pushing his head down with his forearm, and held it with both hands.

"Good, you should be able to hold him still enough like that," I said.

I replaced the otoscope and removed three grass awns, one by one, from the left ear. We switched sides of the exam table, and I removed two more foxtail seeds from the right ear canal.

"Actually," I said, "he doesn't seem to have as much inflammation of the membranes as I expected. I'm going to treat with this tube of mastitis ointment and give you the remainder of the tube to treat both of them with, twice a day. You just squeeze in about five or six drops, like this; then massage the ear from the outside." As I massaged Frack's ears, the dog leaned into my hands making groaning noises of contentment.

"That feel good, old boy? Yeah, I bet it does." The dog's whip-like tail inscribed a figure eight. "Now let's have a look at those paws."

I inspected each paw carefully and found only the one tract between the toes in the left forepaw. Reaching in with the alligator forceps, I removed another foxtail seed and held it up for Gervis to see.

"Here's the culprit."

I squeezed some of the antibiotic mastitis ointment into the wound, and Frack licked off the excess.

"You'll need to put a little of this into the wound a couple of times a day too. It will probably heal over in just a day or two.

"OK, big guy, let's get your bud up here and take care of him," I told Frack.

Gervis gave a tug on Frack's leash, and he jumped lightly to the floor. I lifted Frick onto the table and went through the same process of cleaning the ear canal and removing grass awns from both ears and from between the toes on both front paws and one hind paw. When I finished removing the foxtail seeds, I looked up.

"There's another problem with Frick that we need to address," I said. "Feel his left ear here."

I lifted the dog's ear and guided Gervis's fingers to the middle of the inside surface where it was swollen and soft. "That's a hematoma, the result of him shaking his head and violently flapping his ears against his head. He's managed to bust some blood vessels, and the blood has filled in and separated the skin from the underlying tissues. These things are very difficult to handle and most frequently end up with a scarred and deformed ear. It's the same kind of thing that causes a cauliflower ear in boxers and wrestlers."

"That doesn't sound good," Gervis observed. "What can you do for it?"

"What we usually try first is to drain the hematoma and then bandage the ear tightly with padding to try to prevent the space from filling again with blood or serum. However, that works less than 20 percent of the time."

"What after that?"

"Well, the next thing is to open it up, remove the clot and any excess tissue, freshen all the surfaces, and suture everything back in place allowing for drainage. That works most of the time, but he will still have a scarred ear. Let me try to drain and bandage it first; then we'll see what happens."

"OK, you're the Doc."

I clipped some hair off the ear over the hematoma, cleaned it with soap, disinfected it, and inserted a large bore needle. The first eighteen milliliters of fluid was straw-colored serum. The fluid became blood-tinged as I applied more suction. I massaged the edges of the hematoma, milking as much fluid as possible towards the needle. After I removed the needle, I was still able to express a little fluid through the needle opening. I could feel clotted material inside where the fluid had been but was only able to break it down slightly, resulting in more bleeding.

I covered the inside of the ear with a thick pad of gauze, then placed a roll of gauze on top of the pad, and bandaged the whole thing over the top of Frick's head. Finally, I bandaged his good ear down over the top of the ear with the hematoma.

"I know this looks silly," I said, "but if I leave the one ear free, he's going to keep shaking his head and probably get a hematoma in that ear. "Let's leave this on. When I come out for the pregnancy testing next week, I'll remove the bandages, and we'll see what we have."

Frick seemed puzzled about having his ears bandaged to the top of his head, but he wasn't at all embarrassed. When Gervis pulled on his leash and he jumped to the floor, Frack immediately came to him and started licking his ears. Frick warned him off with a low growl. Frack desisted.

～

It was one of those wonderful sunny, warm fall days. Dr. Schultz and I arrived at the Gervis ranch. The hounds jumped off the front porch and followed us the quarter mile to the corrals holding the cattle. I got out of the truck and both came over to greet me. Frick's bandages were off, and his ear was swollen, larger than before.

Tim Gervis strode over, bandy legged, wearing chaps and high-heeled riding boots. He shook hands with Dr. Schultz and then with me.

"We've got six of them all ready for you in each of the chutes," he said, "so whenever you're ready, we can get started."

"I see Frick shed that wonderful bandage job I did," I observed.

Gervis laughed. "Yeah, Doc. It lasted about two hours after we got home. Between his scratching at it and Frack chewing at it, it didn't last long. Yesterday I noticed the hema-thingamabob was bigger than what you drained. I'll try to get him in next week, and you can have a go at the surgical thing you told me about."

I nodded as I bent to pull on my rubber boots and tuck in the legs of my coveralls.

"OK, we'll see if that will work. I'm afraid his good looks are going to be spoiled though."

Gervis laughed again. "Yeah, well, nobody out here much cares about a hound's good looks, Doc. Maybe we can make up a story about how a cougar got hold of him to explain it."

"Or a porcupine," I rejoined.

While we worked the cattle, the two hounds found a place in the shade to keep watch on the goings-on. I think they enjoyed watching me get stepped on, kicked, and shit upon, especially the latter.

Ten hours later, my coveralls were covered in cow feces, and I was tired and hurting. We had completed rectal exams on 280 cows finding 196 of them over six weeks pregnant. That was a high percentage from a good cattle operation.

"We'll move the rest of the cows in here this evening and be ready for you tomorrow," said Gervis, addressing Dr. Schultz. "Do you think we can finish them all up by early afternoon?"

"If we get an early-enough start," Schultz answered. "We'll plan to be here by six in the morning. That OK with you, Dave?"

"Whatever you say. I'm hoping a hot shower and a decent night's sleep will have revived me by then."

"Good," said Schultz. "We'll be here bright and early and keep going until we finish or can't move anymore." He was enjoying my discomfort as much as he enjoyed the physical labor.

We finished the rest of Gervis's cows the next day. The following week, Frick was back on the exam table. The hematoma was almost twice the original size.

"Have you got some things to do in town?" I asked. "I'll have to anesthetize him to do the surgery. He should be ready to go home in a couple of hours."

"Sure, I can always find something to do for a couple of hours," Gervis answered.

After the rancher left, I anesthetized Frick, prepared his ear for sterile surgery, opened up the hematoma, scraped surfaces to freshen them up, and removed as much of the already forming scar tissue as I could. I sutured through the skin on the inside of the earflap through the cartilage and then back and tied down the "mattress sutures" to close the space between the skin and cartilage as much as possible. Before suturing the skin incision, I inserted a teat tube for a drain at the tip of the incision and secured it with sutures. I planned to remove the drain in two weeks. I taped the ear up over his head again but this time incorporated hair from his neck and the top of his head into the bandage. I hoped he and his brother would leave it alone long enough to heal.

Gervis was back in two hours, and I took him back to the barn where Frick was recovering in the same stall he had occupied after the porcupine incident.

"If he gets the bandage off again, you'll need to remove the drain I put in near the end of his ear at the tip of the hematoma." I showed him a teat tube. "This is what I put in as a drain. If he gets the bandage off, it will act as added weight at the end of his ear and could cause some other problems with his shaking his head and scratching at it. So, you'll have to remove it. It's held in with three sutures, and I left the ends after the knot long so you should be able to find and identify them. Just cut the sutures with a manicure or other small scissors, and the drain should fall out. Think you can handle that?"

"Sure, Doc, won't be a problem. That it?"

"We'll see what happens. Bring him back in ten days if the bandage stays on or not, either way. I'll have to remove the sutures then."

—

This time the bandage stayed on. I removed it and the drain along with the sutures. The ear looked reasonably good, but it was thicker than the opposite ear, slightly gnarled, but not as bad as some other repaired aural hematomas I had seen.

"You OK with this result?" I asked Gervis, a little apprehensively.

"Sure, Doc. It doesn't look too bad to me, gives him some character." He smiled.

I was relieved.

"OK then, that's it. Frick has character, and you can tell the two apart, even if their collars get lost. See you next time they get into something."

Chapter 29:
Separation

Dr. Schultz called me in the evening, but not about any of our patients or clients.

"She told me to get out. Says she wants a divorce. We weren't arguing, just her normal bitching about me being at work all the time and not spending enough time with her and the kids."

When I told Rosalie that I was surprised by what Dr. Schultz had said, she admonished me, "You are so oblivious. It was obvious to me that their marriage is in trouble. She's completely obsessed about finances and how little they make from the practice. At the same time, she does nothing but spend money and complain that he's never home. He, on the other hand, just wants to do the veterinary stuff and take care of his pigs. Surely you've noticed?"

"Yeah, but he's very attached to their five kids."

"Sure, but he doesn't spend much time with them. Her parents have spoiled those kids, giving them anything they ask for. Do you remember the one time she invited us to their house for dinner? Her father and mother were there. She had to have her family's support to put up with us. Her father never missed an opportunity to say something demeaning about Dr. Schultz the whole evening in front of us and their children."

The next morning, I arrived at the clinic and discovered Dr. Schultz dozing on a canvas army cot in the office. I removed my hat and jacket.

Schultz sat up and swung his legs over the edge of the cot.

"You spend the night?" I asked.

"Yeah, my brother-in-law the lawyer explained the facts of my life. You knew Cheryl's dad bought this property from Dick and built the hospital for me?"

"Yeah?"

"Well, I've been making payments on it every month since, but everything is in Cheryl's name. So's that huge house we bought and spent so much money remodeling. I've always let her control all the bank accounts and let her take care of our business and finances. I never dreamed it would come to this. I was happy just practicing veterinary medicine. It turns out the only thing I actually own is the new practice truck." Tears welled up in his eyes.

"You don't have your name on the bank accounts?" I was incredulous.

"Both our names are on the practice account, but she has other accounts. She moves money around a lot."

"I suggest you get down to the bank and find out what's there," I said. "Then you need to open a new account for the practice, one that only you control. You need to deposit everything we take in now into the new account. You also need a good lawyer."

He repeated the same litany he had given me the night before. "I can't believe she kicked me out. Says she wants a divorce. We weren't arguing, just her normal bitching about me being at work all the time."

"I know, but you need to try to rescue what you can from the practice, so she can't drain it. You need to be there when the bank opens."

I finally convinced him, and he left to attend to the shambles of his finances.

"I knew Doc and his missus didn't have much in common, other than the kids," Dick said. "I never did understand what he saw in that woman. She takes after her old man. Not a bit surprised that family managed to take everything Doc owns. They left him his truck though, nice touch. I wonder if he'll even stick around. Seems like leaving him the truck was just an invite for him to clear out. I can't say I'd blame him if he did."

Dr. Schultz leaving town was something I hadn't considered.

I liked Dick and respected him. He was steady, reliable, and calm. He didn't look up during the prolonged silence while we both considered the future.

"You worried about what will happen to you and your wife if Dr. Schultz takes off?" I asked.

"Yeah, I live off my salary but rely on the pet supply business and the free apartment. I have folks depending on me. My parents are getting older, and I have to help them out. I don't think Doc has the balls for it anymore. He would have fought them when he first came here, but that woman and her family have emasculated him."

He handed me a fist full of call slips. I left to get through the demands of the day.

～

When I arrived at the hospital the next day, I found Dick and Don sitting in the office, their heads almost touching. Both men turned as I entered.

"Doc called early this morning from Bismarck," said Dick. "He talked to a classmate of his who works for the USDA. There's a meat inspector job open in Des Moines. He's on his way to Iowa to have a look. He said he wouldn't come back unless he could patch up his marriage."

"How'd he sound?" I asked.

"Depressed. What's the next step for us?" Dick asked. "Do we keep this place going and work for the bitch?"

"Don't know yet, Dick. Do we have a lot going on this morning?" I asked.

That morning it was clear and cold with two to three inches of snow on the ground where the wind hadn't blown it away. Farmers and ranchers were out checking stock. Dick handed me some call slips, not as many as the previous day.

"OK," I said, shuffling through the calls. "Don and I will take care of these this morning, but see if you can keep me clear for a couple of hours this afternoon. Call Mrs. Schultz and make an appointment for me to meet with her. I need to get some sort of agreement, so we'll all know what's going to happen. Also get a hold of Sam Samuelson's office and see if you can make an appointment for me to meet with him an hour or so after my appointment with Mrs. Schultz."

"Good idea," said Dick. "When you deal with the Watts family, you need a shark on your side."

—

"I think we should just continue the arrangement we have. I see no reason to change anything," Mrs. Schultz told me.

She sat at her office table with her brother sitting next to her. I sat opposite them. She did not even offer a cup of coffee.

"As you know," I answered, "when I first negotiated with Dr. Schultz, he offered me five hundred dollars a month. That was the going rate, and most of my classmates who went to work for someone got about the same. However, when I visited, I saw how busy the practice was. I told him I was willing to work for five hundred for fifty hours a week but after I worked two hundred hours each month I wanted 40 percent of anything I billed. He agreed, and that's been our deal."

That negotiation had turned out to be a better deal than I had anticipated. The practice was so busy I routinely worked twelve-plus-hour days. With emergency calls and weekends, I usually reached two hundred hours during the third week of the month.

"I came here as an associate and to learn from Dr. Schultz," I continued. "Now you're asking me to run the entire practice and do the work of two veterinarians. I think we need an entirely new arrangement. If I leave, you'll have to shut the practice down until you can find another licensed veterinarian, if you can find someone. My suggestion is that we arrange for a fair market appraisal for the land, buildings, and equipment. I'll lease everything from you based on that appraisal."

Mrs. Schultz's brother inserted himself into the negotiation. "I'll tell you what," he said. "You sign a five-year lease and pay us 2,500 a month, and we're done."

"The practice couldn't possibly support that much. I know what we take in," I said.

I stood up and addressed Mrs. Schultz. "I didn't think you would bring in legal counsel until after we made some sort of temporary arrangement. Under these circumstances, I'm not prepared to make any commitments, unless I have representation too. Actually, I think it would be best to let the lawyers negotiate with the understanding that our current arrangement is void. My handshake agreement was with Dr. Schultz, and he's no longer involved in the practice. Without Dr. Schultz or myself, there is, in fact, no practice. After my attorney examines all the financial records and determines a fair market value for the buildings and equipment, we can negotiate a fair lease arrangement or not."

Then I addressed the brother. "I'm willing to continue the arrangement I had with Dr. Schultz for one week, no longer. I'll have my attorney contact you."

I turned and started for the door.

"Who is your attorney, Doctor?" the brother asked.

I turned to gauge their reactions and found them both smirking.

"I have an appointment to talk to Sam Samuelson this afternoon."

I was gratified to see a fleeting grimace on the brother's face. Mrs. Schultz frowned.

They're not very good poker players.

—

The next day, Mrs. Schultz turned over the financial records of the practice to Sam. He called me the following morning to tell me that Dr. Schultz had paid back three-fourths of what his wife's father had spent purchasing the property and building the hospital, plus 7 percent annual interest on the unpaid balance each month. All the furnishings and equipment in the hospital were cash purchases from the hospital income.

Sam and I met with Mrs. Schultz's brother the following day, and Sam explained our position. "Even if you can find another veterinarian to take over the practice, it will take some time, probably months, for you do so. Anyone you find would have to be a fool to lease the buildings and equipment or to purchase everything for more than their value. The only thing you can do with an animal hospital is to practice veterinary medicine out of it. Of course, you could renovate it for some other purpose; that's up to your family to decide. Dr. Gross's agreement to continue to work based on his verbal contract with Dr. Schultz expires Monday. Either we have a signed lease agreement, or your client has a building with no veterinary practice. Perhaps she can operate a boarding kennel."

Three days later, Sam and I met again with her brother, plus Mrs. Schultz. Sam took charge.

"Dr. Gross isn't going to continue to run the practice after tomorrow unless we have an agreement. He will continue to practice from his house. He's the only veterinarian in a fifty-mile radius, and he's already well-known and well-liked. Any other veterinarian coming in will have a tough time getting started."

"What about the goodwill, the client list?" asked the brother.

"What goodwill is that?" asked Sam. "Dr. Gross is the one with goodwill. Dr. Schultz has goodwill, but he is not party to these negotiations."

It was a bluff. Rosalie and I hadn't managed to save enough money for me to go into practice on my own. I had very little in the way of instruments or equipment of my own, and no drugs or supplies. I had talked to the representative of the major veterinary supply company that serviced the area, and the company had agreed to extend me credit for a couple of months. However, they wouldn't be able to deliver an order for four or five days.

I needed so much in the way of instruments, equipment, and supplies; I didn't think it would be possible to do enough work and collect enough in fees to pay for everything and reorder what I used. I would have to get a loan, find a place to store everything, and practice out of the Ford. I could probably do it, but it would require a major commitment. Rosalie and I were not certain we were ready to go into debt and shoulder that much responsibility.

"Well, we have no idea of what the building, equipment, and supplies are worth. We'll need time to come up with those figures," the brother responded.

Before the meeting, I had told Sam about our apprehension and the problems I would have trying to practice from our apartment.

"OK," Sam said, "Dr. Gross is willing to continue to run the practice for 40 percent of what he bills but only for another thirty days. To be clear, that means 40 percent of what he bills, not what is collected. That should give us the time we need to set a fair value for everything and negotiate a lease/purchase agreement."

"Forty percent, that's more than we net from the practice now." Mrs. Schultz spoke for the first time that day. She also gave me a very dirty look.

"Well, that's just not the case," Sam rejoined. "Our evaluation of the financial records shows that you and Dr. Schultz have taken out more than 40 percent of the gross on average every month since Dr. Gross has been here, even the first month after he arrived. You should still be able to take considerably more than five hundred a month for yourself and your family."

"We can't live on five hundred a month," she exclaimed.

"It's more than you'll have if Dr. Gross leaves or sets up on his own," Sam answered.

They finally agreed to pay me 40 percent of what I billed for the next thirty days, and I went back to work.

A week and several communications between Sam and the brother did not produce a lease agreement that Sam or I thought fair or beneficial. I was in Sam's office looking over their last offer.

"They started at twenty-five hundred, and they're still at two thousand?" I said. "The practice only brought in how much last year?"

Sam flipped over a couple of pages of the yellow legal pad on his desk. "Took in just under fifty-two thousand in the last twelve months," he said, then looked at me, and shrugged.

"You took home just under eight thousand of that, and Dr. Schultz or, rather, Mrs. Schultz netted almost thirteen, after making payments on the hospital, which, no doubt, she has been banking separately. In any case, the basic problem is that she doesn't really need anything. Her old man can and will support her, and Schultz will almost certainly end up paying child support and maybe even some alimony. I think the real problem is that the old man is too proud to let some young hotshot get the best of his family in a business deal. It would tarnish his reputation in the community, and the word would get out."

Sam smiled, perhaps relishing the thought of spreading that information then he got serious.

"I must tell you that at our last meeting her brother told me, and I'll quote him, 'The family isn't going to let that kike jew us any more than he has.'"

"OK," I said. "That's enough for me. I'm going to find out if I have some other options."

"I think that's a wise and prudent thing to do," Sam replied.

That same evening, I started calling classmates to find out if any knew of jobs available. One of my former roommates, Dick Rezzonico, was working for Dr. Henshaw in Buckeye, Arizona, a small farming community southwest of Phoenix. Dick had joined the air force and was due to report for basic training in a couple of weeks. Dr. Henshaw needed someone for the practice. I called Dr. Henshaw, and we made a deal over the phone.

Rosalie is an only child, and her parents missed her terribly. Neither she nor they ever said a negative word about my carting her off to the wilds of Montana. I presumed they hoped it was just a temporary thing. She missed her parents, and I missed my family. Her mom and dad were ecstatic when we told them were coming home, and my parents were just as happy.

***

It was difficult to leave new friends and loyal clients, but they had survived without us before we came. Dick opened a pet shop in an empty store in town. He had apparently managed to save more than he let on. He and Barbara bought George Kemper's house in town. Don landed a job with the Yellowstone Livestock Company working the sale barn.

    Rosalie and I had accumulated more stuff than would fit in and on the Ford. I bought a two-wheeled luggage trailer, loaded it with all that stuff, and we left Sidney with Mister again in the back seat. A blizzard chased us all the way through Montana, South Dakota, Wyoming, and Colorado. We were happy to hit the Arizona desert and be home again.

About the Author

David R. Gross graduated from Colorado State University's veterinary school in 1960 and was in private practice for ten years. He enrolled in graduate school and earned an MS degree in 1972 and a PhD degree in 1974 from the Ohio State University. He taught and did research at Texas A & M University College of Veterinary Medicine for sixteen years and then became director of the Cardiovascular and Thoracic Surgery Research labs at the University of Kentucky College of Medicine for five years. He retired in 2006 after twelve years as professor and head of Veterinary Biosciences, College of Veterinary Medicine, University of Illinois at Urbana-Champaign.

Dr. Gross is a Fellow of the Cardiovascular Section of the American Physiological Society. He published over ninety papers in refereed scientific journals and over a hundred abstracts in proceedings of scientific meetings. He co-edited three multi-authored textbooks, and the third edition of his single-author text, *Animal Models in Cardiovascular Research*, is in most medical libraries. Since retirement, Dr. Gross has been busy writing both fiction and non-fiction. Visit Dr. Gross's website, www.docdavesvoice.com.